About the Editors

Edésio Fernandes is a Brazilian academic, lawyer and town planner and is currently a senior research fellow with the Institute of Commonwealth Studies of the University of London. His research interests include urban and environmental law and policy, local government and metropolitan administration, and human rights and constitutional law in developing countries. He has been a consultant to many governmental and non-governmental organizations in Brazil and elsewhere. He is the author of *Law and Urban Change in Brazil* (Avebury, 1995) and editor of *Environmental Strategies for Sustainable Development in Urban Areas* (Avebury, 1998), as well as coordinator of the International Research Group on Law and Urban Space of the International Sociological Association.

Ann Varley is a lecturer in geography at University College London. Her interest in the subject of law and urban development dates from the early 1980s, when she carried out research for her doctoral thesis on illegal settlement and land tenure regularization in Mexico. She has written widely on low-income housing questions and more recently on gender and the urban household, and is currently undertaking a major study of gender and housing in urban Mexico funded by the Economic and Social Research Council. Her publications include *Landlord and Tenant: Housing the Poor in Urban Mexico* (with Alan Gilbert; Routledge, 1991) and an edited book on *Disasters, Development and Environment* (John Wiley, 1994).

Other Zed titles on urban development

With relentlessly increasing urbanisation, growing attention to new ways of understanding modern cities and new policy approaches to tackling urban problems, Zed Books is developing a rapidly growing list of Urban Studies titles. These books include the following:

Housing the Urban Poor: A guide to policy and practice in the South
Brian C. Aldrich and Ravinder S. Sandhu (eds)

Our Urban Future: New paradigms for equity and sustainability
Akhtar Badshah

A City for All: Valuing difference and working with diversity
Jo Beall (ed)

Children of the Cities
Jo Boyden

The Challenge of Sustainable Cities: Neoliberalism and urban strategies in developing countries
Rod Burgess, Marisa Carmona and Theo Kolstee (eds)

The Rumour of Calcutta: Tourism, charity and the poverty of representation
John Hutnyk

Greening the North: A post-industrial blueprint for ecology and equity
Wolfgang Sachs, Reinhard Loske and Manfred Linz

Gender and Slum Culture in Urban Asia
Susanne Thorbek

Urban Development Planning: Lessons for the economic reconstruction of South African cities
Richard Tomlinson

Space, Culture and Power: New identities in globalizing cities
Petra Weyland and Ayşe Öncü (eds)

For full details of this list and Zed's other titles, please write to:

The Marketing Department, Zed Books, 7 Cynthia Street, London N1 9JF, UK or email: Sales@zedbooks.demon.co.uk

Visit our website at: http://www.zedbooks.demon.co.uk

ILLEGAL CITIES

Law and Urban Change in Developing Countries

Edited by
EDÉSIO FERNANDES AND
ANN VARLEY

Zed Books Ltd
LONDON & NEW YORK

Illegal Cities: Law and urban change in developing countries was first published by Zed Books Ltd, 7 Cynthia Street, London N1 9JF, UK and Room 400, 175 Fifth Avenue, New York, NY 10010, USA in 1998.

Distributed in the USA exclusively by St Martin's Press, Inc., 175 Fifth Avenue, New York, NY 10010, USA.

The cover photographs top right and top left (Caracas, Venezuela, 1996) are reproduced courtesy of Teolinda Bolívar; the bottom photo (Mexico City, 1991) is reproduced courtesy of Ann Varley.

Cover designed by Andrew Corbett
Set in Monotype Garamond by Ewan Smith
Printed and bound in the United Kingdom
by Biddles Ltd, Guildford and King's Lynn

A catalogue record for this book is available from the British Library

ISBN 1 85649 549 3 cased
ISBN 1 85649 550 7 limp

Contents

Tables and Figures

Tables

Figures

Contributors

Sérgio de Azevedo is Professor of Political Science at the Universidade Federal de Minas Gerais, Brazil.

Antonio Azuela is Mexico's Attorney General for the Environment (Procurador Federal de Protección al Medio Ambiente).

Stephen Berrisford is Director of Land Development Facilitation at the Department of Land Affairs, Government of South Africa.

Teolinda Bolívar lectures in Architecture at the Universidad Central de Venezuela, Caracas.

Emilio Duhau lectures in Sociology at the Universidad Autónoma Metropolitana-Azcapotzalco, Mexico City.

Alain Durand-Lasserve is Director of Research for the National Centre for Scientific Research (CNRS) and Researcher at the Université de Paris VII, France.

Edésio Fernandes is Senior Research Fellow at the Institute of Commonwealth Studies of the University of London, UK.

Kivutha Kibwana is Lecturer in Law at the University of Nairobi, Kenya.

Patrick McAuslan is Professor of Law at Birkbeck College, University of London, UK.

Winnie V. Mitullah is a researcher at the Institute of Development Studies of the University of Nairobi, Kenya.

Rogelio Pérez Perdomo lectures in Law at the Instituto de Estudios Superiores de Administración, Caracas, Venezuela.

Amanda Perry is Lecturer in Law at the University of Sussex, UK.

Omar Razzaz is a member of the Private Participation in Infrastructure Group of the World Banks's Private Sector Development Department, Washington, DC.

Raquel Rolnik lectures in Urban Planning at the Universidade Católica de Campinas and is a researcher at POLIS (Instituto de Formacão e Assessoria em Políticas Sociais), Brazil.

Asteya M. Santiago lectures in Urban and Regional Planning at the University of the Philippines.

Ann Varley lectures in Geography at University College London, UK.

Ayse Yonder is Associate Professor of City and Regional Planning at the Pratt Institute, New York, USA.

PART I

An Introduction to Urban Legal Research

CHAPTER I

Law, the City and Citizenship in Developing Countries: an Introduction

Edésio Fernandes and Ann Varley

Objectives

In the cities of Asia, Africa and Latin America, the urban poor often have to step outside the law in order to gain access to land and housing. If we consider land tenure, infrastructure requirements and building standards, we find that an average of 40 per cent and in some cases as much as 70 per cent of the population of the major cities are living in illegal conditions (Durand-Lasserve and Clerc 1996). Much has been written about the problems the residents of illegal settlements face, but few studies have asked why their housing is illegal, why it matters that it is illegal, or what should be done about it.

This book seeks to answer these questions by exploring the role of law, and illegality, in the process of urban change in developing countries. It analyses the evolution and implications of urban legislation, focusing on the relationship between (legal and illegal) land use patterns and the often elitist and exclusionary legal and institutional frameworks of these countries. Although this book is an edited collection of articles by different authors, the contributors share a common belief that, while law plays a crucial role in the process of urban growth, its role can be understood only in relation to the other social, political, cultural and economic processes which take place in, and structure, urban areas.

This book aims to fill a significant gap in the fields of urban development and legal studies. Both have long underestimated both the legal dimension of the urbanization process and the significance of the various forms of illegality within this process. This is the first book to cover these questions so comprehensively, and from such a broad geographical perspective. We approach the subject of law and urban change from a socio-legal perspective, emphasizing how legal institutions, legislation and judicial decisions affect the social production of urban space. Contributors were asked to consider some of the following issues: property rights and the public control of urban land; land invasions and other 'informal' settlements; the legal management of urban areas; deregulation of land and housing markets; the meaning and political uses of illegality; legal pluralism, customary law and informal regulation of property rights; security of tenure and the regularization of illegal settlements.

In bringing the neglected subject of law and urban change to the attention of a wider audience, this book aims to demystify the subject and to challenge the uncritical treatment it has received in traditional legal studies. It offers a basic introduction to the subject and seeks to provide a critical understanding of the role law plays in the increasingly complex problems facing the people and governments of many of the world's poorer cities.

This book comprises a broad-ranging collection of empirical studies, some of which are more general, others more specific. They touch on issues as diverse as legality and informality, tradition and culture, and resistance to modernization or centralized government, but at least one major theme links the different chapters: that of social conflict around law, property and urban space. In this context, there are three initial points we should make, since they underpin the general argument of this book.

First, far from corroborating the myth that, in a given country, the legal system is based upon a single, unitary, conception of property rights, the literature suggests that different forms of ownership are treated differently by the law. The private ownership of land, especially in urban areas, often proves problematic because the state's ability to impose conditions on the economic exploitation of property in the public interest has long been constrained by liberal legal ideologies.

Second, research has shown that even in countries with a tradition of legal positivism such that the state claims to be sole judge of what is legal or illegal, individual behaviour and social practices are often regulated by other, unofficial, criteria – hence the proliferation of forms of land and housing production which, while illegal, can enjoy greater social and political legitimacy than the official ones. Many studies have also shown, however, that rather than following an exclusive logic of their own, such forms of illegality result from an intimate, though contradictory, dialogue with the official legal system. Although informal law is an important and neglected area of study, it must be viewed in relation to formal law and institutions.

Third, research has also suggested that there are 'degrees of illegality': that is, some forms of illegality tend to be more accepted and/or tolerated than others, by both the state and public opinion. The more acceptable forms are generally those involving the existence of documentary evidence about land ownership or acquisition, such as informal titles or receipts providing some sort of link, however tenuous, to the chain of previous owners. Those situations in which there has been no commercial or legal attempt to preserve the tradition and transference of ownership are more directly subject to repression. In other words, property ownership does indeed seem to be the name of the game.

Two other comments should be made. First: although illegality clearly permeates all sorts of social relations in urban areas – with respect to civil, commercial or criminal law, for example – in this book the emphasis is placed on the illegal aspects of social processes providing access to land and housing. Second: we do not believe that illegality is associated exclusively with the poor. Illegal forms of production of urban land and housing are being observed more and more frequently in the more privileged parts of third world cities. They involve, for instance, closed condominium developments in which gates creating private enclosures may prevent the public from gaining access to the road system as well as to public spaces such as beaches, and the occupation of environmentally protected areas. We believe, however, that, given the quantitative import-ance and social implications of illegality in low-income areas, it is in this context above all that, as a matter of urgency, illegality needs to be understood and addressed.

The need for urban and legal reform in developing countries provides the underlying concern uniting the contributors to this book, which is directed at urban sociologists, development studies specialists and legal scholars as well as public administrators, policy-makers and legislators. We also address issues of interest to those involved with urban social move-ments and non-government organizations (NGOs). We hope to help social and political movements, and the NGOs supporting their work, to gain a better understanding of legal issues, and by so doing to strengthen the diverse movements promoting urban reform in developing countries.

Urban Legal Research in Developing Countries: an Overview

Law in the context of urban studies Since its appearance in the late 1960s, critical social research has progressed enormously in its efforts to understand the factors, agents and processes shaping urban reality in both developed and developing countries. This may primarily be attributed to its interdisciplinary approach and the rich dialogue it has stimulated between the social sciences, to the extent that they now share a common vocabulary for their common subject of study.

The complexity of the subject, together with the limitations of the theoretical framework, particularly in its Marxist variant, have led to endless debate about the nature of the 'urban phenomenon'. Thirty years after the publication of the two landmark works, Henri Lefebvre's *Le Droit à la Ville* (1968) and Manuel Castells' *La Question Urbaine* (1972), however, it can fairly be argued that critical urban research has achieved a satisfactory degree of conceptual clarity with regard to both its critique of the traditional (neo)liberal framework – however dominant that may still be – and its own understanding of the urban phenomenon.

Briefly: within the field of critical urban research the urban phenomenon has been considered as the dynamic result of a complex, and highly contradictory, process of articulation of economic, political and cultural forces, through which both cities and rural areas are currently being redefined in the process of economic globalization. Urbanization produces specific spatial structures and forms supporting the (re)creation of the social relations necessary to the reproduction of capital.

Special emphasis has been placed on the roles played in this contradictory process by a variety of social and political agents and institutions, especially the state and urban social movements. Very little attention has been given, however, to the legal dimension of the urban phenomenon. Very little has been written from a critical perspective about the role of law in urban processes, that is, the role law performs in the social production of urban space. Scant theoretical consideration has been given to the importance of law as an instrument of urban and social change.

We should be particularly concerned about the reasons for such a lack of interest in law on the part of urban sociologists and political scientists, given that they are not so constrained by the positivist tradition as legal scholars. We can more readily understand why, in developing countries in particular, the positivist tradition in legal research, deeply imbued with the ideology of private rights and individualism, refuses to acknowledge – even for academic purposes – the existence of 'urban law'. Dominant legal doctrine still regards the city as no more than a bounded area comprised of demarcated plots of land in individual ownership. Liberal legalism goes little further than the attribution of some administrative powers to public authorities to control urban growth on the grounds that these authorities are responsible for maintaining social well-being.

Yet critical urban research has also largely failed to understand the legal dimension of the urban phenomenon. Law has been either dismissed or taken for granted. On the one hand, not only are the more radical critical analyses, including traditional Marxist ones, unable to provide a satisfactory account of the legal phenomenon in general; they also have almost nothing of significance to say about the intricate network of (il)legal social relations established in the city, particularly those relating to the use of land. Such approaches are very often dismissive of urban law because of their adherence to the narrow perspective of the die-hard Leninist theory of the state, which has conceived law as a mere instrument manipulated by a monolithic (bourgeois) state.

Most urban research, on the other hand, seems to have taken the legal phenomenon for granted, as if it were an independent, and theoretically uncomplicated, domain of knowledge and action. Regardless of the significant advances already made in the formulation of a theory of the state, critical urban research has not gone very far towards identifying the nature of the relationship between the state and its legal apparatus. It has largely, and generally implicitly, conceived of legal relations as being politically and socially neutral. A broad critique of the shortcomings of urban sociology's approach to law is provided by Azuela (1989).

As a result, both progressive urban research and socially oriented projects have very often recommended the enactment of legislation as a solution to urban problems, as if legislation itself were an unproblematic instrument of urban planning and reform. By failing to problematize law, they unwittingly reinforce the positivist position that law is an autonomous, politically neutral, domain of knowledge.

Lefebvre and his followers have always suggested that urban space is a text, waiting to be read. There must be a legal reading of that text – one which, we believe, is fundamental to the constitution of any new, and critical, 'science of the urban phenomenon' (Lefebvre 1971). Given due consideration to its own limitations, this book is an initial attempt to address the neglect of urban law, particularly within the social sciences, for we believe that the legal dimension can disclose new, still unknown, meanings of the urban text.

Is there a 'right to the city'? Among his many other significant contributions to the formation of critical urban theory, some of which are currently being rediscovered by authors such as David Harvey, Mark Gottdiener and Edward Soja, Lefebvre was responsible for coining the expression 'the right to the city', the title of his first (1968) book on the subject of the city. This expression has long been thoroughly assimilated into urban research, to the extent that it has become part of a widely-employed technical jargon. More recently, its constant usage by urban social movements and NGOs in several parts of the world has also turned it into a political claim of sorts, and as such it has been given several differing, and sometimes mutually exclusive, meanings.

In his broad critique of modern society, and especially in his analysis of the city, Lefebvre addressed the role of the main social institutions, particularly the state. However, although he asserted the existence of a 'right to the city', Lefebvre himself paid little attention to the legal meaning of this phrase, the role of law in general, or the role law plays within the city.

Rather than a legal right, Lefebvre seems to have viewed the 'right to the city' only as a criterion for political analysis and a political platform. It would not be a right in the juridical sense of the term, but one like those in the celebrated Declaration of the Rights of Man, by which democracy is defined (Lefebvre 1972). The objectives of such rights would never fully be achieved but they could be used as standards by which to assess the state of a given society. More recently, women's and children's rights have been added to the list. Lefebvre proposed that we should also add 'the right to the city' and, thinking of the different ethnic groups and peoples making up both city populations and human society at the global level, 'the right to difference'.

In one of his last works, Lefebvre developed this point a little further, affirming that, together with other social rights such as 'the right to information' and 'the right to self-management', the 'right to the city' should be incorporated into a new, updated 'social contract' defining new conditions for the exercise of citizenship in contemporary societies (Lefebvre 1990). Again, though, this would be a political right, to be understood within the context of progressive political philosophy.

In a less explicit way, this is also the position of most of the urban researchers, such as Jorge Hardoy, who have subsequently remarked on the fact that, in developing countries in particular, a large number of people are living in illegal conditions. Stressing the consequences of urban illegality, Hardoy was perhaps the first author to employ the term 'illegal city' but neither he nor his collaborators and followers developed a fuller understanding of the nature and operation of the legal system (see, for example, Hardoy and Satterthwaite 1987).

Although authors from Lefebvre to Hardoy have failed to define the legal content of a 'right to the city', in practice growing social and political mobilization around urban issues in many developing countries has already had a significant impact on the official legal order. In Brazil, for example, the latest (1990) version of the Urban Policy bill introduced the notion of a 'right to the city' to be guaranteed by the formulation and enforcement of a national urban policy, comprising measures to improve urban living standards through spatial planning and access to collective infrastructure, services and amenities by the inhabitants of the city.[1]

How can such a 'right to the city' be explained in legal terms? How does it fit into the dominant, liberal, legal order in force in most developing countries? How does it relate to social conflict around urban matters, especially access to land and housing? Although they are important, such questions, along with many others, have not been answered by urban research, largely because they have rarely been asked.

The city in the context of legal studies   Three main paradigms have influenced legal research on the city. Their differing views on the central issue of property rights – influenced by civil law, public law and the more recent socio-legal tradition – account for their different approaches to the nature of the city, state action and the relation between the two.

In many developing countries the dominant paradigm has been the liberal and individualistic approach typical of civil law, which leaves little room for state intervention in the control of the use, occupation and development of urban land. From this viewpoint, in legal studies the city is often implicitly considered as a set of privately owned plots of land.

Urban law is responsible only for governing relations between individuals (especially neighbouring property owners) and approving administrative restrictions limiting, in the interests of social welfare, the full exercise of property rights. The process of urban development is largely left to be decided by market forces.

In countries with a more consistent public law approach to property rights, legal studies usually link the notion of the social function of property with that of the public interest, enabling the state to control land use and property development through legal instruments such as zoning laws or compulsory land acquisition. On the whole, however, by stressing the instrumental nature of law such studies fail to raise a number of important questions and are unable fully to explain the role of law in urban development. Confined within the tradition of liberal legalism, albeit with redefined boundaries, such studies tend to share the positivism and formalism of the private/civil law approach, especially as they too regard the law as an objective, self-contained system. They also fail to question the role of state intervention in the process of urban development, viewing the state as a neutral agent in charge of protecting the public interest and social welfare. There is no critique of social reality, nor a basic under-standing of the political economy of urban development. Moreover, still constrained by the traditional dichotomy between civil and public law, such studies fail to appreciate the political nature of urban law, thus restricting their ability to interpret progressive laws. Above all, they tend to focus exclusively on the legal city, ignoring the illegal city where the majority of the city's residents live, daily reinventing their social practices in response to the exclusionary legal system. References to shanty towns, *favelas*, *barrios* and suchlike are not to be found in such studies.

A different tradition of urban legal studies began in the 1970s, drawing from, and combining, critical urban research, the 'Law and Development' movement and legal pluralism in its efforts to understand the relation between law and urban development. A whole tradition of studies on legal pluralism in urban areas is indebted to the seminal work of Boa-ventura Santos (1977), who sought to understand the relation between the official legal system on the one hand and, on the other, the existence of informal rules and popular mechanisms for dispensing justice. Such studies also made it possible to reflect upon the nature of state action, and on attempts to legitimate it. The important, thought-provoking work of Antonio Azuela (1989) deserves special mention. More recently, following this tradition a number of studies have been published on the specific issue of land tenure regularization.

Few studies, however, have sought to build a bridge between the legal and illegal cities or to establish a general analytical framework to explain the role of law in the process of urban development in developing countries. Among these, Raquel Rolnik (1997) and Edésio Fernandes (1995) have analysed the role of urban law in the socio-economic, political and ideological aspects of urban development.

We would argue that the developments of Lefebvre's urban philosophy, critical urban theory and critical legal studies have already suggested several ways in which law, the state and ideology interact in the production of urban space, and put forward some valuable ideas about the logic of social attitudes to law and (in)formal justice, especially as regards access to urban land. Notwithstanding its limitations, such as an inadequate understanding of the complexities of the political process, we believe that such a framework yields arguments which are sufficiently interesting as to justify deeper reflection on the role of law either in urban social segregation or in the process of urban reform. Contributors to this book seek to understand the 'right' to the city in the context of the social production of urban space and urban society. In addition, they wish to find out to what extent urban law can serve as one of the instruments of the progressive 'urban strategy' proposed by Lefebvre (1971), seeking to achieve a truly democratic administration of city life.

The contributions to this book are set in the context of two hypotheses. The first is that, far from being merely an instrument, automatically determined by economic processes, or simply a repressive element of the state superstructure, urban legislation also performs important functions in both the production and structuring of social space as a whole, and in shaping the conditions of everyday life in the city. The second is that there is an intimate, albeit contradictory, relationship between public policies, decisions and laws concerning the city, on the one hand, and, on the other, the social attitudes, conventions and rules of everyday life contributing to the emergence of various forms of 'informal justice' in developing countries.

In this context, we seek to understand the production of urban legislation from the perspective of the interests that have turned third world cities into a stage for capitalist accumulation, without ever losing sight of the responses and alternatives – the practices of resistance – produced in everyday life by those who have traditionally been excluded from the production of this legislation: the vast majority of urban dwellers.

Rather than a technical matter to be understood within the limits of the legal universe, we regard the production of urban law as a political process, one fundamental aspect of the social conflict which lies at the heart of the city. As we see them, city and citizenship are different aspects of the same subject.

The Structure of this Book

The structure of this book reflects its main objectives: to provide a general introduction to the subject of law and urban development, review the existing literature on developing countries and discuss critically some key aspects of the legal dimension of urban development, particularly those referring to illegal settlements. Given our belief in the need for an interdisciplinary understanding of law and urban change, the contributors include jurists and researchers from other backgrounds who share a common interest in the role of law in urban planning, policy and management. They include leading professionals and international specialists in the field, and although their earlier, individual, publications have established the basis for our understanding of the subject-matter of this book, this is the first publication to bring them together and to some small extent to integrate their ideas.

The book is international in scope. While the situation in nine countries is examined in some detail – Turkey, Jordan, India, the Philippines, Venezuela, Brazil, Mexico, Kenya and South Africa – the authors of three overview chapters also draw on their professional experience and previous research in a wide range of other countries. This allows them to go beyond the specificities of the case studies to identify the main characteristics and implications of the action of law in urban areas. It also enables them to identify the main trends in policy and legal reform, and the main themes for future urban legal research.

In Chapter 2, Patrick McAuslan surveys the record of research on legal aspects of urbanization since 1960 and suggests some directions that urban research might usefully take in the years to come. Following his discussion of the origins and development of the 'Law and Development' movement, which first suggested the need to understand the legal dimension of urban development, McAuslan focuses on the main issues that have dominated urban legal research to date. These are land management and housing in informal settlements in Latin America and Asia; customary tenure in the South Pacific and Asia; and 'formal' or 'official' legal issues including the operation of traditional Town and Country Planning Laws in Africa and compulsory acquisition of land in both Asia and Africa.

McAuslan then offers a general assessment of urban legal research, suggesting that researchers should extend the critical Latin American tradition to Africa and Asia. There is an urgent need for further research, as law pervades urban development, urban management and the processes of urbanization. The central issue of the current research agenda is that of governance, including the development and organization of processes and procedures for managing a city and its activities. On the basis of his extensive international experience in dealing with urban legal issues, McAuslan is convinced that the main challenge is the development of legitimacy in urban governance.

Nine case studies follow McAuslan's overview. Contributors naturally focus on those issues which are more significant to their own research interests, but the general framework mentioned in the first section of this introduction underlies the formulation of all the chapters.

In Chapter 3, Ayse Yonder discusses the development of informal settlements resulting from the double standards which have long prevailed in Turkey's housing policy. She describes the structure of Istanbul's land and housing markets, emphasizing the importance of illegal settlement processes in the provision of access to land and housing for low-income groups and in the growth of the overall urban land supply. She goes on to discuss the evolution and implications of government policies relating to informal settlements since 1946. Criticizing the scant attention given to low-income housing needs, she defends the need to increase the supply of affordable and serviced land in order to guarantee the sustainability of the city as a whole.

Chapter 4, by Omar Razzaz, discusses property disputes resulting from the absence of ownership rights in Jordan. It highlights the functioning of illegal markets and conflict resolution in cases of illegal subdivision and the subsequent sale of individual housing plots. While corroborating the hypothesis that formal legal rules and procedures fail to provide fair principles for dispute settlement, thus generating the proliferation of informal rules, Razzaz suggests that the development of such informal rules have to be understood in their intimate, if contradictory, relation to the formal ones.

In Chapter 5, Amanda Perry examines the role of law in the major issues raised by urban growth in Bangalore, India: the provision of housing, regulation of land use, protection of the environment and provision of adequate levels of infrastructure and civic amenities. Arguing that law must be considered an integral part of the process of urban development, she demonstrates how, in the last instance, the law is a tool for the use of those who are most able to manipulate it – which, in India, rarely means the urban poor living in illegal settlements.

Urban legislation in the Philippines is the subject of Chapter 6, by Asteya M. Santiago. The author discusses in detail the range of policies and laws affecting illegal settlements in the country since the 1940s, and assesses their consequences. Although there is a wide range of legal provisions for improving urban living standards, urban legislation has failed to produce the intended results, especially in so far as the urban poor are concerned. Santiago argues that, although legal reform is undoubtedly important, it is the obstacles to the implementation of laws that most urgently need to be overcome.

In Chapter 7, Rogelio Pérez Perdomo and Teolinda Bolívar discuss the nature and implications of legal pluralism in the *barrios* of Caracas, Venezuela. Following an exploration of the meanings of illegality – its 'swings and roundabouts' – they proceed to challenge the mythical notion that living in illegal areas leads to violence. On the contrary, they suggest that, however precarious such forms of urban land occupation tend to be, they produce specific and to some extent positive and co-operative forms of conflict resolution which should be taken into account in promoting the reform of the official legal order.

In Chapter 8, Edésio Fernandes and Raquel Rolnik discuss the relation between law and the process of urban change in Brazil. Following a brief overview of the main characteristics of the country's urban order, they analyse the logic underlying the evolution of urban legislation from the viewpoint of two conflicting paradigms concerning the definition of property rights. They then evaluate the innovative chapter on urban policy approved in the 1988 Constitution, suggesting that, while it has the potential to become a new paradigm guiding state action and a new relationship between the state and society, especially with regards to landowners and illegal settlers, its translation into practice will depend on how far broader political changes manage to ensure increased popular participation in urban decision-making.

In Chapter 9, Antonio Azuela and Emilio Duhau evaluate the experience of land tenure regularization in Mexico, which has one of the most ambitious legalization programmes in the world. Following a description of the antecedents and major characteristics of this programme, they undertake an analysis of the role played by regularization in both the constitution of private property and the consolidation of public order, in the light of which they defend the importance of conferring property titles on the residents of illegal settlements.

Chapter 10, by Ann Varley, also concerns land tenure regularization in urban Mexico. It complements the previous chapter by tracing the workings of legalization as a strategy employed by the Mexican government to maintain political stability in urban areas. In seeking to demonstrate the political uses of illegality and legalization, this chapter challenges the narrow perspective adopted in much international work on the consequences of regularization for the housing conditions of the urban poor, which fails to acknowledge either dissent from the orthodox view that legalization promotes housing improvements or the political costs of this strategy.

In Chapter 11, Winnie V. Mitullah and Kivutha Kibwana examine the legal and policy framework guiding urban development in Kenya, with special emphasis on Nairobi. Following a brief description of urbanization in Kenya, they describe the rise and main characteristics of Nairobi's 'legal' and 'illegal' cities. Recognizing that the production of illegality has been historically linked to the needs of economic production, they believe that urban policies formulated to deal with the challenge of rapid population growth have failed to address the housing needs of the poor properly; it is in this context that they proclaim the need for an urgent reform of both policy and law in Kenya.

In Chapter 12, Stephen Berrisford examines the complex and extremely significant case of South Africa. Following a discussion of the nature of

South African urban law and the crucial role it played during apartheid, Berrisford evaluates the shift in urban policy resulting from the recent political transition and the main characteristics of the new legislation it has brought about. He then considers the many critical legal questions which are currently being discussed, especially those related to the constitutional protection of private property and to land use regulation. Berrisford suggests that, although there is consensus on the need to replace the previous legal framework, the emergence of a new, progressive framework is still dependent on the outcome of ongoing reorganization of social, economic and political forces.

The case studies are followed by chapters offering systematic overviews of the main research and policy themes raised by the book. In Chapter 13, Alain Durand-Lasserve draws on the previous case studies and his own experience of research on land regularization programmes throughout the world to identify the main trends and issues at stake. Durand-Lasserve discusses the main options for and limitations on management of the 'illegal city', including settlement integration policies, the importance of local government and the nature and role of formal laws. He proposes that the formal and informal orders should be reconciled within the context of a legal reform enabling new instruments and procedures to generate new socio-legal practices. This, however, depends on a broader redefinition of the conditions of urban management and the implementation of a decision-making process which takes into account the needs and demands of the urban poor.

Finally, in Chapter 14, Sérgio de Azevedo also looks at the previous case studies and focuses, from a political viewpoint, on the questions raised by Durand-Lasserve and some of the case studies concerning the democratic management of urban areas. Following a reflection on the role of the state in developing countries in the changing economic climate resulting from globalization and the widespread adoption of privatization policies, Azevedo discusses the potential of different forms of popular participation in city management. He then analyses the prospects for urban planning in metropolitan areas as well as the challenges facing the state in its efforts to devise appropriate legal strategies for intervention in urban areas. Azevedo emphasizes the original point raised by McAuslan: the main urban challenge is indeed the development of legitimacy in urban governance.

Themes for Further Research

As we have stressed, this book provides only a general introduction to the subject of law and urban change. While we have addressed several of its main aspects, we hope that the studies presented here stimulate further research into these and other issues.

Amongst the themes which deserve better understanding, we believe that more empirical studies should focus on the importance of the legal system, both formal and informal, for the internal workings of the land and housing markets. Special attention should be paid to the socio-economic and cultural implications of traditional legal instruments such as zoning and construction laws, including a critical evaluation of their underlying concepts and methodologies. In addition, the efforts that in recent years have been directed towards understanding the 'urban question' in the light of problems in rural land structure and development processes should be extended to include the relationship between urban and agrarian law.

Urban researchers should not forget that the phenomenon of illegality is not restricted to the urban poor: many illegal forms of land occupation and construction can be observed among the more privileged groups in society. What do they say about law, especially the role it plays in the allocation of urban space between different social groups? What reactions do they provoke, by the state and by society?

While many important studies have recently highlighted the gender dimension of the urban development process, they have not on the whole questioned the gender implications of the role of law in this process. We know little about how the impact of the issues discussed in this book varies by gender. Like some progressive urban research, some early feminist concern with equal rights saw legislation as the way to address the problem of gender inequalities; again, the role of law itself was not problematized. When it was realized that trying to impose legal equality on a situation of pre-existing social and economic inequality risked entrenching that inequality, some feminists adopted a sceptical or even cynical attitude towards the law. Just as some currents in critical urban research dismiss law as the instrument of a bourgeois state, some feminists regard it as irredeemably masculine, by definition a manifestation of male power. There is, nevertheless, a productive dialogue under way at present between critical legal theory and feminist perspectives which do regard the law as a valid subject of research and political debate; yet very little work has been done on housing or urban issues in this context. This is a field which demands attention in future research.

The same applies to the environmental implications of state intervention, through legislation and the enforcement of existing laws, in the processes of urban growth and change. The potential conflict between legalization policies and environmental protection, for example, deserves to be better understood, especially as the environmentalist stance has been frequently espoused by conservative interests opposed to regularization.

To stay with the theme of land regularization: there is by now a rich empirical literature to provide the basis for more comparative and analytical studies of what such policies really mean in practice. To what extent do they genuinely promote settlement consolidation and incorporation into the 'official' city, and the socio-economic integration of their inhabitants with the rest of the urban population? How likely are they to produce contradictory outcomes by encouraging further uncontrolled settlement or population displacement from areas that have been legalized? We may also question whether and to what extent they have contributed to structural changes in the official legal system and ideologies, or whether they are basically forms of short-term political accommodation.

Another central question concerns an apparent paradox. The studies presented in this book – like most studies on the subject of law and urban change – underline the need to redefine traditional urban property rights and ideologies to widen the scope for urban policy to improve living conditions for all of the city's inhabitants. As Sérgio Azevedo notes, however, most developing countries have recently been undergoing significant political and administrative reform in the context of economic liberalization and privatization policies. How can such policies be reconciled with a more progressive notion of property rights?

A better understanding of the role of judicial power is also of considerable importance. How has judicial power responded to changes in the legislative and executive branches of government? What exactly is the importance of 'die-hard' legal ideologies which still seem to restrict judicial interpretation of progressive legislation and social policies? Such questions raise the issue of legal education for legal professionals, law-makers and judges, as well as urban and environmental NGOs and government agencies. A failure to understand how law and urban change are connected is arguably to blame for much of the resistance, even on the part of 'progressive' organizations, to seeing law as relevant to their concerns. In this context, an interdisciplinary dialogue is needed: while legal professionals clearly need to understand more about the relationship between law and the city, urban researchers also need to learn to speak the language of jurists.

Last, but not least, we would stress the crucial importance of deeper reflection on the issue of law and urban politics. On the one hand, emphasis should be placed on examining the relations between central and local governments, and particularly the implications of decentralization for the legal aspects of urban management. On the other hand, and more importantly, we need to achieve a better understanding of recent trends in urban governance, including the experiences of participatory decision-making, and their implications for the reform of the urban and legal orders.

The studies presented here have demonstrated that, given the nature of the relationship between law and urban space, urban reform is to be attained only through a more encompassing and democratic political process. We believe that the fight for the approval and enforcement of a more progressive legal paradigm concerning access to urban land and housing is a crucial element of that democratic process.

Note

1. Urban Policy bill, no. 5,788 (1990), Articles 2 and 3.

References

Azuela, A. (1989) *La Ciudad, la Propiedad Privada y el Derecho*, El Colegio de México, Mexico City.

Castells, M. (1972) *La Question Urbaine*, Maspero, Paris.

Durand-Lasserve, A. and V. Clerc (1996) *Regularization and Integration of Irregular Settlements: Lessons from Experience*, UMP Working Paper no. 6, World Bank, Washington, DC.

Fernandes, E. (1995) *Law and Urban Change in Brazil*, Avebury, Aldershot.

Hardoy, J. E. and D. Satterthwaite (1987) *La Ciudad Legal y la Ciudad Ilegal*, Grupo Editor Latinoamericano, Buenos Aires.

Lefebvre, H. (1968) *Le Droit à la Ville*, Anthropos, Paris.

— (1971) *Everyday Life in the Modern World*, Allen Lane, London.

— (1972) *Espace et Politique: Le Droit à la Ville II*, Anthropos, Paris.

— (1990) *Du Contrat de Citoyenneté*, Syllepse et Periscope, Paris.

Rolnik, R. (1997) *A Cidade e a Lei: Legislacão, Política Urbana e Territórios na Cidade de São Paulo*, Studio Nobel, São Paulo.

Santos, B. de S. (1977) 'The law of the oppressed: the construction and reproduction of legality in Pasargada', *Law and Society Review*, Vol. 12, no. 1, 5–126.

CHAPTER 2

Urbanization, Law and Development: a Record of Research

Patrick McAuslan

Traditions of Legal Scholarship

This chapter surveys the record of research on legal aspects of urbanization over the period 1960–90 and, in the light both of that survey and of current research and policy concerns, suggests some possible lines for future urban legal research.

At the outset, however, we must confront a paradox: in the real world of urbanization, law and urban development are almost synonymous, while in the world of research on urbanization, law has never been accorded a central role. We find in the colonial history of the developing world some form of legal regulation accompanying, indeed in some cases preceding, the coming together of people in a settlement which we can identify as the beginning of the modern city; examples may be found in every major world region. With urbanization now an overwhelming fact in virtually all of the countries of the developing world, we retain a remarkable faith in the efficacy of law as an indispensable attribute of it. It is commonly considered that, if only the correct legal framework for managing, controlling or facilitating urban development could be found, put in place and implemented, the problems of urbanization would be on their way to solution. Why, when practitioners have this long-standing faith in law as a tool of urban management, has there been so little investigation of this tool by the urban research community? A major factor, and one worth discussing in attempting to answer the question, is the nature of legal scholarship in general and its evolution within and in relation to the developing world.

Until some thirty to thirty-five years ago (longer in the United States) legal scholarship in the developed world of the colonial powers was overwhelmingly doctrinal in nature. This meant that legal scholarship discussed the actual laws, regulations and codes, and the statements by judges (judgments) on the meaning of those laws. That was the material that lawyers worked with in practice, so what they wanted and were prepared to pay for and recognize as scholarship were books and articles about 'the law' – a reasonably well-defined subject.

It is true that there were some differences in legal scholarship between civil law and common law countries, between France, the Netherlands, Spain, Portugal, Germany and Belgium on the one hand, and the United Kingdom on the other (I confine myself at the moment to the colonial powers), but these need not concern us here. The legal scholars from both systems had one attribute in common: the identification of the practising lawyer and judge as their reference points or role models, not the community of scholars (economists, political scientists, sociologists and the like). Legal scholars were interested in influencing the development of the law – that relatively self-defining body of concepts, ideas, words and phrases which had been constructed by lawyers in practice – and that meant influencing lawyers in practice. In turn that meant writing about the law in practice and nothing else. So most legal scholarship in the colonial powers of Europe was, by choice of its practitioners, more or less cut off from all those disciplines which were to form the foundation of research into the phenomenon of urbanization. Furthermore, those disciplines themselves acquiesced in the approach to law put forward by legal scholars: that it was an unproblematic phenomenon which had no connection with the social sciences, and which could be understood only through doctrinal analysis proffered by professional lawyers.

At the same time as this model of legal scholarship was emerging in the mid-nineteenth century, the role of law in the development of European towns and cities was becoming firmly established. Urban local governments were being established by law; public health legislation was being introduced and, as gas and electricity were developed, so a legal framework was built for their use and management in urban areas. The growth of urban transport contributed to the development of the law relating to contracts and civil wrongs (tort) as well as to regulatory law. The transition from a rural agricultural to an urban industrial society, led by the United Kingdom in the nineteenth century but followed rapidly by other European countries, was also the transition from a minimal state, and therefore minimal law and lawyers, to the modern regulatory state, with its plethora of laws and a formal legal profession.

This, then, was the model imposed on colonial possessions in Africa and Asia in the nineteenth and early twentieth centuries, and the model that was followed in Latin America: formal laws which provided the legal foundations for urban settlements, and doctrinal legal scholarship which provided an interpretation of those laws within the restricted intellectual framework discussed above. In many cases the laws governing urban activity – industrial, commercial, social and so on – were copied from the laws of the metropolitan country or were applied directly, so that any colonial legal scholarship, to be taken seriously, had necessarily to follow the same intellectual traditions as that of the metropolis. Probably the best example of this comes from the Indian sub-continent where, following the introduction of codified versions of parts of the English common law in the 1870s and 1880s, legal texts began to appear, sometimes co-authored by English and Indian lawyers, consisting of commentaries on the new codes, commentaries which included discussions of the extent to which English cases, applying principles of English common law, could be used to interpret a code based on that common law. The books did not (and still do not) include discussions of the appropriateness of imposing English common law on Indian society. This approach to legal scholarship in India, Pakistan and Bangladesh is still dominant.

Presented with such unpromising legal scholarship, it is not surprising that writing on the colonies, whether undertaken in the metropolis or in the colonies themselves, which started from a different intellectual tradition – anthropological, economic, geographical – should leave the law alone. It was a 'given', much like the 'given' of the colony itself, and there was plenty of indigenous material to be investigated and written up without reference either to the law or to the existence of the colony.

The case of the anthropological perspective is of particular interest. Anthropologists came early to the field of social scientific scholarship in the colonies (indeed, they were often employed by colonial authorities) and, in investigating 'tribal' or 'primitive' or 'traditional' societies, recorded customs and practices governing social conduct and public affairs which to the uninitiated might seem deserving of the name of law. That was indeed the name given by the anthropologists to these customs and practices. The corollary of this was that these 'laws' should receive some recognition from the colonial authorities and that in turn might mean that traditional societies could protect themselves by reference to their 'laws' against the depredations of the colonial authorities. Help was at hand. These were not really 'laws', said the lawyers; at best they were customs – and they began to be called customary law – which were subordinate to, and subject to being overridden or ignored by, 'the law', that is, the formal laws introduced by the colonial authorities. Anthropological work on customary law was thus relegated to the status of social science, rather than elevated to the status of legal scholarship, and could therefore safely be ignored by the practising lawyer. To the extent that it was referred to by the formal legal system, reference was made in connection with the colonial administration of traditional rural society; it did not impinge on urban administration.

We turn now to the American traditions of legal scholarship. These have had a profound effect on legal scholarship in general in the last thirty years or so, and in particular on developing world legal scholarship. The approach to legal scholarship and education in the USA, which derived its legal system from the common law traditions of England, began to diverge from the traditions of English legal scholarship and education. There was a greater willingness on the part of American lawyers to investigate and write about non-legal phenomena and ideas, and to incorporate these into their legal writing. There was a willingness to 'go behind' the words of the judges and investigate what 'really' made them decide cases as they did; the movement was called 'legal realism' when it emerged in the 1930s. There was, in short, less reverence for and more scepticism about the judicial and legal process in the USA than in England or in the other colonial powers of Europe. It was perhaps a reflection of the greater commitment to democracy in the USA, in both theory and practice, than existed in Europe including the UK.

This more open, social-science-oriented, approach to legal scholarship initially had little effect on European legal scholarship, and even less effect on legal writings in and about the colonies in Africa and Asia. It had little effect also in Latin America, which continued to regard the European tradition – doctrinal commentaries on the texts of the written laws – as being the proper approach to legal scholarship. In the 1960s, however, this new approach began to make inroads both on European legal scholarship and on legal scholarship in and about legal phenomena in the developing world. The 'Law and Development' movement was born.

The 'Law and Development' movement Several factors impelled this movement's development. In Latin America, the Alliance for Progress unleashed American lawyers, often academic lawyers, on countries within the region to investigate and propose administrative and other reforms in the public and private sectors. These lawyers approached their tasks as they would have done in the USA; the first step was to find out what was really happening behind the formal barriers of laws, administrative decrees and judicial statements. Where lawyers showed the way, others followed. Social scientists, also from the USA, began to investigate legal phenomena in the region.

In Africa, particularly in anglophone Africa, it was the coming of independence in the early 1960s and the establishment of law schools in newly independent countries which triggered the release of the new wave of legal scholarship. No law schools had existed in British colonial Africa; virtually all legal education had taken place in the UK, at either London University or the Inns of Court School of Law, the professional training school for barristers, or at both institutions. In the first decade of independence in the 1960s, university law schools were established in Tanzania (to serve that country, Kenya and Uganda), Ghana, Nigeria and Zambia. Of these schools, those in Tanzania and Ghana spearheaded the new approach to legal scholarship, both in terms of the orientation of the regular staff they attracted and of the welcome they provided for legal scholars from the USA, which helped to reinforce the socio-legal approach to legal scholarship.

In Asia, there was no cause similar to those in Latin America or Africa. American influence after World War II was the dominant one in the

Philippines, South Korea and Taiwan, and by the 1960s many lawyers in both practice and academia had been exposed to US legal education and scholarship, and many American lawyers had worked in those countries. Even so, there was no early flowering of the Law and Development movement there. In other Asian countries – those in the Indian sub-continent, Sri Lanka, Malaysia and Singapore – the English tradition was dominant, and legal education and scholarship, whether in the sub-continent where it had long existed or in Malaysia and Singapore where it was established in the 1960s, followed the more traditional English mode, little influenced by US-inspired ideas.

What are the characteristics of Law and Development research? In 1972 the International Legal Center, a New York-based Ford Foundation-funded body, invited 'a distinguished, international group of scholars – a Research Advisory Committee – to study the progress and problems of research on "Law and Development" ' (ILC 1974: 9). The report of the group, published in 1974 as *Law and Development: The Future of Law and Development Research*, is a useful starting point for non-lawyers to come to grips with the field. The committee opined that:

> Research on law would make a greater contribution to development if it … examined the social origins and functions of law, explored the relationship between legal rules and institutions and specific developmental efforts and examined the actual and potential impact of law on developmental goals … This type of study is concerned with what law does as well as what it 'is'.
>
> Law and Development research will involve other types of studies as well. Thus LD (Law and Development) researchers will be concerned with understanding the actual structure of decision-making in a society and evaluating the impact of this structure on developmental goals and processes. LD scholars will want to know who has access to legal processes and how decisions are actually made … [S]uch research could demonstrate the many ways in which legal processes can be used to distort development goals, delay the implementation of development programs and mask inaction and the maintenance of privilege behind a formal facade of change and legal equality.
>
> Unlike much doctrinal research, LD studies will look at all the 'legal communities' in a nation, not merely its formal national legal system. LD researchers will be concerned with … informal 'legal systems' like the unofficial court, that exist in many Latin American squatter systems on the one hand and the national law on the other. Finally LD research must be concerned with the impact of all forms of change on legal systems. (ILC 1974: 20–1)

Given this mammoth agenda, it is no surprise to learn that the committee considered that 'LD research must employ all the available methods of scholarship to understand what law does in society, and how legal processes and institutions function' (ILC 1974: 22).

Thus lawyers, while reaching out to those members of the social science community engaged in development studies research, at the same time claimed a rather special status. Law and Development research, as the above extracts demonstrate, was to be of direct relevance to the decision-makers and policy-makers; indeed, the researchers themselves might have to answer normative questions and resolve issues. In taking this stance, the committee was in fact following the traditional path of doctrinal legal scholarship from which, as indicated by its constant references thereto, it could not quite emancipate itself. The aim of legal scholarship is to influence the 'real' world of law; doctrinal scholarship aims at the professional lawyers in practice; Law and Development scholarship appears to be aimed at everyone else involved in the real world of law. Another, equally important, point was the recognition that Law and Development research was too important to be left to lawyers alone; social scientists (lawyers were apparently not social scientists) would need to be involved.

At the time, the report's reception was mixed. In retrospect, one can say that it was perhaps overly ambitious in trying to set out an agenda for research and in assuming that Law and Development studies were in some way special; that the 'ultimate test of LD research' was 'its capacity to contribute to the development effort'. In the twenty years since the committee deliberated, while studies on Law and Development have proliferated and are regarded increasingly as a sub-set of socio-legal research, and while journal outlets for their publication have likewise burgeoned, the aims of such research have become more modest. The practitioners of such activity do not see it as particularly special, nor indeed do the policy- and decision-makers. It has taken its place in the world of social science research and is judged on its merits. (For a recent discussion of the present state of Law and Development studies, see von Mehren and Sawers 1992.)

Notwithstanding this more realistic approach to Law and Development research, however, the criticism which the committee made of 'development researchers' – that they 'have failed to understand the potential contribution that legal studies might make to a better understanding of development' (ILC 1974: 17) – still holds true for research on urbanization. As will be discussed below, there is now a considerable literature of the Law and Development, or socio-legal, genre in the area of urbanization in all regions. This literature is rarely cited by social scientists. It would appear that the perceptions of law and legal scholarship on the part of urban social scientists have not adjusted to the new realities of urban legal scholarship.

Before consideration of the substance of the literature, some further points must be made on its classification. Thirty-odd years ago it was still possible to make two fairly clear-cut distinctions; first, between doctrinal legal scholarship and development legal scholarship; and second, between research by lawyers which addressed legal issues and research by social scientists which did not. Neither distinction is so clear-cut today and this makes the question of classification of the literature somewhat complex.

On the first distinction, doctrinal legal scholarship has taken on board some of the ideas, concepts and language of socio-legal scholarship. In literature (including reports from official law reform agencies) which is concerned primarily with expounding or describing the rules applicable to, say, compulsory acquisition of land, discussion will often be found of how the rules operate in practice, their justice and how they could be improved. The same point may be made about judicial decisions in the common-law world. They are now, to a much greater extent than is appreciated by the social science community, a major source of information of a socio-legal kind on many important societal issues. So doctrinal work on urban legal issues can no longer be so readily dismissed as irrelevant to an understanding of urbanization.

On the second distinction, a growing number of social science scholars now write about law and legal issues, not just mentioning law in passing while writing about something else, but making legal phenomena the central issue of their research, or at least recognizing much more explicitly than in the past that there are legal issues involved in their subject and that these must be confronted rather than brushed aside. Here, too, the socio-legal approach has been taken on board. While this is all to the good, it has made it much more difficult to determine what, for purposes of this chapter, constitutes literature on law and urbanization. I have decided to concentrate on literature culled from legal or socio-legal journals, because these sources are often neglected by urban social scientists, but I have also included literature on the margins from other journals.

One final point: this review must be seen as no more than an introduction to the field; its intention is to alert the urban social science research community to a field of literature, the product of research and scholarship over a thirty-year period which has hitherto been neglected, to the detriment of urban research as a whole. The survey of journals, books, official reports and documents from national and international sources has shown that urban land and housing are the subjects which have generated by far the largest amount of writing; these, then, will form the largest part of this survey.

Informal Settlements: Land Management and Housing

Latin America Lawyers and others have written a steady stream of articles on property rights and their protection in informal settlements. One of the earliest, on urban squatters in Peru, was by Kenneth A. Manaster (1968), a lawyer. The focus of his article was the Barriadas Law which, he concluded,

> combines traditional Civil Code and constitutional provisions with new legal

devices and modes of exercising government power – all for the purpose of giving effect to the policy choices which have been made regarding the redistribution of urban property rights in the Barriadas areas. In all its features, the Barriadas Law of Peru is a strong example of the important process by which law is adapted and developed ... The kind of pragmatic, imaginative adaptation of old legal concepts to new problems which we see in this law is the kind of first step which Peru and many other countries must take if they wish to begin to confront the squatter crisis effectively, peacefully and fairly within the framework of legal systems which are both progressive and just. (Manaster 1968: 60–1)

At one level, we would be right to compliment the approach and conclusions of a relatively youthful author; at another level, we cannot but wryly reflect that this article would be damaging evidence for the case against the LD research effort being able to achieve its 'ultimate test: the capacity to contribute to the development effort', for, thirty years on, precisely the same sentiments would not be out of place in respect of articles on urban squatters in many countries in the developing world.

Manaster's article was focused on a law, and may be seen as a species of doctrinal work, albeit one in which an effort was made to relate the law to its social context. A 'purer' example of a social scientific approach to legal research is to be found in the article by Kenneth L. Karst (1971) reporting on work that he, a lawyer, and two co-directors, non-lawyers, had done on the *barrios* of Caracas:

The study's main objective was to describe the norms and sanctions governing the lives of the barrio residents in four substantive areas of law. The legal areas chosen were, family obligations, rights in land and housing, protection of the person and simple contractual obligations. In addition the study examined a barrio institution called the junta – the leadership group that acts in many barrios as a resolver of disputes and a law making body. (Karst 1971: 551)

The article is a thorough and clear account of the development of tenure security in the *barrios*, which 'has made *barrio* housing a developmental success story in Caracas'. The security was not, however, founded on land titles but 'has instead been the product of an informal legal system in which rights and immunities are created and defined by such actions as the government's provision of water pipes or the junta's settlements of a boundary dispute'. This security in turn assisted in growth and reinforcement of a 'development mentality' among *barrio* residents – risk taking and self-improvement.

Almost a decade later, another socio-legal study of housing in the *barrios* of Caracas by Rogelio Pérez Perdomo and his colleagues came to much the same conclusions on the role of the *junta*. They termed the system:

an informal official system of regulation in the barrios. We use the term 'official' because those who run it and who prevent and resolve conflicts are public servants ... We use the term 'informal' to contrast it with the formal law which is easy to identify ... the system as it operates has solved many of the basic problems connected with dwellings, including security of tenure and ease of conveyancing. (Pérez Perdomo and Nikken 1980: 393)

A very different perspective on law in informal settlements was taken by Boaventura de Sousa Santos (1977) in one of the best known and most forceful pieces of work of this genre. The author, a professor of sociology, worked on the subject in Rio de Janeiro in 1970 for his doctoral thesis for the Yale Law School. The work is primarily on dispute settlement and was seen by the author as being a work of legal anthropology which, with other work of the same kind, 'may establish the basis for a social theory of legal pluralism and a social theory of legal reasoning and argumentation' (Santos 1977: 8). The thrust of the work, then, is not specifically the kinds of issues discussed by Karst or Pérez Perdomo and Nikken and their colleagues, but one inevitably learns a good deal about the way the informal legal system works in the *favela* and the way housing rights are protected thereby. In addition, this is a detailed study of legal pluralism, the co-existence within one urban society of more than one legal system. This raises many issues about the nature of urban society and the direction that policy should take in those societies where legal pluralism exists, as in many African cities. Despite the daunting length and, at times, language of the article, it is one to which all urban researchers should pay more attention.

This fruitful line of socio-legal research does not seem to have been pursued by lawyers in other regions, despite there being ample scope and, one would have thought, good policy reasons for developing it. As noted above with reference to Pérez Perdomo and Nikken's work, it continued in Latin America, and here it is pertinent to mention Antonio Azuela de la Cueva's (1987) work on the urban poor and the law in Mexico City. His general comments on law and urban research are worth quoting *in extenso*:

> The interdisciplinary movement that has developed in the field of urban studies during the last 15 years has on the whole ignored the law as one of the conditioning elements in urban social processes. This is true also in the specific area of low income settlements. Although case studies almost invariably include legal issues as part of the explanation of concrete situations, when it comes to theoretical, or in any other sense general propositions, legal categories disappear from the academic discourse; or else they appear in such an ambiguous way that they become blurred amongst other explanatory elements. (Azuela 1987: 522)

The paper containing this quotation demonstrates that the legal situation of land before its development will influence both the concrete forms of its appropriation for urbanization and the process of legitimization of property relations once the land is developed. A general conclusion follows:

This argument presupposes a more general issue in urban research today, namely the presence of law as a conditioning element in urban social processes ... [T]he concept of forms of legitimisation or any other category which tries to account for law as a conditioning element of a social process should be the subject of a theoretical debate ... it will have to be admitted that, contrary to the way it is usually regarded in the field of urban research, law is more than a mere reflection of actual social relations or an 'instrument in the hands of the state'. (Azuela 1987: 539–40)

His later work on legal and institutional aspects of urban land management in three cities in Mexico, undertaken for the UMP, brings out very clearly the interrelationship of law and urban social and political processes in the evolution of urban land management practices in Mexico (Azuela and Duhau 1989).

Asia We now turn to studies on urban land issues in Asia. First, reference may be made to the work of Alan Smart (1986; 1988) on the squatter property market in Hong Kong; one of the rare empirical studies outside Latin America which focuses on legal issues. In Smart's own words:

My research in Hong Kong suggests, I believe, that the legal aspects of transactions in squatter property are crucial and that in the absence of a legal foundation for such transactions, government policy towards squatter settlements plays a major role in structuring the squatter market. However, just to look at government policy and implementation is not enough, because without the regulatory actions of the squatter residents, a systematic market of the type found in Hong Kong could hardly exist without legal foundation. (Smart 1986: 42)

He later (Smart 1988) draws parallels between organized crime and squatter property in Hong Kong as examples of the informal regulation of illegal economic activity, describing the operation of the market for squatter housing and arguing that 'community norms' provide the backing for contract enforcement where such becomes necessary.

These conclusions are very similar to those arrived at in respect of informal settlements in Latin America, and lend added force to the arguments of those – Akin Mabogunje (1995) for example – calling for more effort to be made to base urban management on informal associations in African cities.

A second study comes from Pakistan. Written by Peter Nientied and Jan van der Linden (1990), it looks at the role of the government in the supply of legal and illegal land in Karachi. After examining the operation of both systems, the authors conclude that the government's involvement in illegal subdivision is very evident:

Firstly, the government through the Karachi Development Authority is actively promoting illegal subdivision by systematically failing to provide an alternative

... Secondly ... many highly and lowly placed persons in the government apparatus are crucial actors allowing and facilitating the system and profiting substantially by it. In the third place, the legal and bureaucratic systems are instrumental to – among other things – illegal subdivision of government land ... In conclusion, the non-functioning legal and the flourishing illegal systems for land supply neatly complement each other and the government is much involved in both. (Nientied and van der Linden 1990: 237–8)

As to why this system is allowed to continue, the authors point out that it relieves the public agencies of their obligation to provide plots while posing no threats to vested interests which, on the contrary, can make substantial profits from it, as can vast numbers of low-paid government employees. Finally:

to many politicians and government officers, the illegal subdivisions constitute an arena, where they can operate and get their votes and profits from without ever having to challenge the system or to make a fundamental demand. Since the whole operation is illegal, demands by definition are always for favours, rather than for rights. And because all the actors depend on each other, they are careful not to disturb the balance in the system. (Nientied and van der Linden 1990: 238)

The structure and function of the law, then, facilitates 'illegal' activity. A law designed and administered to curb illegality which did not at the same time ensure an adequate supply of low-income plots would, the argument must be, cause instability – lawlessness of another kind. This conclusion has important implications for law reform in the area of urban land management.

A further study which may be noted is by Harold Brookfield, Abdul Samad Hadi and Zahara Mahmud (1991) on Malay reservation land in Kuala Lumpur, in many respects a model socio-legal study (none of the authors is a lawyer). In the authors' words:

This book addresses two issues. The first ... concerns the effect of explosive growth of great cities on their rural peripheries ... The second issue is specific to Malaysia, even to Peninsular Malaysia though it has parallels in some other countries. It relates to peculiarities of the Malaysian land code in the context of *in situ* urbanization ... Codification of land tenure was an early object of the British colonial administration, initially with the purpose of creating a land market and of regulating and deriving revenue from that market. A concern that indigenous Malays were too readily parting with their land for cash under the new system led early in this century to the creation of Malay reservation areas, within which land could not be transferred to non-Malays. A significant group of these reservation areas is now caught up in the process of *in situ* urbanization in which the labour market knows no boundaries but in which the land code, until now little changed for more than 50 years has greatly restricted the land market. (Brookfield et al. 1991: v–vi)

The study then examines the effect of a specific legal restriction on land development and land markets, and on the people for whose benefit the restriction was originally created. The study was based on an examination of land records and on interviews with persons living in the Malay reservation villages. Its conclusions make sombre reading for the protagonists of control of land as a means of aiding the urban poor:

> It has been evident throughout this book that the continued application of the 1913 Malay land reservation system and of its amendments particularly that of 1933 has had unfortunate consequences. It has not protected the traditional use of Malay land as a basis for a valued lifestyle ... It has impeded rational planning and has permitted the creation of islands of depressed, even crowded and slum-like conditions within the urban and peri-urban fabric. Its sole principal benefit for the Malay landholders has been to offer them the security to house themselves for participation in the urban economy and to accommodate migrant workers and their families as tenants. The level of services and of planning control, has remained low so that insanitary conditions have come to prevail. (Brookfield et al. 1991: 169–70)

As the authors note, the practice of land reservation to protect indigenous peoples from exploitation by aliens was a common feature of British colonialism (although it must be noted that the aliens who were deemed likely to exploit indigenous peoples tended to be Asians rather than Europeans) and can be found for instance in Uganda, Tanzania and Fiji as well as in Malaysia. There has been legal writing on the subject but only with this study has an effort been made to understand the effect of the law on the people and their development. Further studies along these lines, particularly in Africa, are badly needed.

Customary tenure in the South Pacific and Africa The Brookfield study provides a way in to the consideration of studies, principally but not exclusively from countries in Africa, on the relationship between customary land tenure and urban development. This is not the place to discuss the intricacies of customary land tenure, but one or two points need to be made in order to understand the problems which arise from the relationship. First, customary land tenure is, for the most part, unwritten law which governs the relationship between a particular group (tribe) of people and the land on which they customarily reside or farm or pasture cattle. Second, there are long-standing disputes in this literature over the issue of whether, to what extent and subject to what conditions, customary land can be transferred temporarily or permanently away from the control of the tribe to some other person or group, all of whom, in the eyes of the controlling tribe, are alien. Third, there is the issue of whether customary land tenure and customary law disappear or are set aside when *in situ* urban development overtakes rural or peri-urban land subject to customary tenure. Allied to that is the fourth issue of the continuation in fact of unofficial customary tenure in towns and cities in Africa and elsewhere where customary tenure still exists.

Given the prevalence of customary land tenure in Africa, it is a matter for critical comment that so little work of a socio-legal nature has been done on these issues. Work has been done in francophone Africa, for instance by R. Verdier and A. Rochegude (1986), but lawyers in anglophone Africa have not hitherto been interested or indeed qualified (in terms of the research techniques) to undertake such work, while anthropologists have apparently preferred to work on these issues in rural areas. We therefore know far too little about the interaction between customary land tenure and urban development, although we do know something of its effects.

There are some studies on customary tenure evolution in an urban setting on which we may comment. John P. Lea (1983) looked at the position in Port Moresby, Papua New Guinea, concentrating on the 'participatory mechanisms which are necessary to resolve land and housing conflicts'. He highlighted the basic problem of urban land tenure in customary societies, first identified by H. D. Evers (1974) as being the difficulty for new migrants to a city in finding land for housing. Acquisition of customary land is restricted to members of the local lineage group, and the upshot is a variety of 'informal and usually "illegal" direct leasing arrangements with migrants as mutually agreeable means of overcoming the many formal constraints facing the landless' (Evers 1974: 55). He describes the tensions and difficulties of accommodation between migrants and landowners in Port Moresby and ends his article with some useful general points of which he says: 'The tentative nature of these interim conclusions are a reflection of the small amount of comparative research into the problems of incorporated urban customary land which exists. The historical precedents involved and the range of issues are not new as Cobban's investigations in Java have established' (Lea 1983: 69).

Another study, this time from Africa, to which the same comment applies is by August C. M. van Westen (1990), who examined the land supply mechanisms in Bamako, Mali. To do this he examined the formal French-inspired land tenure system and the customary land tenure system, and their interaction over the historical evolution of Bamako. He notes that the dualism in land tenure created by colonial land tenure legislation – a formal juridical system existing alongside tenure arrangements of pre-colonial origin – 'prepared the way for conflicts between the two modes of land supply when the city started to expand into rural areas, as happened after independence' (van Westen 1990: 89). There were in practice three modes of land supply after independence: the market mechanism, the public allocation of land and spontaneous settlements based on customary tenure. The public allocation of land which was reformed in 1978 had procedures which 'proved much too complex to be applicable', provoked fierce opposition from investors, 'stopped peripheral allotments – as it was supposed to do – but also had a devastating effect on the regular supply of new plots of the district of Bamako' (van Westen 1990: 95). In the case of spontaneous settlements which 'proved to be the most dynamic part of the urban fabric', van Westen observes that:

> By definition, all tenure practices in Bamako's spontaneous settlements are illegal. This does not mean that land rights are not observed in this area. Actually, customary ideas about tenure are usually scrupulously complied with. Squatting with that disregard of existing claims on land and invasions of the kind that are known from several Latin American examples are exceptional in Bamako. In principle, all aspirant house owners in the spontaneous settlements will proceed according to customary rule. (van Westen 1990: 97)

In other words, permission is obtained from the person who 'exerts traditional use-rights to the land'. In van Westen's view, the dualist system of land supply is likely to continue to exist in Bamako, but gradual regularization of the spontaneous settlements will occur with their resultant incorporation into the formal land markets.

The dualistic urban tenure system is a feature of all sub-Saharan African cities, as is their encroachment on to rural land at their periphery. One might therefore suppose that the situation in Bamako analysed by van Westen would also exist in other African cities. To suppose, however, is not enough. The problem is a major one and needs to be addressed by policy-makers. But in most countries, since researchers have not investigated the position, policy-makers are groping in the dark as to what to do, and often decline to recognize the continued presence and vitality of customary law. Here, then, is an area where research could have an immediate and beneficial impact on policy.

'Formal', or 'Official', Legal Issues

A much more voluminous area of legal research and writing on urban land issues is on what may be called 'formal', or 'official', legal issues. These embrace aspects of formal laws – rent control, town planning, slum clearance, land tenure and transactions – and, in terms of the nature of the legal writing, cover socio-legal and doctrinal aspects, and a mixture of the two. Here again there can be no claim to be comprehensive but rather to indicate the kind of work that has been done over the three decades covered by this survey.

Asia

Urban land issues in India Within Asia, emphasis will be placed on legal writings from India, since several collections of papers on urban land and legal issues have been produced there over our period. The first was *Law and Urbanization in India* edited by S. N. Jain (1969) for the Indian Law Institute (ILI), a pioneering collection of papers by lawyers, public administrators (both practising and academics) and planners. Topics included rent control, town planning, compulsory acquisition of land, land taxation, the administrative structure of urban development, industrial licensing, and aspects of labour and welfare. The overall conception of the collection – that law was an important instrument in the process of urban development and that there both could and should be developed a unifying conceptual approach to law in this area – was in many respects far ahead of its time. It is a matter of regret that law schools in India did not follow up on that initiative by developing courses and academic writing on urban law; when the National Law School of India University at Bangalore began to develop a course on law and urban development in the late 1980s, it had to start from scratch. Yet the outlines of research and education in this area had been shown twenty years previously.

Nine years after the ILI collection, H. U. Bijlani and M. K. Balachandran (1978) edited a collection of papers on *Law and Urban Land* for the Centre for Urban Studies (CUS), Indian Institute of Public Administration. The majority of authors contributing to this collection were not lawyers; they were practising administrators and planners from urban development authorities, local, state and central governments. The papers concentrated on the four areas of compulsory acquisition, town planning, land taxation and the recently introduced Urban Land (Ceiling and Regulation) Act 1976. The papers displayed considerable concern at the complexity of the law and the long-windedness of legal and judicial procedures – a constant refrain of urban administrators in India – but it too failed to spark any detailed socio-legal work on the actual operation of many of these laws in specific cities.

Three years later, the journal of the CUS, *Nagarlok*, devoted a special issue edited by T. N. Chaturvedi and Abhijit Datta (1981) to 'Town planning legislations [*sic*] and their implementation'. Again, the majority of contributors were practising urban administrators and planners as opposed to lawyers. The special issue recorded the proceedings of a seminar held to consider a report prepared by the CUS on 'existing planning legislations with the object of evaluating their effectiveness in facilitating the process of urban planning and implementation and for making suitable suggestions for formulating a sound legal structure for the town planning and development programmes in the country' (Chaturvedi and Datta 1981: editorial preface). This seminar, too, expressed concern at the nature of town planning laws in India but, in the absence of any detailed study of how the laws were used and abused, the overall impression of the collection is that of frustrated administrators wanting changes but lacking the detailed case that needs to be made for specific changes.

A decade later, two more collections of papers on aspects of urban land law became available, both being the product of seminars and workshops which took place in Bangalore (Bijlani et al. 1992). The first seminar, held in June, was the last in the series on urban land issues sponsored by the National Housing Bank, the Ministry of Urban Development and USAID, and concentrated on four themes, on each of which papers were prepared: namely, land assembly, land transfers, land taxation, and planning and development legislation. Each theme paper itself covered a wide range of topics so that the seminar was in a position to review the legal framework on urban land management in India on a more comprehensive basis than had been the case for many years. As with the other meetings which had led to the collections noted above, the majority of participants in this seminar were practising administrators rather than lawyers or academics. The focus was on the need to move away from a compartmentalized approach to urban land reform: 'The complexities of urban land management tasks are such that a comprehensive view must be taken on the overall urban development purposes and legislative reforms must be conceived with due regard for the same. This would help eliminate the built-in conflict' (Bijlani et al. 1992: 100).

The second Bangalore workshop, held in December 1992, was a joint activity of the UMP and the National Law School of India University, one of the few law schools in India committed to the development both of the socio-legal approach to legal research and education, and to the study of urban law. As might be expected, a higher proportion of lawyers were present at this workshop, but the majority of participants were still urban administrators and planners.

A general reflection on all these collections may be made. None of them contained any papers which investigated the law in action, what was really happening on the ground. Administrators' reflections and frustrations are a necessary but not sufficient basis for a full understanding of the role of law in urban land management. Reform can be effective only if it is based on a thorough understanding of the real world of urban law.

A good illustration of the kind of work of which more needs to be done in India is provided in a recent article by Rejan K. Gengaje (1992). The summary of the article indicates its purport:

> This article examines the growing concern for urban fringe land management in the light of the legal framework and the procedure for land transfer ... [A]s the public authorities in most of the growing cities in the developing world have been unsuccessful in supplying land for housing for lower income groups, the smaller lots outside the legal framework are gaining importance in city land markets. As a result large scale transfer of lands in the fringe areas are affected. In anticipation of future profits, land developers have engaged in malpractice, including the outwitting of legislative provisions, bribing of local officials and cheating landowners. Such land transactions undoubtedly exploit landowners

and defeat the objectives of the legislation meant to safeguard the interests of the ordinary citizen. This article looks at the fraudulent nature of such land transactions, along with the *modus operandi* of land dealers in the light of the current legal framework. (Gengaje 1992: 272)

The author sets out the steps which need to be taken to effect a transfer of land in Maharashtra State, and the laws (in tabular form) regulating land transfer in the state. He then examines, via the records and interviews, the actual processes of land transfers which have taken place. The author's conclusions and recommendations have a down-to-earth feel about them to which few of the papers in the collections referred to earlier can aspire:

> On the face of it the procedure for land transfer and for maintenance of village land records as evolved and governed by a plethora of enactments, as well as statutory bodies and officials, appear to be foolproof. However ... the loopholes in this system outnumber the safeguards. This emphasises the need for learning the different workings of both formal and informal market forces and their effects upon one another. (Gengaje 1992: 285–6)

Town and country planning law We turn now to consider some studies on town and country planning law, starting with the Malaysian town and country planning system. Two particular authors should be referred to here: David Willcox (1978) and Michael J. Bruton (1982). Both have acted as consultants in Malaysia on land policy and town and country planning, and take rather different positions on Malaysia's approach to the latter topic. Willcox draws attention to the long-standing and well-understood system of conditional titles in Malaysia which are granted under the National Land Code; his point is that the powers under the Code provide a better way to regulate land development than does the use of development control powers under the 1976 Town and Country Planning Act. Regulation through the powers of the landlord can be more effective and more flexible than regulation by public authorities under planning law.

Bruton is a planner and was one of the consultants used by the Malaysian government in the development of the 1976 Act which, *pace* Lik Meng Lee (1992), is very closely based on the reforms introduced in England in 1968. Bruton is naturally a protagonist of the 1976 Act and considered that, while it had had a slow beginning, it was proving a useful addition to the armoury of Malaysia's land use planners. Later studies, however, especially by M. K. Sen (1986) and Goh Ban Lee (1988), have suggested that the rigidities in the housing supply associated with the long and unpredictable regulatory process for developing land pushed housing prices beyond the reach of all but the wealthiest groups, even with subsidy.

Two further and detailed studies of the legal framework of the land use planning and management systems in, respectively, Pakistan and India, were commissioned by the UMP. They provide further evidence of the long, drawn-out process of obtaining permission to develop land in those countries whose planning systems are based on the British model. The Indian case study was conducted by Christopher C. Benninger and colleagues (1990–92) in respect of Maharashtra State, focusing both on the state in general and on three cities therein: Thane, Aurangabad and Kothapur. A history of town and country planning legislation in India and in Maharashtra State is combined with detailed discussions of the practical workings of the system and, in the third volume of the study, a detailed set of recommendations. The central theme of these is:

> to bridge the large gap between the existing needs and means of the people to increase procedural accessibility to the system and to relax the legal definitions of what can be considered permissible ... To this end, urban land management and development organization, implementation procedures and statutory instruments must be restructured. This restructuring will ensure that resources and efforts are channelled towards constructive development rather than towards the consumption of scarce resources in cumbersome administrative procedures, lengthy legal disputes, policing and costly procedural delays. (Benninger 1990–92: 8–9)

These recommendations are well thought through but the thrust of much work on urban land in India suggests that a good deal more than a reform of the town planning laws and procedures is needed to free up the process of land development.

The Pakistan study was undertaken by Shahid Kardar (1990) and was a case study of the institutional and legal arrangements for the administration of land in Lahore. This excellent study put the legal and institutional aspects of land development into the wider socio-political contexts of Lahore. Thus:

> [O]ver 95% of land in Lahore is privately owned. The structure of land ownership and the legislation governing land acquisition does not facilitate availability of land as a solution to the housing problem. In a situation of joint ownership of property, Islamic law of inheritance, family disputes and pre-emption rights recognised in law it becomes exceedingly difficult to sort out ownership rights – as there can be several claimants to the same area.
>
> ... Determination of market value of land and compensation for standing crops and buildings on land can become a complex and long-winded exercise in a fairly corrupt bureaucratic system, a social system that appears to encourage prolonged litigation and a judicial system characterised by the lack of infrastructure (personnel and resources) required for it to fulfil its obligations speedily and effectively. The cost in terms of energy time and finance are huge. (Kardar 1990: 5.3, 1.4)

Later on, the study explicitly makes the connection between the lack of access of the poor to urban land and the fact that the 'policy-makers come from middle class background. Because of their ideological leanings the policy structure that they formulate ultimately serves the interests of the dominant groups in society' (Kardar 1990: 1.10). Hence, when the author addresses possible reforms, he recognizes the connection between institutional and legal reforms on the one hand, and wider socio-political reforms on the other. Looking at the system from the top and from the formal perspective, these sentiments echo those of Nientied and van der Linden (1990) who examined the land development system in Karachi from a bottom-up, informal perspective.

Africa

Urban land issues There is a considerable legal literature of a fairly traditional kind on urban land issues in anglophone Africa. For the most part, these are textbooks on 'modern' statutory land law and planning law which operates in urban areas but, though traditional in approach, some of these works are of considerable scholarship which should not be ignored either in any survey of urban legal research or by urban researchers in general who wish to examine urban land issues. B.O. Nwabueze (1972) on Nigerian land law, and Kwamena Bentsi-Enchill (1964) on Ghana land law are two works which may be noted.

There is, however, a different stream of texts which deserves a fuller mention. First, there are those books written by Rudi W. James (1971; 1987) on Tanzanian and Nigerian land law and policy. As the titles imply, these books attempt to go behind the laws of the countries concerned and discuss the reasons for the radical policy and legal changes which those countries had introduced into their land tenure arrangements. Probably the better of these books is James's first, from 1971, on Tanzanian land law and policy. Through its use as a legal education textbook it had a considerable effect on the way lawyers and policy-makers viewed land tenure issues in Tanzania.

The other more policy-oriented works to which attention may be drawn are those from Ghana, in particular the work of Samuel K. B. Asante. His major work, *Property Law and Social Goals in Ghana 1844–1966* (1975), examines the evolution of customary land law in the light of the far-reaching social and economic changes which took place in Ghana. A major historical and scholarly work, it set a standard for legal scholarship on land issues not only in Ghana but for anglophone Africa generally which has not, alas, been emulated. It is no accident that the antecedents of Asante's book lie in work for his PhD in the Yale Law School, one of the major centres of the Law and Development movement in the USA in the 1960s.

In anglophone Africa as in India, reference may be made to several collections on urban, social or legal themes where aspects of land law are discussed. A collection of essays edited by James Obol-Ochola (1969), devoted specifically to *Land Law Reform in East Africa*, featured only one paper on urban land tenure, a disappointing survey of the position in Uganda by E. M. S. Kate. Much more interesting is the paper by Lal Patel (1972) on legal and social aspects of landlord/tenant relations in Mombasa, where legal and social issues were discussed together and their inter-relationship clearly demonstrated.

A collection of papers dealing centrally with urban legal issues was that edited by George W. Kanyeihamba and Patrick McAuslan (1978). Eleven of the fourteen papers were by lawyers and among the topics covered were planning, housing, including housing finance, rent control, rural–urban migration and the administration of justice in an urban environment. The final paper, by the editors, discussed the prospects and problems connected with urban legal research. Some of its conclusions are worth highlighting. First, it noted that urban legal problems embrace more than the difficulties arising out of the operation of laws about planning, housing and land tenure in the city. If this present paper does not go much beyond those subjects, it is because, with limited exceptions (for example, some of the papers in the volume under review), lawyers have not in fact gone much beyond those subjects when writing about urban legal issues. The second conclusion was that 'lawyers cannot neglect questions of social justice, the allocation of urban resources and the need for fair administrative procedures in managing the urban environment' (Kanyeihamba and McAuslan 1978: 285). Third, it was stressed that, 'Emphasis needs to be placed on the interest of the urban poor and disadvantaged and how they are affected or ought to be affected, if at all, by the laws, the legal processes, the structures and powers which play roles in urban growth and management' (Kanyeihamba and McAuslan 1978: 287). Fourth, the point was made that the case for urban legal research would stand or fall on the quality of what was produced, and legal researchers would need commitment and a willingness to emancipate themselves from traditional modes of legal research.

Twenty years on, not much has changed. Many of the lawyer authors of those papers have left the academic world and are now in government or private practice. The political climate in Eastern Africa has not been propitious for research focusing on the urban poor and on the unequal application of the laws; but one cannot escape the feeling that more could have been done had the commitment and interest been present. One can, after all, point to critical work undertaken and published by other social scientists in this period – see, for example, the references in Halfani (1994).

The Land Use Act is a major and radical piece of reforming legislation in Nigeria which in effect nationalized all land in the country and placed its administration under public authority control. Not surprisingly, it has generated an enormous amount of literature, among which may be noted the collection of papers edited by J. A. Omotola (1982), which may be discussed in the general context of work on the Act. The collection was principally one of legal papers, and, like James's work (1971) and the work of other lawyers, concentrated on the Act and how it was being interpreted in the courts. What is interesting, however, is that lawyers in Nigeria have not attempted in any systematic way to go behind the words of the Act and write about the reality: how developers (with the aid of lawyers) get around the Act, and the practical effect of the Act on urban development.

Work along these lines has been done and one example may be given. David C. Williams (1992) set out to investigate the effectiveness of the Act in Oyo State in order to test the different propositions put forward by commentators about its significance for state–society relations in Nigeria. He used records of the Lands Office in Ibadan, the state capital of Oyo State, interviews with officials from the Lands Office and with lawyers, information from newspapers on who owns what lands in Nigeria, and survey data. Based on these sources, he concluded:

> The Land Use Decree provides a potentially important means for influencing state society relations via certificates of occupancy ... the regulatory control of the state bureaucratic apparatus has been extended down to one of the most intimate levels of social interaction. Well over a decade later, however, there is considerable evidence that most transactions in land continue to proceed outside of the authority of the states in Nigeria ...
>
> Those awarded certificates of occupancy seem to rely heavily on traditional rulers and customary court decisions in obtaining security of title ... [T]he manner in which both land administration and private transactions are now carried out brings to light new rules surrounding tenure that must be discovered by individuals seeking to adapt to the uncertain legal dispensation initiated by the Land Use Decree. (Williams 1992: 607–8)

The contrast between these articles and lawyers' work on the Land Use Act is both striking and painful. These pieces of research investigate the real world of the Land Use Act using techniques and information readily available to lawyers; indeed, some of the information comes from lawyers. Using their traditional techniques and skills, the lawyers produce information which is, to all intents and purposes, completely irrelevant to any attempt to understand the operation of the Act on land transactions, and completely irrelevant therefore to any policy debate on the reform of the Act. In this respect, legal writing on the Land Use Act in Nigeria resembles much legal writing on the Urban Land (Ceiling and Regulation) Act in India.

Town and country planning law Most of the discussion on research and publications on legal aspects of urban land issues in Africa has concentrated on land tenure matters. There are two other subject areas to which some attention may be given. The first is town and country or urban planning law; the second, compulsory purchase or eminent domain law. There is a considerable amount of writing by planners and other social scientists on urban planning in Nigeria, most of which acknowledges the existence of town planning laws and development control. Many of these papers do attempt to investigate and discuss the effect of development control on urban development, and come to the conclusion that development control has had a deleterious effect where it has had any effect at all, but that more often than not, development has proceeded in disregard of town planning laws. Among articles which may be referred to in this regard are those by Donatus C. I. Okpala (1984) and G. Omuta (1986). One paper which may be highlighted deals not with individual case studies of specific urban development but with the whole corpus of the law. This is by Thomas A. Gihring (1976), and it questions the whole elitist basis of town planning law in Nigeria. Gihring's argument is that there is a need to reform the basic town planning law on the basis of certain assumptions about Nigeria's future. These assumptions are that democratic ideals will prevail in society, an indigenous body of planning theory and practice will arise and, via the continuation of the federal system of government, the principle of local self-determination will be secured. He makes the point that:

> Development controls should not restrict development initiative, but rather should themselves adapt to the natural process of urban growth ... Both British and Nigerian experience has demonstrated that the cumbersome process of reviewing applications often results in curtailing development progress ... The existing legislation has achieved no higher purpose than the reinforcement of elitism in the exercise of power ... The law of non-accountability has produced the effect of withdrawal of the planning function from the realm of the public welfare. (Gihring 1976: 419–21)

This conclusion has wider import. The planning laws of most anglophone African countries are, like those of Nigeria, based on English models – with one important difference. Whereas in England the laws operate within and reflect the existence of a local government system where elected members play a crucial decision-making role, in many African countries local elected councillors have little or no say in planning decisions which are controlled by central government. Equally, there is no public participation in the making of plans, or of decisions on development control. The elitist nature of the planning law in Nigeria is therefore paralleled throughout anglophone Africa and has been extensively commented on by lawyers. Articles and reports which may be noted are those by William T. McClain (1978) on Zambia, George W. Kanyeihamba (1980) and H. McCoubrey (1988) on anglophone Africa generally, and Catherine Farvacque and Patrick McAuslan (1992). This universal elitism helps explain why so little fundamental reform of that law has taken place anywhere;

as in Nigeria so elsewhere, the elites are perfectly satisfied with a law which serves their interests.

Mention may also be made of the study commissioned by the UMP of the legal and institutional aspects of urban land management in Ghana, concentrating on three cities. This was undertaken by Ebenezer Acquaye & Associates and Kasim Kasanga (1990) and focused on both tenure and town planning matters, drawing attention to their interrelationship and their combined effect on land development. Disputes over tenure issues had rendered large amounts of land sterile; land could not be developed until ownership issues had been resolved and this could take years. Equally, the complex process of acquiring permission to develop land and acquisition of the land itself, which involved both customary and statutory authorities, added more years to the process. The study was a valuable addition to the literature on the law in action.

Compulsory acquisition of land One matter which crosses regional boundaries is compulsory acquisition of land and compensation therefore. An important and too little regarded study, one which attempts a global synthesis, is that on *Land Acquisition in Developing Countries* by Michael G. Kitay (1985). His introduction states: 'The primary purpose of this book is to provide models of land acquisition laws, policies, procedures and institutions. These models in the context of the inevitable urban population explosion are intended to stimulate dialogue that will lead to substantial reform of existing laws and institutions for land acquisition' (Kitay 1985: xvi). One of his hypotheses is that 'few developing countries possess adequate laws, procedures, policies, trained personnel or institutions capable of performing the land acquisition function in an effective fashion' (Kitay 1985: xvi). This hypothesis is borne out by several country studies contained in the book.

The most recent, and probably the most comprehensive, discussion of the processes of land acquisition under the Land Acquisition Act 1894 of India, a model for much legislation in anglophone Africa and Asia, took place at the first 1992 Bangalore workshop on the legal and institutional framework for urban land management in India. The deficiencies of the 1894 Act were rehearsed once again but, in keeping with the top-down nature of the whole series of urban land management workshops, there is absolutely no reference to the effects of compulsory land acquisition on the urban, or urban fringe, poor whose land or housing is to be acquired. One facet of the Indian work to which attention may be drawn is the sharp contrast between the administrative view of the Act, as typified in virtually all the writing to which attention has hitherto been drawn, and the legal view. This is summarized in a recent paper by M. P. Singh:

During the last decade, no serious difficulties have arisen for the state in its exercise of the expropriation power. Largely this is because most of the reforms likely to generate impassioned response had already been achieved, at least by statutory enactment if not in fact as well ... Inordinate delays are, at present, the most pressing cause of injustice both procedurally and even substantially. The frustration that delays can breed, has on occasion even spawned malpractice, as one or other of the parties attempts to bulldoze the case through completion. (Singh 1990: 55–7)

For the administrator, then, it is the law, lawyers and courts which are at fault; for the lawyer it is administrators and administrative procedures which are at fault, a classic situation where some empirical work on the operation of the law would seem to be very necessary for achieving some unity of policy on reform.

In African countries compulsory acquisition has always raised particular concern, since loss of land is regarded as a good deal more than merely loss of property, and the administrative procedures and practices for setting about the exercise have always left a good deal to be desired. Work on the law here falls into three broad categories: surveys of the relevant statute law, case studies of practice and, finally, policy-oriented discussion involving legal and philosophical issues. On the first category, three articles of considerable value may be noted: Charles McDowell (1975) on Nigeria; James Read (1975) on Kenya, Tanzania and Uganda; and Clement Ng'ong'ola (1992) on Botswana, Malawi, Zambia and Zimbabwe. This last is a particularly good piece of writing, combining a historical with a comparative survey of the law which will remain for some time an essential starting point for any discussion of the law or its practice in the countries covered by the article.

The second category of work may be instanced by two papers from Nigeria. The first is from the classic study by Peter Marris (1961) of rehousing in Lagos in the 1950s. One chapter deals with the slum clearance scheme in Broad Street, Balogun Street and Victoria Street. The intention of the scheme was to rehouse 200,000 people over a period of five to seven years. The chapter deals in detail with the actions of the Lagos Executive Development Board (LEDB), its proposals for compensation, for reallocation of plots to owners once the scheme was under way and for relocation. Despite the attempts to meet what the LEDB considered were the demands of the residents in the area, riots ensued once a notice setting out the objection to the scheme and the Board's answers were published. Some of the objections, particularly to the issue of compensation, highlighted the inadequacy and inappropriateness of the compensation offered. For some, the loss of their family land where their forebears were buried and where shrines to them existed as was the custom, was too much for them to bear: 'So there were many stories of old people who had died heartbroken within a few months of dispossession' (Marris 1961: 92). Notwithstanding the problem, the scheme went on and, according to press reports quoted by Marris, by 1958 people were clamouring for houses in Suru Lere where relocation had taken place.

The second paper is Francis Okafor's (1988) study of the resettlement of villagers from the site of Abuja, Nigeria's new capital; here again, speed of execution in resettlement was preferred to participation by the persons being dispossessed of their land. These studies draw attention both to the limits and to the importance of law. Law is a necessary but by no means sufficient precondition for fair administration of compulsory acquisition of land. Too often lawyers in their writing assume that a well-designed law is both necessary and sufficient. These case studies provide a useful antidote to that attitude.

A final piece of work in this second category is an interesting case study from Barbados. Written by Marva Alleyne, Arthur Archer and Gordon Walters (1984), it discusses the resettlement of a squatter community in Bridgetown to make way for the construction of a sewage treatment plant. It shows how a heavy-handed approach to forcible relocation produced a hostile reaction, not only from the community concerned but from several sections of the Barbadian community. A more participatory approach was then adopted, with the community being involved in the planning of the relocation and the facilities to be provided at the new site. Relocation then proceeded more smoothly and with greater understanding on both sides. The positive lessons of this case study could usefully be learned in many countries. Finally, the third category of work – policy-oriented, even polemical, papers – may be noted. These come from South Africa and the nature of the debate is well summarized in the editorial comment to the special issue of the *South African Journal on Human Rights* on 'Debating the land issue':

> The form and substance of a new legal order necessarily encompass all aspects of social existence and are not merely 'legal issues' to be resolved by lawyers. Legal considerations mingle with economic, political and historical facts and policies. The 'land' debate is a case in point. The 'right to land' involves consideration of the history of land dispossession; of the principle and modalities of affirmative action to redress past racially structured economic and political discrimination and of the impact of legally enforced racial geography. It also involves complex policy considerations in relation to land tenure … It raises new perspectives on the question of 'just compensation' for those who hold title, purchased in good faith as well as those who have been deprived of the rights to do likewise. (Haysom 1990: v)

The issue of 'just' compensation for compulsory acquisition is discussed by Keith McCall (1990). After setting out clearly the way in which the apartheid state expropriated, without compensation, land and homes from the majority for the benefit of the minority in the pursuit of apartheid in urban areas, McCall quotes the South African Law Commission's proposal that legislation may provide that private property may be expropriated 'against payment of reasonable compensation' and comments:

> I have heard it suggested in discussion that 'reasonable compensation' will not necessarily mean 'market value' in a South African context. This is because there will be insufficient funds to pay market value for the land needed to redress the overwhelming imbalance in land ownership and to provide land for housing ... Whatever course South Africa decides in the future, it should not ignore the unfairness of taking property without market-related compensation ... The burdens should not be placed unjustly and disproportionately on the shoulders of the few regardless of the historical reasons which may have led to their acquisition of land. (McCall 1990: 273–4)

Whatever one may think of the philosophy implicit in that statement, it shows a touching if misguided faith in the concept of 'market value'. Empirical work has shown only too clearly that, even in a society where legal procedures are observed, government officials can manipulate market value in their practice of expropriation so as to reduce compensation payable for the loss of homes.

This survey of research on legal aspects of urban land management in developing countries will conclude with references to two overview works. The first is by Patrick McAuslan (1991) and was commissioned as a background paper by the UMP. It reviews the legal and institutional framework in a range of countries, examines the systems at work, discusses the different public and private law tools available for urban land management and, after a discussion of the various options for approaching the issue of law reform, suggests the principles which should be used in any reform programme. Parts of the paper were incorporated in another UMP paper (Farvacque and McAuslan 1992) on reforming urban land policies and institutions in developing countries.

The second overview is more in the nature of a call to action; it is Scott Leckie's (1992) International Institute for Environment and Development (IIED) paper on housing rights and the role of international law in giving effect to those rights. This approach to urban shelter issues has now assumed considerable practical importance with the appointment of UN expert Rajinder Sachar, a former judge, by the UN Commission on Human Rights to review the position on housing rights and come forward with a programme of action to give them greater effect. Leckie's purpose is stated in his preface:

> This report seeks to provide an introductory and accessible framework for non-lawyers to be used in understanding and grasping the many diverse issues associated with housing rights as they are currently found under international human rights law ... This study aims to provide a variety of possible means of empowerment for the hundreds of millions of victims of housing rights violations (such as evictions) by revealing not only where housing rights exist and

which governments are bound by law to respect them but also how these can be enforced and protected. (Leckie 1992: I)

Leckie discusses what is happening on the ground, how housing rights came to be incorporated into the different human rights conventions, how housing rights can be enforced and what NGOs exist to assist with documenting their violation and their enforcement. Interestingly too, the report devotes a section to the role of lawyers in the enforcement of housing rights; it notes that in the future there will be

> a need for lawyers to develop, for instance, collective community knowledge and capacity to use the law with a social purpose or intent. Such a perspective stipulates not only a willingness on the part of the lawyer, but also the provision of traditional legal aid to impoverished peoples as well as building up their community strength, knowledge and capacity to use the law. (Leckie 1992: 69)

Apart from practical action on the ground, this approach to lawyering would also imply a more sociological and contextual approach to legal research and writing than is currently the case.

An Assessment of Urban Legal Research

Although, for reasons of language, fewer individual pieces of research from Latin America have been discussed than from Asia or Africa, the quality of what has been produced makes up for the lack of quantity. Whether the work has been by American legal scholars or by scholars indigenous to the region, the subjects that have been researched and the quality of the analysis and comment indicate that there is more receptivity to, and more understanding of, the relevance and importance of socio-legal research on urban issues in Latin America than in other regions. Why should this be so?

There are perhaps two principal reasons. The first lies in the influence of foreign models of legal education and research on indigenous systems; the second, in the evolution of the process of urban development. On the first point, the principal contrast is between the American and British systems. The argument is this: American legal education and research, with its emphasis on the need to 'go behind' the statements of judges and legislators to find out the underlying reasons for formal legal decisions, has had a greater impact on Latin American legal research than it has on either Asian or anglophone African legal research and education. The early socio-legal work of American legal scholars on law in informal urban settlements pointed the way forward for such scholars as Rogelio Pérez Perdomo, Boaventura de Sousa Santos, Antonio Azuela and Fernando Rojas. As already noted, however, the American influence has never been so strong in Asia and anglophone Africa. There, the dominant influence remains the traditional British approach and this tradition has continued to be passed on to law teachers and graduate law students from the Commonwealth through postgraduate legal studies in the United Kingdom and through the thin stream of visiting British law teachers who still venture into African and Asian law schools.

The second point concerns the nature of the urbanization process. Latin America is more urbanized than either Asia or Africa. I would argue that there is a greater intellectual depth and sophistication in respect both of urban social movements and of research and writing about the processes of urbanization and urban development in Latin America than in either Asia or Africa. The process has been going on longer and has penetrated society more deeply; it should not therefore be surprising, and it certainly reflects no discredit on scholars in Africa and Asia, if research and writing about the process reflects that greater depth of societal penetration. Since legal scholars and lawyers in practice are a part of society themselves, they reflect and demonstrate this deeper penetration; they have perceived the need to address the urban question in their writing and their work, and bring to bear on the issues a greater – one might almost say, a more natural – awareness of their urban background and culture than is the case with their counterparts in Asia or Africa. I would not wish to be misunderstood on this. Much valuable work from which a great deal can be and has been learned has been undertaken in Africa and Asia, and this work can and should be built on. My point is really directed to the fundamentals of this whole research exercise: who can learn what from whom? In a process of the cross-fertilization of ideas, approaches, methodologies and assumptions, in which direction should the flow move? In respect of urban legal research, I would answer: from Latin America towards Africa and Asia.

A Research Agenda

Two arguments may be advanced as to why urban legal research should be supported. First, while there can be no claim that the material discussed in this chapter is comprehensive, the evidence shows that what has been produced over the last thirty to forty years is a considerable body of work, covering many areas of importance. Rather than turn away from this body of work, we should bring it into the fold of social scientific urban research and support it both intellectually and financially together with other social scientific disciplines.

Second, as other research reports have acknowledged, law pervades urban development, urban management and the processes of urbanization. If so much of this law is perceived to be unsatisfactory and in need of radical reform, does it make sense to put obstacles in the way of learning more about what makes laws unsatisfactory, or satisfactory; where they seem to work or not to work; and how they can be put to more equitable and efficient use? In particular, support from urban legal research in the developing world will facilitate the South–South two-way learning process in law and law reform, and will possibly reduce the North–South one-way tutelage process.

What, then, should be supported and how? What should be the future research agenda? I would argue that it has to be related to the wider issue of the urban agenda as a whole. What are the crucial urban issues facing governments, both local and national, and people in the cities of the developing world? Urban legal research, no less than urban research as a whole, has to have regard for those issues and has to locate its agenda within that context.

From the perspective of a legal academic manqué who was for three years a participant-observer of a programme directed to assist the improvement of urban management in the developing world, I have at one and the same time an advantaged and a biased viewpoint. I was on the inside but was concerned with only one view of the cathedral while there. Due notice must be taken of that. With this caveat on the record, I suggest that the central urban issue for the foreseeable future is governance: the development of processes and procedures for managing a city and its activities which have at their core the participation and involvement of all citizens and their organizations; which provide for transparency and accountability; which aim to facilitate sustainable economic activity yet monitor and regulate it in the interests of environmental and social protection; and which develop and assist in the development of practical programmes for tackling urban poverty and restoring effective citizenship rights to the urban poor. In a word, the urban challenge is the development of legitimacy in urban governance.

In this context, the next question is: what is the the role of lawyers in the development of an urban governance of sustained legitimacy? Simply, to develop innovative legal frameworks and processes to enable a participatory form of urban government to be established; and to operate, establish and implement a framework for the right of citizens to basic services, and the responsibilities of providers to set up mechanisms to enforce those rights and responsibilities; to construct regulatory mechanisms which ensure transparent, accountable and effective administration and management; to provide a legal framework within which economic activities can be conducted with due regard for public health, public safety and environmental protection; and finally to provide, or join with others in providing, legal services to all citizens to enable them to enjoy in equal measure the facilities, rights and urban services available in the city.

This is a substantial yet practical agenda. It provides the entry point for urban legal research as we head towards the next millennium. On every one of the tasks outlined in the preceding paragraph, much more needs to be known about what works, what does not and why, before realistic proposals for reform can be put forward. More work needs to be done on rights to urban services to build on the pioneering work of Leckie. More work needs to be done to flesh out the ideas of Mabogunje (1995) for locating more of the urban governance tasks for African cities in institutions such as Hometown Voluntary Associations. What roles do non-governmental organizations have at present, especially in informal settlements? What framework of law and customs at present apply and can these be built on?

The work of Pérez Perdomo and Nikken (1980), Smart (1986) and Burman and Scharf (1990) are models to follow here. Where can we find modern regulatory mechanisms which seem to work quite well and appear to be the keys to success? How can access to justice for the urban poor be made more of a reality? Is the way forward the provision of fairly traditional legal aid services such as are described by Olukunke A. Bowen (1987) and Murtaza Jaffer (1989) in African cities or is a more innovative approach such as is discussed by Fernando Rojas (1988) more likely to succeed? What could be transplanted and subject to what limitations?

These are just a few of the more obvious issues on the face of the practical agenda outlined above. But there are less obvious issues which also need to be addressed and which are, when properly understood, also of a practical concern. Let us recall Azuela's and Duhau's identification of: 'a more general issue in urban research today, namely the presence of law as a conditioning element in urban social processes ... The concept of forms of legitimation or any other category which tries to account for law as a conditioning element of a social process should be the subject of a theoretical debate' (Azuela and Duhau 1989: 38). Their point is that law has too often been taken for granted as a relatively unproblematic phenomenon in urban social processes; or it has been ignored altogether. Law needs to be seen as an important, if not on occasions a central, determinant of the form and operation of urban social, economic and political processes. A deeper, more theoretical, understanding of law is a *sine qua non* for all social scientists who try to make sense of the role of law in urban processes of all kinds. This is not a luxury: it is a necessary precondition for understanding the present and formulating future legal processes and frameworks.

There is a sense of urgency about this agenda. In the 1960s there was, as David Trubek and Marc Galanter (1974) have pointed out, a somewhat naive belief in Western aid circles that the transplant of a law from the West where it worked well (the assumption was always that it had worked well, even if little research could be adduced to support such an assumption) to a developing country, would in some mysterious way result in the same 'success' being replicated. This has rarely happened, and much research has been devoted to showing why and how it does not. Alas, the lessons of this research are in danger of being ignored. In pursuit of such policies as deregulation and privatization, both of which are being urged on city and national governments in the developing world as appropriate solutions to urban management problems, legislative and other law-based models from the West are being touted as equally appropriate to adopt. They are unlikely to be any more successful this time around than before. Whereas the last time, research followed the introduction of the law, this time around, with a much better intellectual resource base in the South, it will be essential to ensure that research precedes the intro-duction of the law and is intellectually persuasive enough to ensure that any law that is introduced takes full account of existing urban processes. Such research must be grounded in a defensible theory.

Conclusion

It must be reiterated that this survey cannot be seen as comprehensive. It is an attempt to introduce urban social scientists, and legal scholars who would not regard themselves as urban social scientists, to a hitherto neglected but none the less fairly substantial body of work on urban law. The survey concludes that, though uneven in quality and range, this work is of sufficient magnitude and merit to warrant both being taken more seriously by the urban research community, and being given further support as part of the general support for urban research in the developing world. There is now a greater appreciation of the intellectual and practical merits of socio-legal research among lawyers the world over, so there is a better likelihood now than was the case thirty years ago that urban legal research will have practical as well as intellectual pay-offs. There is no necessary conflict, therefore, between supporting socio-legal and traditional legal research into urban legal phenomena, and urban legal issues of concern to practising lawyers and urban policy-makers. For this to become a reality, however, there is a need not only for support from donors for such research but also support from the urban research community itself, as well as a coming forward by and commitment from the community of legal scholars in the developing world.

Note

This chapter was originally written as part of a Ford Foundation-funded project and published in R. Stren and J. K. Bell (eds) (1995) *Urban Research in the Developing World. Vol. 4: Perspectives on the City*, Centre for Urban and Community Studies, University of Toronto, Toronto.

References

Acquaye, E. & Associates and K. Kasanga (1990) *Institutional Legal Requirements for Land Development in Ghana*, UNCHS, Nairobi.

Alleyne, M., A. B. Archer and G. Walters (1984) 'The resettlement of residents from Emmerton, Bridgetown, Barbados', *Environments*, Vol. 16, no. 3, 162–70.

Angel, S., R. W. Archer, S. Tanphiphat and E. A. Wegelin (eds) (1983) *Land for Housing the Poor*, Select Books, Singapore.

Asante, S. K. B. (1975) *Property Law and Social Goals in Ghana 1844–1966*, Ghana University Press, Accra.

Azuela, A. (1987) 'Low income settlements and the law in Mexico City', *International Journal of Urban and Regional Research*, Vol. 11, no. 4, 522–42.

Azuela, A. and E. Duhau (1989) *Institutional and Legal Arrangements for Administration of Land Development in Urban Areas: the Mexican Case*, Report submitted to UNCHS, Nairobi.

Benninger, C. C. (ed.) (1990–92) *Applications of Land Regulations and Development Control Mechanisms in India: The Maharashtra Case*, 3 vols, Centre for Development Studies and Activities, Poona, India.

Bentsi-Enchill, K. (1964) *Ghana Land Law: An Exposition, Analysis and Critique*, Sweet and Maxwell, London.

Bijlani, H. U. and M. K. Balachandran (eds) (1978) *Law and Urban Law*, Centre for Urban Studies, Indian Institute of Public Administration, New Delhi.

Bijlani, H. U., P. S. N. Rao and M. Desbandhu (eds) (1992) *Report of the Regional Policy Seminars on Urban Land Issues in India*, National Housing Bank, New Delhi.

Bowen, O. A. (1987) 'An operational assessment of the Nigerian legal aid scheme', in J. A. Omotola and A. A. Adeogun (eds), *Law and Development*, Lagos University Press, Lagos, 259–80.

Brookfield, H., A. S. Hadi and Z. Mahmud (1991) *The City in the Village: The In-Situ Urbanization of Villages, Villagers and their Land around Kuala Lumpur, Malaysia*, Oxford University Press, Singapore.

Bruton, M. J. (1982) 'The Malaysian planning system: a review', *Third World Planning Review*, Vol. 4, no. 4, 315–34.

Burman, S. and W. Scharf (1990) 'Creating people's justice: street committees and people's courts in a South African city', *Law and Society Review*, Vol. 24, no. 3, 693–744.

Chaturvedi, T. N. and A. Datta (eds) (1981) 'Town planning legislations and their implementation', *Nagarlok*, Vol. 13 (Special Issue).

Evers, H. D. (1974) 'Changing patterns of Minangkabau urban land ownership', *Bijdragen tot de Taal-Land-en Volkenkunde*, Vol. 131, 107.

Farvacque, C. and P. McAuslan (1992) *Reforming Urban Land Policies and Institutions in Developing Countries*, UMP Paper no. 5, World Bank, Washington, DC.

Gengaje, R. K. (1992) 'Administration of farmland transfer in urban fringes: lessons from Maharashtra, India', *Land Use Policy*, Vol. 9, no. 4, 272–86.

Gihring, T. A. (1976) 'From elitism to accountability: towards a re-formation of Nigerian town planning law', *Quarterly Journal of Administration*, Vol. 10, no. 1, 411–21.

Halfani, M. (1994) 'Urban research in Eastern Africa: Tanzania, Kenya and Zambia – towards an agenda for the 1990s', in R. Stren (ed.), *Urban Research in the Developing World. Vol. 2: Africa*, Centre for Urban and Community Studies, University of Toronto, Toronto, 113–91.

Haysom, N. (1990) 'Editorial comment', *South African Journal of Human Rights*, Vol. 6, no. 2, v–vi.

ILC (International Legal Center) (1974) *Law and Development: The Future of Law and Development Research*, Scandinavian Institute of African Studies, Uppsala.

Jaffer, M. (1989) 'The role of legal aid in the administration of justice', in L. G. Muthoga (ed.), *Law and Society*, International Commission of Jurists, Nairobi, 68–73.

Jain, S. N. (ed.) (1969) *Law and Urbanization in India*, N. M. Tripathi and Indian Law Institute, New Delhi.

James, R. W. (1971) *Land Tenure and Policy in Tanzania*, University of Toronto Press, Toronto and Eastern Africa Literature Bureau, Nairobi.

— (1987) *Nigerian Land Use Act: Policy and Principles*, University of Ife Press, Ile-Ife.

Kanyeihamba, G. W. (1980) 'The impact of received law on planning and development in anglophonic Africa', *International Journal of Urban and Regional Research*, Vol. 4, no. 2, 239–66.

Kanyeihamba, G. W and P. McAuslan (eds) (1978) *Urban Legal Problems in Eastern Africa*, Scandinavian Institute of African Studies, Uppsala.

Kardar, S. (1990) *Institutional and Legal Arrangements for Administration of Urban Land: The Case of Lahore*, UNCHS, Nairobi.

Karst, K. L. (1971) 'Rights in land and housing in an informal legal system: the barrios of Caracas', *American Journal of Comparative Law*, Vol. 19, 550–74.

Kate, E. M. S. (1969) 'The relevance and implications of land tenure to urban development in Uganda', in J. Obol-Ochola (ed.), *Land Law Reform in East Africa*, Milton Obote Foundation, Kampala, Uganda, 297–302.

Kitay, M. G. (1985) *Land Acquisition in Developing Countries: Policies and Procedures of the Public Sector*, Oelgeschlager, Gunn and Hain in association with Lincoln Institute of Land Policy, Boston.

Lea, J. P. (1983) 'Customary land tenure and urban housing land: partnership and participation in developing societies', in S. Angel, R. W. Archer, S. Tanphiphat and E. A. Wegelin (eds), *Land for Housing the Poor*, Select Books, Singapore, 54–72.

Leckie, S. (1992) *From Housing Needs to Housing Rights: an Analysis of the Right to Adequate Housing under International Human Rights Law*, International Institute for Environment and Development, London.

Lee, G. B. (1988) 'The future of urban planning in Malaysia', *Habitat International*, Vol. 12, no. 4, 5–12.

Lee, L. M. (1992) 'Town planning law in Malaysia', *Habitat International*, Vol. 15, no. 4, 105–14.

McAuslan, P. (1991) *Institutional/Legal Options for Administration of Land Development*, UNCHS, Nairobi.

McCall, K. (1990) 'The use of expropriation to bring about a re-distribution of land in South Africa – with particular reference to "group areas", "homelands" and "housing requirements"', in G. M. Erasmus (ed.), *Compensation for Expropriation: A Comparative Study. Vol. 2*, Jason Reese, Oxford, 245–74.

McClain, W. T. (1978) 'Legal aspects of housing and planning in Lusaka', in G. W. Kanyeihamba and P. McAuslan (eds), *Urban Legal Problems in Eastern Africa*, Scandinavian Institute of African Studies, Uppsala, 63–84.

McCoubrey, H. (1988) 'The English model of planning legislation in developing countries', *Third World Planning Review*, Vol. 10, no. 4, 371–87.

McDowell, C. M. (1975) 'Compensation for compulsory acquisition of land in

Nigeria', in J. F. Garner (ed.), *Compensation for Compulsory Purchase: A Comparative Study*, UK National Committee of Comparative Law, London, 107–26.

Mabogunje, A. L. (1995) 'Local institutions and an urban agenda for the 1990s', in R. Stren and J. K. Bell (eds), *Urban Research in the Developing World. Vol. 4: Perspectives on the City*, Centre for Urban and Community Studies, University of Toronto, Toronto, 19–45.

Manaster, K. A. (1968) 'The problem of urban squatters in developing countries: Peru', *Wisconsin Law Review*, Vol. 1, 23–61.

Marris, P. (1961) *Family and Social Change in an African City: A Study of Rehousing in Lagos*, Routledge and Kegan Paul, London.

Ng'ong'ola, C. (1992) 'The post-colonial era in relation to land expropriation laws in Botswana, Malawi, Zambia and Zimbabwe', *International and Comparative Law Quarterly*, Vol. 41, 117–36.

Nientied, P. and J. van der Linden (1990) 'The role of government in the supply of legal and illegal land in Karachi', in P. Baross and J. van der Linden (eds), *The Transformation of Land Supply Systems in Third World Cities*, Avebury, Aldershot, 225–42.

Nwabueze, B. O. (1972) *Nigerian Land Law*, Ocean, New York and Nwamife, Enugu, Nigeria.

Obol-Ochola, J. (1969) *Land Law Reform in East Africa*, Milton Obote Foundation, Kampala, Uganda.

Okafor, F. C. (1988) 'Resettlement and ecological disruption in Abuja, Nigeria', *Land Use Policy*, Vol. 5, no. 2, 175–9.

Okpala, D. C. I. (1984) 'Urban planning and control of urban physical growth in Nigeria: a critique of public inputs and private roles', *Habitat International*, Vol. 8, no. 2, 73–94.

Omotola, J. A. (ed.) (1982) *The Land Use Act: Report of a National Workshop*, Lagos University Press, Lagos.

Omuta, G. (1986) 'Minimum versus affordable environmental standards in third world cities: an examination of housing codes in Benin City', *Cities*, Vol. 3, no. 1, 58–71.

Patel, L. (1972) 'Mombasa housing problems: legal and social aspects', in J. Hutton (ed.), *Urban Challenge in East Africa*, East Africa Publishing House, Nairobi, 235–57.

Pérez Perdomo, R. and P. Nikken (1980) 'Law and housing ownership in the barrios of Caracas', *Urban Law and Policy*, Vol. 3, 365–402.

Read, J. S. (1975) 'Aspects of the East African experience', in J. F. Garner (ed.), *Compensation for Compulsory Purchase: A Comparative Study*, UK National Committee of Comparative Law, London, 127–48.

Rojas, F. (1988) 'A comparison of change-oriented legal services in Latin America with legal services in North America and Europe', *International Journal of the Sociology of Law*, Vol. 16, 203–56.

Santos, B. de S. (1977) 'The law of the oppressed: the construction and reproduction of legality in Pasargada', *Law and Society Review*, Vol. 12, no. 1, 5–126.

Sen, M. K. (1986) 'Problems and obstacles from the view of the construction industry', in Institute of Strategic and International Studies (ed.), *Target 80,000: Malaysia's Special Low-Cost Housing Scheme*, ISIS, Kuala Lumpur, 9–24.

Singh, M. P. (1990) 'Expropriation in India', in G. M. Erasmus (ed.), *Compensation for Expropriation: A Comparative Study. Vol. 2*, Jason Reese, Oxford, 34–57.

Smart, A. (1986) 'Invisible real estate: investigations into the squatter property market', *International Journal of Urban and Regional Research*, Vol. 10, no. 1, 29–45.

— (1988) 'The informal regulation of illegal economic activities: comparisons between the squatter property market and organized crime', *International Journal of the Sociology of Law*, Vol. 16, 91–101.

Trubek, D. M. and M. Galanter (1974) 'Scholars in self-estrangement: some reflections on the crisis in Law and Development in the United States', *Wisconsin Law Review*, Vol. 4, 1062.

van Westen, A. C. M. (1990) 'Land supply for low-income housing in Bamako, Mali: its evolution and performance', in P. Baross and J. van der Linden (eds), *The Transformation of Land Supply Systems in Third World Cities*, Avebury, Aldershot, 83–110.

Verdier, R. and A. Rochegude (eds) (1986) *Systèmes fonciers à la ville et au village*, L'Harmattan, Paris.

von Mehren, P. and T. Sawers (1992) 'Revitalizing the law and development movement: a case study of title in Thailand', *Harvard International Law Journal*, Vol. 33, 67–101.

Willcox, D. L. (1976) 'Malaysia's system of conditional land titles as a potential policy instrument', *American Journal of Comparative Law*, Vol. 26, 321–32.

— (1978) 'New planning wine in old bottles: the case for a greater utilization of existing legal resources in Malaysia', *Urban Law and Policy*, Vol. 1, 275–305.

Williams, D. C. (1992) 'Measuring the impact of land reform policy in Nigeria', *Journal of Modern African Studies*, Vol. 30, no. 4, 587–608.

PART II

Case Studies

Implications of Double Standards in Housing Policy: Development of Informal Settlements in Istanbul, Turkey

Ayse Yonder

Informal settlements have provided access to urban land and housing for large numbers of people in most cities of the developing world. Research from different parts of the world over the past decade has shown that providing full legalization is neither necessary nor sufficient to improve low-income access to housing. In the context of 1980s' structural adjustment programmes and an increased focus on urban efficiency and macroeconomic productivity, however, regularization policies have continued to emphasize full legalization for tax purposes as well as cost recovery in delivery of services and an increased role for the private sector. Recognition of informal processes and settlers as part of the urban economy may mark an important shift in policy-makers' perception of these problems. Yet, narrowly defined economic and legal measures are bound to be ineffective since they fail to deal with the political and institutional complexities of informal processes or the issue of affordable housing – the reason these processes emerged in the first place.

First, legalization is not a simple straightforward transition from illegal to legal status (Azuela 1987; Leaf 1994). It is a complex process conditioned by the intricacies of land ownership and tenure legislation, and the involvement of diverse actors and interests in informal housing processes affecting implementation of government programmes under different political and economic conditions, as well as the distributional impacts (Azuela 1987; Connolly 1982; Doebele 1994; Rakodi and Withers 1995; Varley 1993). Second, legalization is not necessary to increase investments in housing and payment for services by settlers, to attract outside investors, or to increase property prices (Amis 1988; Ward et al. 1994, Varley 1987; Yonder 1987). In fact, consolidation may be secured by the amount of investments made on land (Razzaz 1993). Nor is legalization a measure designed to improve low-income access to land or to prevent new settlement formation (Yonder 1987).

Turkish cities provide interesting cases for studying the impact of regularization policies. More than half the population in the three largest cities – Istanbul, Ankara and Izmir – live in settlements formed through two types of informal processes, squatting (*gecekondu*) and unauthorized subdivision (*hisseli tapu*). A series of legal and administrative reforms in the 1980s, including a general amnesty for all unauthorized buildings, transformed the housing sector and reduced the share of informal processes in overall housing production. The impact of these policies has not been the same in all cities. In Istanbul the legalization of existing settlements has broad environmental implications. The lack of commitment to low-income housing production to meet the increasing demand led to new informal settlement development within the city's fresh water reservoir areas and concern with the environmental impacts of rapid development in these areas served only to remarginalize new settlement development.

This chapter discusses the evolution of informal settlement policies in Turkey, with a focus on the 1980s' regularization measures, in relation to the development of Istanbul. The purpose is to show that ignoring the distributional implications of regularization policies may have an adverse impact on overall urban 'efficiency' and sustainability. After a short contextual section on Istanbul and the factors that have contributed to the development of informal settlements in Turkish cities, the development of informal settlements in Istanbul will be discussed in relation to the evolution of the political and institutional context. The implications of 1980s' urban reforms will then be considered in detail.

Context: Istanbul and the Structure of Metropolitan Land and Housing Markets

Istanbul is the largest metropolitan centre in Turkey. Until after World War II, under state-led industrialization policies, public investments were targeted away from Istanbul – the old capital and symbol of the Islamic Ottoman legacy – to build up the new capital city, Ankara, and develop new centres throughout Anatolia. When Istanbul regained its centrality under the new economic liberalization policies in the late 1940s, it was no longer a primate city. As the leading harbour and major industrial, financial and cultural centre, it attracted private and public investments and grew rapidly, with massive flows of migration mainly from rural areas. Istanbul's population increased from fewer than one million people in 1950 to three million in 1970 and over seven million in 1990. It is estimated that about ten million people now live in the Istanbul metropolitan area, which still accounts for 20 per cent of the total urban population.

Historically, settled areas in Istanbul were confined to a narrow strip

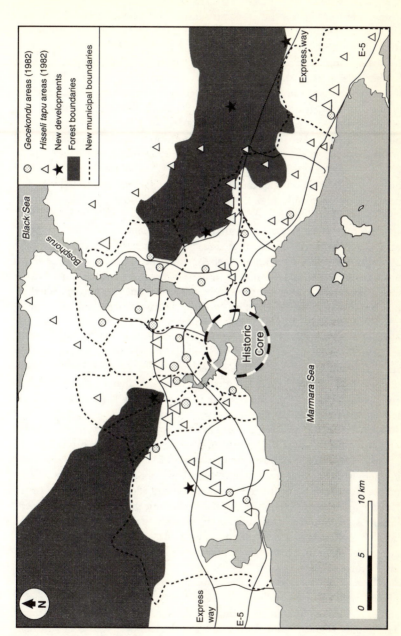

Figure 3.1 Main areas of *gecekondu* and *hisseli tapu* in Istanbul, Turkey, as of 1982

along the coast of the Sea of Marmara and the Bosphorus (Figure 3.1). Forest areas protecting the city's precious water reservoirs and a lack of roads restricted growth further inland. Until the late 1970s, Istanbul grew through two distinct types of development: density increases and middle- to high-income development along the coast, and low-income settlements further inland, near the industrial areas located along the E-5 highway. Construction of the first Bosphorus bridge in the 1970s facilitated a similar pattern of growth on the Asian side of the city. During the 1980s, this pattern of socio-spatial segregation started to change. An increasing number of upmarket (and often gated) housing communities (*sites*) were created inland, on the 'periphery' formerly populated only by low-income groups. These *sites*, which represent new forms of segregation (between different middle- and upper-income groups) are directly connected via the new expressway to new high-rise office buildings, shopping malls and the city centre. Even though different income groups now live in greater spatial proximity to each other, their contact is minimized.

The rapid growth of Istanbul since the 1950s has been accompanied by a speculative boom in urban property markets. It has been argued that until 1980 the urban land market was 'the most dynamic sector of the urban economy, a major distributive and redistributive arena' in all the major cities of Turkey and that 'nearly all major social and economic groups' benefited from this 'tumultuous expansion' (Öncü 1988: 38–9). A number of interrelated factors gave rise to this speculative boom and facilitated informal development processes. In addition to demand pressures and supply constraints, there were two other factors: the clientelist nature of local government politics and issues related to the transition from the Ottoman land system, that made urban land and building regulations prone to contestation.

High levels of demand for urban land and housing were sustained, first, by rapid rates of urbanization. The proportion of the population living in urban areas increased from 18.1 per cent in 1950 to 56.3 per cent in 1990, with the annual growth in the urban population peaking at a rate of over 6 per cent in the period 1965–70 (Turkiye Ulusal Komitesi Danisma Kurulu 1996). Second, rapid and cyclical economic growth in Turkey under import substitution policies during the postwar period was accompanied by high and sustained rates of inflation. Urban real property became an attractive 'inflation-proof' asset in which all income groups sought to invest their savings.

The supply of housing and new urban land was limited by a number of constraints. First, public funds were directed to public works projects and to subsidizing 'productive' sectors, such as industry, rather than housing. The public sector accounted for much less than 10 per cent of all housing investments in Turkey until the 1980s. The limited amount of public credit and housing provided ended up in the hands of middle-income groups.

Second, financial institutions were not well developed, and confined to direct credits to commerce and industry. Large construction firms stayed out of the housing sector, concentrating on public works projects. Private sector investments were dominated by small development firms which had limited capital and used traditional construction techniques. Production was geared towards upmarket redevelopment of central areas of the city, (Yonder 1987). Third, land use and building codes that imposed a strict and often irrelevant set of regulations, and the cumbersome process for approving partial master plans required for new development outside central areas of the city, further discouraged new urban land and housing production through the formal sector. In the late 1950s, the formal sector accounted for a little over 55 per cent of housing production. By the mid-1970s, its share had declined to only one-third of housing built in the three largest cities (Heper 1977).

Informal settlement processes not only provided access to land and housing for low-income groups, but also expanded the overall urban land supply in the market. Settlements were formed on land which would have been impossible to develop through the formal market because of restrictions in the Reconstruction, Public Health or Forest Laws. Unauthorized subdivisions, moreover, followed a leap-frog pattern of development on rural land. Once the settlements became consolidated and received services, land prices in neighbouring areas increased (Yonder 1982).

The clientelist nature of party politics at the local and national levels fuelled both the speculative building boom and informal settlement formation.[1] During national elections all parties promised title deeds and delivery of services to informal settlements, and building amnesties were issued for unauthorized construction in the established middle-income districts. At the local level, municipal governments responsible for delivery of infrastructure services and enforcement of land use and building regulations lacked the financial or technical capacity to undertake these functions (Yonder 1987). Selective enforcement and relaxation of regulation thus became 'the most expedient way of dispensing patronage' in return for votes in both the formal and informal districts of the city (Öncü 1988: 45).

The transition to private property was fully established in Turkey with the 1926 Civil Code. The state inherited substantial amounts of land from the Ottoman system.[2] The lack of long-term policies for the administration of public lands, as well as the slow pace of land title registration, created ownership disputes throughout the country and making land claims therefore became a profitable activity, especially in urban areas (Yavuz 1980). Even in Istanbul, where cadastral records were better organized than in the rest of the country, it took over fifty years – until the late 1970s – to complete (Erturk 1991). Changes in the mapping techniques used created inconsistencies between cadastral documents and current maps and hence further disputes.

Public lands and lands in dispute became the prime target of squatters. During the title registration process, individuals could claim ownership of holdings they cultivated or on which they lived (Yavuz 1980; Payne 1982) and *zilyedlik senedi*, popularly known as the 'village' ownership document, was used in transfer of property in areas where cadastral registration was incomplete. These traditions became the basis for claiming and transfer of land in informal settlements.

Evolution of Government Policies and Development of Informal Settlements

Several pieces of legislation issued in relation to *gecekondu* and low-income housing during the post-World War II period included both demolition measures and provisions to assist low-income housing development. In practice, underlying policy has simply been to condone informal settlements as the main option for low-income housing. The specific measures adopted and their enforcement depended on the changes in the political and institutional context. The development of informal settlements in Istanbul can therefore be considered in three distinct periods, described below.

Foundations of urban policy and establishment of *gecekondu* in Istanbul (1946–60) This period is marked by initial policy efforts to regulate rapid urbanization under the multi-party system. Initially the government approach was to demolish *gecekondu* as a violation of property rights and the modern city image (Law no. 5431 of 1949), but Law no. 6188 of 1953 set the tone for later legislation: existing *gecekondu* would be consolidated, new construction demolished, and municipal land would be provided on easy terms of payment to encourage new housing construction (Keles 1993). Complementary measures authorized credits through the Bank of Real Property (1948) and the transfer of State Treasury lands to municipalities to assist housing construction (1959). Since the new migrants and the urban poor could not, however, qualify for or afford the terms of payment, it was middle-income groups which benefited from these measures.

Legislation issued after 1948 gave municipalities the primary responsibility for dealing with *gecekondu* and encouraging new housing construction. Yet even after the municipal administration in Istanbul started to be elected in 1956, its operations were restricted by limited revenues and strong central government tutelage. The new Reconstruction and Resettlement Law (no. 6785 of 1956), followed by the establishment in 1958 of a Ministry of Reconstruction and Resettlement charged with co-ordinating various urban functions, reinforced this central control. In fact, during the mid-1950s, the prime minister was directly involved in the major road construction and 'beautification' programmes in Istanbul, which further dislocated large numbers of people from the city centre; these people joined the squatters.

Gecekondus (squatters) first appeared in Istanbul in the late 1940s, gradually occupying mainly public land.[3] Even though the term is also used to describe hastily-built shacks, legally it refers to occupation of someone else's land and construction without permits. The term *gecekondu* ('landed by night') derives from the fact that units had to be completed, often overnight, with a roof, and inhabited before government forces arrived, in order to prevent demolition. A court order would then be required to demolish the building and the settler would have to be compensated for improvements made on the land. The overwhelming number of appeals by settlers, procedural delays, lack of municipal funds, and the fact that judges and government forces were often sympathetic to those in need, rendered demolition measures ineffective.

By 1960, the number of *gecekondus* had increased to over 60,000 (from 5,000 in 1949), and the largest settlements in the city were already established. Some of these settlements were initiated by various state agencies. In Gultepe and Kagithane, the municipality directed people displaced from the city centre during the massive road construction activities to build their homes on land in dispute.

The rapid growth of *gecekondus* was mainly due to the determination of earlier squatters, who rebuilt their houses several times after each demolition and used various tactics to legitimize their claims to land. The tactics ranged from contestation – as in the case of Taslitarla, where settlers claimed land near public housing built for resettlement of Balkan immigrants – to seeking patronage from prominent public figures, as in the case of Zeytinburnu. In this case the settlers occupied public and *wakf* land as well as land that belonged to minorities who had left Turkey. Despite periodic demolitions in the area, settlers received support and building materials from their employers in nearby factories, some of them state-owned. As their numbers increased, votes became the major tool for negotiating with political parties. By the late 1950s, *gecekondu* processes had become quite organized. According to Hart (1969), in Zeytinburnu only half of the units were self-built, and renting was common.

Refinement of the institutional framework and expansion of informal development processes (1960–80) From the mid-1960s to 1980, informal development processes became fully commercialized as both *gecekondu* and the new *hisseli tapu* settlements spread rapidly in a more favourable political and institutional framework. The 1961 Constitution guaranteed democratic freedoms, and increased governmental accountability towards low-income groups. Low-income families' right to housing was established as part of the right to health (Item 49). The first two five-year development plans (1963–72) recognized the need to increase 'mass housing' construction, as well as upgrading of existing settlements. Within this framework, the *Gecekondu* Law (no. 775) of 1966 provided a comprehensive programme based on the earlier legislation. Good *gecekondus* would be upgraded while those in poor condition would be cleared, giving the residents priority access to the new housing which would be provided in *gecekondu* prevention areas (Yonder 1987). Most of the existing settlements in Istanbul were designated as upgrading areas, but deadlines were continually extended to exempt newly constructed settlements, as elected officials responded to their growing squatter constituencies (Danielson and Keles 1985).

In 1973 specific programmes, such as *Koykent* (rural centres) and *Akkondu* (sites and services), were formulated by the 'left-of-centre' Republican People's Party (RPP), following the populist reforms within the party itself. Three years later, a 1976 amendment to *Gecekondu* Law no. 775 legalized *gecekondus* built after 1966. During the 1970s, all the mayors in Istanbul (the majority of whom were from the RPP) started to give priority to servicing the informal settlements where half the city residents lived (Yonder 1982).

The *Gecekondu* Law provided increased security of tenure to a large number of settlers, facilitating improvements and delivery of services to existing settlements. By 1980, however, only about 10 per cent of the *gecekondus* in upgrading areas in Istanbul had received full title to their land (Yonder 1987). The municipal Housing and *Gecekondu* administrations charged with implementing this law lacked the resources to do so adequately. Differences between the municipal and *wakf* administration policies towards disposing of public land, as well as cadastral problems, slowed down the procedures. The law also failed in its goal to prevent speculation in consolidated settlements. Areas such as Dikilitas, which received title deeds, became middle-class districts. Zoning limitations until upgrading plans were prepared proved ineffective. Densities increased even in centrally located settlements without full title deeds to land, such as Zeytinburnu and Caglayan. In addition, due to insufficient funding, only three out of the twelve *gecekondu* prevention areas could be prepared for new housing (Danielson and Keles 1985). Since alternative housing was not provided, most *gecekondu* clearance could not take place.

By the mid-1960s, squatting in the traditional sense of the term had disappeared in Istanbul. Settlers had to pay local strongmen for the right to occupy even public land. In the mid-1970s, entrepreneurs with underground connections started controlling public lands in certain districts of Istanbul, selling land and monopolizing all construction activity. When settlers attempted to occupy *gecekondu* prevention areas, however, as in Umraniye and Alibeykoy, violent confrontations with government forces resulted. Confrontations also occurred when the occupied land was part of or adjacent to large private development projects, as in Umraniye (Yonder 1982; 1987).

Unauthorized subdivisions (*hisseli tapu*) became widespread during the 1960s and 1970s, mostly on rural land, as a more expensive alternative to *gecekondu*. In *hisseli tapu*, settlers hold title deeds to shares (*hisseli tapu*) of a large parcel of land, which is legal according to the Turkish civil code, although the land subdivision and construction are unauthorized according to the Reconstruction Law of 1956. *Hisseli tapu* settlements developed in an ambiguous legal context during this period. While a Supreme Court decision in 1976 endorsed the legitimacy of *hisseli tapu* according to the civil code, a government decree the next year required land registrars to warn purchasers about its 'illegal' status under the Reconstruction Law.

Settlers' security of tenure was higher than in *gecekondu*, since they held title deeds to land. However, they too had to negotiate with the local government to build their houses and to receive services, and there were no public funds for delivery of services to unauthorized subdivisions. A wide range of agents was involved in these processes, from formal sector developers to small agents working on commission, since there was no risk in selling rural land with shared title deeds. The same was not true for the purchasers. Sale agreements with maps were often endorsed by the public notary in order to prevent encroachments, but a shelter had to be built rapidly to avoid losing one's plot.

In municipalities with development plans, local councils could legalize such subdivisions if legal and technical issues could be resolved. Thus, twenty new municipalities were established (mostly by *hisseli tapu* residents, once the settlement population reached 2,000) around the central municipality of Istanbul during this period. Given the constraints on formal sector production, informal settlement development became the major means by which new housing was provided for low- and moderate-income groups in the 1970s. Legalization policies encouraged haphazard urban sprawl on public and private land, without any provision for social or infrastructure services (Yonder 1987).

1980s urban reforms and informal settlement development Within the framework of structural adjustment programmes, the 1980s was a period of transformation in land and housing markets in Istanbul. First, the military regime of 1980–83, soaring rates of inflation that had started in the late 1970s and the private banks' crash of 1982 significantly slowed down market activities. Second, the pressures that had accumulated since the 1970s led to major urban reforms, and the government established new legislation and institutions that changed the structure of the housing sector.

The urban reforms increased the planning, enforcement and services-provision capacity of local governments. First, the metropolitan government system was reorganized in 1984. The jurisdiction of municipalities was expanded to control new development areas. The financial capacity of municipalities and infrastructure agencies was significantly improved and a cost recovery system was adopted in services provision in 1981. All water and sewerage services were centralized under the Istanbul Water and Sewage Authority (ISKI) and its budget was increased substantially, from local revenue and international credit sources. Improvements in the local revenue sources of municipalities were intended to reduce their dependency on the central government (Laws no. 2380 and no. 2464 of 1981). A major step in improving municipal revenues was to charge them with the collection of real estate taxes within their jurisdiction. Second, real estate tax reform in 1982, replacing the self-assessment system with centralized assessment of minimum property values, increased tax revenues, as well as the costs of real property ownership. Third, a new Reconstruction Law (Law no. 3192 of 1984) was adopted in 1985. The new law decentralized plan approval from the ministry to the metropolitan level, and introduced a number of new items. These included prohibiting unauthorized subdivision sales at the land registrar's office, with penalties for sellers; exempting small structures from the building permit process; enabling the government to earmark up to 35 per cent of the land for public uses during new plan preparation; and phasing out the infrastructure requirement for large-scale projects located outside master plan boundaries.

Within the framework of a new item in the 1982 Constitution, which expanded the housing right to all citizens, two sets of housing strategies were developed.[4] The first set of strategies was geared to stimulating formal sector production, and fully established a favourable legal, administrative and financial framework for large construction companies to enter housing production. These strategies included the establishment of the National Housing Authority and Mass Housing Fund, with substantial funding to finance housing and infrastructure development. NHA credits and loans helped produce 350,000 new housing units throughout Turkey from 1984 to 1986. This was substantially higher than the total number of units built over the preceding thirty-eight years through other credit sources. NHA credits were mainly directed to mass and co-operative housing initiatives, i.e. for people with savings and formal sector employment. Over recent years there have been efforts to extend credits to reach low-income housing, but these efforts have been directed away from Istanbul (Turkiye Ulusal Komitesi Danisma Kurulu 1996).

The second set of housing strategies, which was directed to low-income housing, simply involved consolidation of existing informal settlements as usual. A general building amnesty was issued in 1983, followed by a number of (sometimes contradictory) amendments until 1989, to upgrade existing settlements and to prevent new informal processes. These measures were similar to the 1966 *Gecekondu* Law, but for the first time included *hisseli tapu* in the amnesty.

These policies led to formal sector housing production almost doubling by the mid-1980s, while informal sector housing production fell by almost half in the same period.[5] The reasons for this were, first, that the expansion of municipal boundaries led to increased controls on unauthorized subdivisions on rural land or land whose ownership was disputed. Public land was strictly protected for new large-scale projects. Second, housing and land prices increased in existing informal settlements. The price increases may be explained by a number of factors, including the decline in new informal housing production and the new real estate tax reform increasing the cost of holding property.

Still, informal housing production did not disappear. It has continued through infill development and density increases in existing settlements through incremental development of even multi-unit structures. With the expansion of municipal boundaries, new settlement formation has been pushed further out to the edges of the new municipal areas.

The implications of government policies Informal development processes have always involved environmental problems, but these problems intensified in the 1980s. The lack or inadequate provision of clean water and sewage systems has always caused outbreaks of certain diseases and posed serious health threats to residents, especially the children. Haphazard development created problems during consolidation, in finding space for parks or schools for example. Given that Istanbul is located on a first-degree earthquake zone, dense, unregulated construction and development on steep slopes has always been a risky process.

In the 1980s, densities started to increase rapidly in existing settlements with rising land values. The centralization of infrastructure-provision functions, which were taken away from the municipalities, and the priority given to building up major facilities slowed down daily upkeep and servicing in informal settlements. With increased controls, new settlement formation was pushed further inland, to the boundaries of the expanded municipal areas, in areas which also contain the city's sources of fresh water. Lack of infrastructure services, which used to be the settlers' problem, now poses health hazards to the city in general. Even though new reforms initially slowed down new informal settlement development processes, by the end of the decade it was business as usual, and the environmental implications of new development had become critical.

Conclusion

Despite some long-awaited improvements in the institutional framework of urban land and housing markets, low-income housing continues to be an afterthought in Turkey. The marginal attention paid to low-income housing demand has serious distributional, spatial and environmental implications. Consolidating existing settlements and exempting small structures from the permit process have not been sufficient to accommodate new demand for low-income housing. The old housing and environmental health problems continue, exacerbated by increased costs of access and maintenance of access to land and housing, demand pressures, high rates of inflation, and the priority given to developing Istanbul's 'global city' image by city governments.

It is critical to consider the distributional and environmental implications of housing policies. Increasing the supply of affordable serviced land and housing for low-income groups is critical for the sustainability of the city as a whole. This is also necessary to protect low-income households from being exploited by subdividers. It is necessary, moreover, to monitor density increases in newly consolidated areas. Finally, it is necessary to provide small credits to low-income households without regular employment in order to encourage the construction of sturdy housing structures.

Notes

1. Since 1950 the political regime in Turkey has been a multi-party democracy. Military regimes during 1960–61, 1971–73 and 1980–83 marked periods of economic and political crisis and structural adjustment measures.

2. There were five categories of land in the Islamic Ottoman system: (1) *Mulk* or privately owned land, a small category concentrated mainly in cities; (2) *Miri* or sultan's property, which made up 80 per cent of all arable land in the country and was distributed to villagers on usufruct for cultivation; (3) *Wakf* land, belonging to the deity, was administered by pious foundations established by the palace or families; (4) *Metruk* land in public or communal places (streets, the village green, etc.); and (5) *Mevat* or non-arable land. The state inherited all unclaimed *miri* land, as well as *metruk* and *mevat* lands. The semi-autonomous *Vakiflar* Administration was charged with the management of non-family *wakf* land. The state also received land during the exchange of Turkish and Greek populations following the Lozanne Treaty.

3. The first squatters included old city residents displaced from their homes, immigrants from the Balkans and rural migrants (Hart 1969).

4. Item 57 of the 1982 Constitution states that the state shall take measures to meet housing needs, within the framework of a plan which takes into account the characteristics of cities and environmental conditions and supports large-scale housing initiatives.

5. Findings from author's study of land prices and construction permits issued in Bakirkoy, the largest and fastest-growing municipality in Istanbul in the early 1990s. This study involved examination of 1975 and 1985 building census data, municipal permits, property tax assessments and interviews with real estate agents in both the formal and informal sectors.

References

Amis, P. (1988) 'Commercialized rental housing in Nairobi, Kenya', in C. V. Patton (ed.), *Spontaneous Shelter: International Perspectives and Prospects*, Temple University Press, Philadelphia, 235–57.

Azuela, A. (1987) 'Low income settlements and the law in Mexico City', *International Journal of Urban and Regional Research*, Vol. 11, no. 4, 522–42.

Connolly, P. (1982) 'Uncontrolled settlements and self-build: what kind of solution? The Mexico City case', in P. M. Ward (ed.), *Self-Help Housing: A Critique*, Mansell, London, 141–74.

Danielson, M. N. and R. Keles (1985) *The Politics of Rapid Urbanization*, Holmes and Meier, New York.

Doebele, W. (1994) 'Urban land and macroeconomic development: moving from "access for the poor" to urban productivity', in G. A. Jones and P. M. Ward (eds), *Methodology for Land and Housing Market Analysis*, UCL Press, London, 44–54.

Erturk, M. E. (1991) *Imar uygulamada kadastro ve tapunun rolu*, Yildiz Mimarlik ve Muhendislik Akademisi, Istanbul.

Hart, C. W. M. (1969) *Zeytinburnu Gecekondu Bolgesi*, Ticaret ve sanayi Odalari Yayini, Istanbul.

Heper, M. (1977) *Gecekondu Policy in Turkey*, Bosphorus University Publication no. 146, Istanbul.

Keles, R. (1993) *Kentlesme Politikasi*, Imge Kitabevi Yayinlari, Istanbul.

Kerem, Z. (1992) 'Gecekondu Surecinin Incelenmesi: Alibeykoyde (Istanbul) bir Alan Arastirmasi', Unpublished PhD thesis, Istanbul Teknik Universitesi.

Koksal, S. (1990) 'Ticarilesen Gecekondu ve Kent Yoneticileri', *Marmara Universitesi Iktisadi ve Ticari Bilimler Fakultesi Dergisi, Prof. Mubeccel Kiray'a Armagan*, Vol. 7, 260–76.

Leaf, M. (1994) 'Legal authority in an extralegal setting: the case of land rights in Jakarta, Indonesia', *Journal of Planning Education and Research*, Vol. 14, no. 1, 12–18.

Öncü, A. (1988) 'The politics of the urban land market in Turkey: 1950–80', *International Journal of Urban and Regional Research*, Vol. 12, no. 1, 38–64.

Payne, G. K. (1982) 'Self-help housing: a critique of the gecekondus of Ankara', in P. M. Ward (ed.), *Self-Help Housing: A Critique*, Mansell, London, 117–39.

Rakodi, C. and P. Withers (1995) 'Home ownership and commodification of housing in Zimbabwe', *International Journal of Urban and Regional Research*, Vol. 19, no. 2, 250–71.

Razzaz, O.M. (1993) 'Examining property rights and investment in informal settlements: the case of Jordan', *Land Economics*, Vol. 69, no. 4, 341–55.

Stephens, C. (1995) 'Health, poverty, and environment: the nexus', in I. Serageldin, M. Cohen and K. C. Sivaramakrisnan (eds), *The Human Face of the Environment*, Environmentally Sustainable Development Proceedings Series no. 6, World Bank, Washington, DC, 173–8.

Turkiye Ulusal Komitesi Danisma Kurulu (1996) *Turkiye Ulusal Rapor ve Eylem Plani – National Report and Plan of Action for Turkey*, Report for United Nations Human Settlements Conference, Habitat II, Istanbul, June 1996.

Varley, A. (1987) 'The relationship between tenure legalization and housing improvements: evidence from Mexico City', *Development and Change*, Vol. 18, no. 3, 463–81.

— (1993) 'Clientilism or technocracy? The politics of urban land regularization', in N. Harvey (ed.), *Mexico: Dilemmas of Transition*, Institute of Latin American Studies, University of London, and British Academic Press, London, 249–76.

Ward, P. M., E. Jiménez and G. A. Jones (1994) 'Measuring residential land-price changes and affordability', in G. A. Jones and P. M. Ward (eds), *Methodology for Land and Housing Market Analysis*, UCL Press, London, 159–78.

Yavuz, H. (1980) *Kentsel Topraklar*, Siyasal Bilgiler Fakultesi Yayinlari no. 452, Ankara.

Yonder, A. (1982) 'Gecekondu policies and the informal land market in Istanbul', *Built Environment*, Vol. 8, no. 2, 117–24.

— (1987) 'Informal land and housing markets: the case of Istanbul, Turkey', *Journal of the American Planning Association*, Vol. 53, no. 2, 213–19.

CHAPTER 4

Land Disputes in the Absence of Ownership Rights: Insights from Jordan

Omar Razzaz

Legality and illegality have preoccupied scholars working on urban housing and land markets in developing countries. This is hardly surprising given that more than 50 per cent of the urban dwellers of many major cities of the developing world occupy housing which, in one form or another, violates laws and regulations. The focus on legality and illegality as mutually exclusive categories, however, has led many scholars to extend these categories beyond the law to describe urban dwellers, developers and neighbourhoods as either 'legal', or 'illegal'. Hardoy and Satterthwaite (1989: 6), for example, describe third world cities as divided into 'legal' and 'illegal' parts with a 'gap' separating the two. As a result, 'most poor people have little faith in laws. Many may know little or nothing about existing laws' (Hardoy and Satterthwaite 1989: 32).

The poor may know little about the letter of the law, but they are often conscious of its function (Azuela 1987; Holston 1991). Recognizing that squatters are conscious of the law does not, however, mean that they conform to it, nor does it mean that law determines their actions. In a seminal article, Santos (1987: 298) captures the porous boundaries of legality and illegality: 'We live in a time of porous legality or legal porosity, of multiple networks of legal orders forcing us to constant transitions and trespassings.'

Most studies of urban land legality and illegality focus on the implications for residents *vis-à-vis* the state: the likelihood of eviction, demolition, regularization of title, delivery of services and so on. I have dealt with these questions elsewhere (Razzaz 1992; 1993; 1994). This chapter examines a different problem: in the absence of *de jure* property rights, how do illegal markets function and how are local disputes resolved in cases where land is being subdivided, sold, bought and developed illegally? In a seminal work on dispute settlement between neighbouring cattle farmers, Ellickson (1991) provides evidence of how little formal legal rules and procedures matter in providing norms of fairness and principles for dispute settlement. He shows that people largely govern themselves by informal rules which develop over time to fit their own circumstances. This chapter provides support for Ellickson's thesis about the significance of informal rules in determining transactions and dispute resolution. It suggests, however, that the development of these rules cannot be understood in isolation from formal rules. That is, informal rules evolve to undermine, accommodate, complement or re-enforce formal rules. Furthermore, bargaining, negotiation and dispute settlement processes take place in the shadow of formal rules. While, as Ellickson correctly argues, people often choose to turn a 'deaf ear' to the law, they also invoke it as a threat in their informal transactions, and, indeed, resort to it when informal rules fail them.

Yajouz: the Contested Land[1]

While Jordanian law (and before it British and Ottoman laws) recognized cultivators' claims to land, it did not recognize claims by pastoral communities. As a result, cultivated land in Jordan was formally registered to its traditional holders, while pastoral land was registered, for the most part, as state land. For several decades this did not create problems, as pastoral communities continued to use the land for residence and herding and were not interested in formally claiming legal ownership, as they were aware of the registration fees and property taxes that registration would bring.

This *détente* was not long lived, however, in areas close to urban centres. Yajouz, now a low-income suburb to the north-east of Amman, was part of the pastoral domain of the Bani Hasan tribe, one of the largest tribes in Jordan. In the 1970s, the eastern suburbs of Amman grew to within close proximity of these lands. There was considerable pent-up demand by lower-income groups for affordable land on the eastern and north-eastern outskirts. Members of the tribe attempted to register the land formally so that they could 'cash in' on growing urban demand, but the government was not responsive to their demands: granting the land to the tribes would create a precedent that the government was unwilling to establish, and the government had its own plans for developing the north-east with large-scale industrial and public service areas.

The rival claims of the state and the tribe quickly degenerated into conflicts on the ground, claims and counter-claims of corruption and greed, and a competition between the government's ability to enforce property rights over vast areas of land, and the tribe's ability to create *de facto* possession which is legally very difficult to reverse. Economic and political factors during the 1970s and 1980s made it extremely difficult for the government to follow a consistent policy on the issue, and tribal members developed elaborate mechanisms to undermine enforcement and manipulate laws and regulations. By the end of the decade, the government had been able to fence and develop limited segments of land along the main roads. The rest of the landscape was littered with small, 'illegal', housing plots and farms which tribal members had managed to subdivide and sell to lower-income groups who could not afford land and housing elsewhere in the city. As I demonstrate in the following sections, neither the vendors of plots (the Bani Hasan members) nor the buyers (mostly Palestinian refugees from nearby camps) had *rights* to the land or rights to transfer it. What they had were property *interests* which were supported not only by informal norms and rules but also by the selective use and application of formal rules, procedures and state agents (Razzaz 1991a; 1991b; 1992; 1994).

Elements of an Informal Land Market

Territorial clusters and the role of middlemen Territoriality and the clustering of communities are important means to minimize the risk of future conflicts. In one of my visits to Yajouz, I was searching for the house of a man involved in a dispute I had been investigating. There were no street names, no house numbers, and very few landmarks. All I knew was the man's name, and that he lived north of Yajouz road. I stopped by a grocer on the main road and asked him if he knew the man. He asked: 'Is he from Hebron? ... his family name sounds like he is. Most of the [people from Hebron] live up on that hill. You should ask there.' Indeed, once I reached the hill, I was immediately shown to his house.

The man I was visiting explained: 'It is important to know who your neighbours are, a good and trusted neighbour can save lots of headaches in the future ... One bad neighbour is like a bad tomato, he could ruin the life of everybody around.' He gave as an example how everybody in the neighbourhood pitched in to get a contractor to cover a muddy road with gravel. He said: 'If our hearts were not together, this would have never happened.' It turns out that Yajouz has several kinship- and place-of-origin-based neighbourhoods.

One of the main community roles in facilitating clustering is that of a *wasta* (a go-between). A *wasta* is an outsider to the Bani Hasan tribe who buys land from the Bani Hasan, moves in, and then takes on the role of a trusted go-between, arranging land deals between the tribal land holders and members of the *wasta*'s community. The *wasta* does not generally charge for his services. He gains simply by getting 'good neighbours' around him who share family ties or a common geographical background. If financially able, a *wasta* might sometimes buy the land adjacent to his plot from tribal members and sell it to relatives, people from the same village or acquaintances. Buying land through the *wasta* minimizes the problem of information asymmetry in such a market.

Another emerging role in the area is that of the *mu'azib*. A *mu'azib*, literally a host, is a tribal member with a reputation for honest dealing. He usually has land of his own to sell, but is also known to direct buyers to and facilitate deals with trustworthy members of the tribe. One of the well known *mu'azib*s boasted that none of the land sales he had seen through had been abrogated, attributing this to his earnest efforts to resolve any problems by making sure the buyer is satisfied. He said: 'When a dissatisfied buyer comes back to me asking to annul the sale, I don't even ask for reasons. I return his money and take back my land.' Although there is some exaggeration about the extent to which vendors are willing to accommodate buyers, there is no question that by making such claims, tribal members try hard to allay any fear or hesitation on the part of buyers.[2]

The *mu'azib* acknowledged that disputes do sometimes occur, but argued that they are rare, and that they can be avoided by applying some caution. He mentioned as an example of a bad strategy those who choose a suitable plot first and then seek out its owner. In Yajouz, it is more important to find a trustworthy *mu'azib* or *wasta* first and a suitable plot second.

The roles of the *mu'azib* or *wasta* have evolved over time and changed in importance as the market has developed. The *wasta*'s role is based on mutual trust. In addition to material benefits in cases where the *wasta* is party to the transaction, the *wasta* benefits by helping to forge a cluster of neighbours with family and village links thus increasing the chances for co-ordinated action and lowering the probability of disputes within the cluster. The *mu'azib*'s role vis-à-vis prospective buyers is based not so much on trust (since no connections bind him to buyers) as on reputation. The role has evolved to address the asymmetric information problems relating to the honesty of the vendor, the location of the plot and settling of *ex-post* disputes.

Contractual obligations: the *hujja* In the process of establishing land markets with no *de jure* rights, not only have community roles had to develop to address new needs, risks, and opportunities, but land sales contracts have had to acquire a new role and meaning. Historically, the *hujja* was the only document required for land transactions between buyers and vendors in the region. Ottoman reforms, however, and later British-based laws required that a title deed be obtained along with the *hujja*. Today, the use of *hujja* for land transaction, without transferring the title and obtaining a title deed is illegal.[3] In Yajouz, however, the *hujja* continues to be used as the only document for transferring possession of land. As land markets in Yajouz have evolved, the *hujja* has acquired a new meaning and new functions, including new conditions that were never part of the 'traditional' *hujja*.

While formal land sales contracts in Jordan represent discrete transactions, the *hujja* in Yajouz has increasingly become an on-going relational contract. A tribal member explained:

> We do not think of a *hujja* as a regular sales contract. It is more like a marriage contract, binding both the buyer and vendor for good. I am expected to intervene whenever there is any dispute over the ownership of any piece of land that I have sold ... In some cases I am called upon to re-establish the boundaries, in others I am called upon to identify the person who bought the land and paid me for it ... If I stopped performing this role, I would be reneging on my commitment in the *hujja*, and people would have no trust in me, I wouldn't be able to sell.

The tribal vendor is thus a lifetime guarantor of the buyers' possession of the land. This is almost always explicitly mentioned in *hujjas*: 'the vendor is responsible for the protection of the buyer against the intrusion of tribal members and adjacent neighbours.' Modifications to this provision, however, started appearing after 1977: 'with the exception of the state' was added to the provision, absolving the vendor from protecting the buyer against demolition or appropriation of land by the state. By the mid-1980s, almost all *hujjas* examined included this distinction.[4] This change came at a time when the state had stepped up its policing of the area in an attempt to prevent further expansion of settlement.

Thus, the *hujja*, in its content and function, has not been a 'continuation' of a traditional or customary practice. It has evolved, rather, to address changing conditions and to reflect realistic obligations between contracting parties. In its form, the *hujja* has increasingly resembled official sale contracts: two witnesses are required to sign the *hujja* along with the buyer and vendor. Increasingly, standardized *hujja* 'forms' in which specific information can be included (such as names, dates, location) are sold in the market. In some cases, a *hujja* is hand-written on paper bearing the state emblem, with the wording and arrangement of text resembling official contracts. Sometimes official stamps used as fees for administrative documents are added to the *hujja*. All these elements – the standard form, the state logo and the stamps – provide an aura of officialdom to the ratification process. The inclusion of such symbols 'is aimed at investing transactions with a load of normativity which will increase the security of contractual relationships' (Santos 1977: 51).[5]

The *hujja* asserts the legitimacy of land transactions in Yajouz in more than one way. First, it spells out in a functional way the mutual obligations of buyer and vendor and serves as a reference for future disputes. Second, by using the traditional term for land sale contract '*hujja*' instead of the generic legal term '*aqd*', the contracting parties invoke the historical legitimacy of this form of contract, while at the same time appealing for official recognition by endowing the *hujja* with the symbols of legitimacy of the modern contract.

In content, the only 'traditional' aspect of the *hujja* is the term itself. As with the emerging community roles of *mu'azib* and *wasta*, the *hujja* is essentially a 'modern' response to the new needs, opportunities and risks posed by the market and the conflict with the state. As I show in the next section, however, the Yajouz community is not 'self-contained' within its own institutional arrangements but can selectively appeal to and invoke rules and enforcement mechanisms from a wider context, including formal rules, procedures, and state actors. Indeed, transacting 'in the shadow of the law' has unintended effects: the threat of formal intervention acts as a deterrent to internal strife and strengthens local arrangements.[6]

The role of the state The presence of the state's coercive power not only influences power relations between state agencies and Yajouz residents, but also influences power relations among residents themselves. In an interview with one of the new buyers in the area, I asked him why he thought the tribal vendor was going to fulfil his obligations made in the *hujja*. The buyer said: 'the last thing tribesmen want is to have me complain to the governor or the police. They know that the authorities are looking for excuses to clamp down on them.'

The authorities' sentiments were reflected in the barrage of anecdotes I was confronted with on my visits to the governor's office or the Department of Lands and Surveys. Bani Hasan members were portrayed as usurpers of state land. The situation in Yajouz was described as chaotic, a 'grave threat to law and order', a 'potentially explosive situation where disputes between neighbours, heirs, and contesting claimants, could turn bloody and set the place on fire'. These portrayals of 'lawlessness' and chaos serve to justify the various measures used by authorities to clamp down on the residents 'in defence of law and order and the public interest' (Razzaz 1993; 1994).

Ironically, such a campaign to undermine tribal control over land proved effective in deterring land vendors from cheating.[7] In fact, it seems to have contributed to an 'offensive' of good-will in which tribal members and families compete to prove their worthiness as dependable parties to deal with. This suggests that external coercive power triggered by local complaints can unintendedly serve to strengthen local obligations and arrangements.

The role of the courts Going to court over property is largely a last resort used when all else fails. 'Litigation over property is not very common in Yajouz', a lawyer said, 'but it is on the rise.' People in the area agree. A shopkeeper who was suing the vendor of his property said: 'I never knew I could take someone to court over land in Yajouz. We were always warned by the government that if we buy land through a *hujja* and without proper registration the sale would be unrecognized by the government and would have no legal value.'[8] People have, however, become aware that despite the 'illegality' of the transaction, there are avenues for restitution available, especially in cases of *hujja* abrogation and obtaining injunctions against encroachment. In fact, many lawyers seeking clients have been promising restitution in return for 10 per cent of the damages collected as their legal fee. A series of Supreme Court decisions during the late 1970s and early 1980s have helped to enhance the legal positions of buyers *vis-à-vis* vendors in these settlements (Razzaz 1991a). These shifts in the legal status of the buyer, together with an increased awareness of the legal options available, seem to have influenced the outcome of disputes processed outside the courts. As one settler put it: 'Previously, when a vendor was stubborn and refused to negotiate, he would say contemptuously: sue me in court why don't you? Now he would have to think twice before saying that.'

Thus, it is not only through litigation, but through the *threat* of litigation, and the relative power of disputants, that the outcomes of some disputes are determined.

Contracts, Disputes and Dispute Processing

The land market institutions and the roles of the various actors in Yajouz have evolved to address problems of information, fulfilment of contract, enforcement of contract conditions, and dispute processing. A better understanding of the functioning of these institutions can be obtained only through examining contractual relations and dispute processing in action. The following cases were selected out of forty-one cases documented in the field. The cases selected do not reflect frequency of occurrence, but rather the range of issues to be addressed in informal land transactions. With no legal title or proof of ownership, how does a vendor prove his legitimate claim to the plot? How does the buyer verify that the vendor has the power to transfer the land? How does the buyer ensure that the vendor will not renege on the sale after the transaction is complete, or sell the same plot to someone else? How does the buyer verify the location of the plot he or she bought? How can the buyer be protected from future intruders? This section will show that all these issues can and do lead to disputes. The norms, rules, procedures, and enforcement mechanisms invoked in these disputes vary tremendously.

Disputes over reversing the land sale

CASE NO. 1[9] A, a returning migrant looking for a piece of land to buy, stopped by B's restaurant to inquire about plots for sale. B showed him a 500 m² piece of land he was planning to sell. They bargained extensively over the price, and finally agreed on JD 2,000.[10] The buyer had only JD

1,000 in cash, which he gave B as a down payment. B gave him a receipt, but refused to give him a *hujja*. B commented to me: 'To give a *hujja* is to transfer the land. How can I guarantee that he will pay me the remaining amount once he has received the *hujja*?'

The migrant came back one week later, bringing along JD 1,000, only to realize that B had sold the plot to someone else for a higher price (or that at least is what B claimed). When the migrant protested that he had made a down payment, B told him that he could have his JD 1,000 back, but that he had no other claims to make.

The fact that the returning migrant was a stranger and did not seek a *wasta* or a *mu'azib* contributed to the abrogation of this deal: B did not know the migrant, and did not trust him enough to give him a *hujja* before the full amount was paid; and once B sold the land to someone else, the migrant could not activate any community pressure on his behalf.

It is well established that a written *hujja* is an essential element in land transactions in the area. As the following case will show, however, the *hujja* is necessary but not sufficient to conclude a transaction.

CASE NO. 2   A bought a plot from B, a Bani Hasan member, and has been living on it for ten years. In 1987, A decided to buy two more *dunums*[11] adjacent to his plot from the same person. A did not pay cash but agreed with B that he would pay him the money within six months. They wrote a *hujja* that declared the transaction of land but had no mention of the form of payment. A was hoping to sell the two *dunums* at a considerable profit within six months, pay B back, and pocket the difference. However, A's hopes did not materialize. He said:

> As I bought the land in the spring, I was sure I would be able to sell it quickly and at considerable profit by summer and pay [B] back. Just as I bought the land, however, the municipality opened a road through it leaving only 1.5 *dunums* that I could sell. I became worried they might open another perpendicular road that would eat up even more of the plot, so I quickly subdivided it into three plots of half a *dunum* each. Then I sold two of them at no profit to two newcomers who were planning to build immediately. Once they build, I thought, no side road can go through, and I would have a half *dunum* plot left to sell and make my profit on.

A soon also found himself entangled in B's family affairs. A woman showed up at his shop one day and said she was B's first wife. She said that when B decided to marry his second wife, she had asked for a divorce, but B had promised that if she stayed, he would give her the plot of land and build a separate house for her and her children. She later discovered that B had sold the plot to A, and was coming to claim it back.

A told the woman that he was not responsible for any promises B might have made her. He told her he had a *hujja* for the land from B and that neither she nor B could take the land back at that point. He also explained to her that he had already sold most of the land, and that he was not about to return the remaining plot as it offered his only hope to making up the loss on the first two.

This, however, was not the end of it, as B appealed to A's partner and some of his (A's) friends. A group of them visited A at home and told him that B's first wife had requested a divorce, and nothing would change her mind unless the remaining plot was given to her through a *hujja* in her name and her son's name. They urged A to return the remaining part of the plot to 'safeguard and keep intact B's family'. Under significant moral pressure, A agreed to return the remaining plot. He insisted, however, that in exchange for returning the original *hujja* (proof of his purchasing the two *dunums*) he and B would write two new *hujjas*, each recording the sale to A of half a *dunum* (which he had already sold to two different people).

A admitted that his position was made more difficult since he had not yet paid the price of the plot, but he insisted that, had moral issues not been raised, the *hujja* would have given him the right to keep the plot and pay later. His main reason for returning the remaining plot was his 'reluctance to be the cause for a divorce and hardship for B's family'. He also explained that he had to insist on writing two new *hujjas* so as to protect the rights of the two brothers who had bought the other two plots from him.

Several significant points come across from this case. First, social norms (such as 'the priority of preventing the break up of a family') and issues of honesty and reputation occupy a major part of the dispute settlement discourse. In this case, these arguments transformed the dispute from one about rights and obligations emanating from the contract itself to one about A's moral responsibility to prevent family strife. Such transformation was achieved through the intervention of a third party (partner and friends).[12] Second, A's insistence on getting two new *hujjas* for plots he had already sold and which were of no direct interest to him underlines the significance of his continuing responsibility towards the buyers.

Disputes over the location, size and boundaries of a plot

CASE NO. 3   A, a well-known *wasta*, purchased a 5-*dunum* plot from B, a tribe member, in 1981. A described the deal:

> B took me to see the plot before buying it. He owned one side of a steep and rocky hill that flattens out into a plateau. I wanted to buy a piece on the plateau. We agreed on the location and price. We wrote a *hujja* and I paid him in cash. Several months later, I sold the plot to a potter [C] who was looking for a flat and accessible plot suitable for a pottery workshop. One day he came running to me and accused me of selling him land that did not belong to me in the first

place. He said [B] had seen him moving building materials to the plot and accused him of trespassing on his land. B threatened C that unless C removed all his building materials right away, B would confiscate everything on 'his' plot. I told C not to worry as his rights were protected.

A then appealed to a close friend and associate, a member of the same tribe as the vendor, to mediate the dispute. They decided to go to B to try to settle the issue in a friendly manner. A took along his original *hujja* as proof of his purchasing the plot from B, who admitted to selling A a plot of land, but insisted that its location was not the flat part (which A in turn sold to C), but the hilly and steep part to the north of that part. A was outraged at such a claim but had little evidence to show concerning the agreed location. He told me:

> There were no buildings, roads or land marks to help identify any specific boundaries in the *hujja*. But most of all it was a matter of trust. I had always purchased land without worrying about recording the exact location. A man's word used to be better than pencils and papers [meaning a written document]. But as the saying goes: you are often assaulted where you least expect.

B seemed unwilling to negotiate. He also accused A of cheating C into thinking he was buying a flat plot when in fact A knew it was steep.

The mediator then tried to convince C (the final buyer) to settle for the steep plot instead of the one he thought he had bought. C said that he was not being intransigent but that steep and rough terrain was simply not suitable for a pottery shop.

A did not give up. He approached an influential *mu'azib* from the Bani Hasan tribe to intervene. The elder agreed to intervene but, when the disputants met, took the side of his fellow tribesman. A regarded this as an aberration of a convention of intervention:

> When you approach an influential figure for intervention, it is known that he is being asked to intervene on your behalf. He does not have to accept such a role. But if he does, then he is obliged to speak on your behalf. In this case, not only did he not speak for me, but he did not remain neutral either. He stood by his fellow tribesman against me. He undermined his reputation as a man of credibility.

Frustrated by the futility of his efforts to get B to negotiate via third party intervention, A changed his strategy to a more personal one: 'Not only did this guy [B] turn out to be a fraud but a drunkard too. I saw him leaving the park once completely intoxicated. I had the whole neighbourhood waken up to watch him swinging right and left to his home.'

A also threatened B with further 'exposing' him. He would not disclose to me the exact nature of his threat, but said it finally brought B to the negotiating table.

A wanted B to cancel the *hujja* and return the money so that A could, in turn, cancel his *hujja* with C and return his money. B said he had already spent most of the money and could only pay A back in instalments. A refused, citing B's bad record on ethical dealing. B then made another offer, suggesting he swap the flat for the steep plot, but for an additional JD 3,000. C was excited about this option but said he could not pay the whole amount. After long bargaining among the three, B settled for JD 2,000 (JD 1,600 to be paid by C, and JD 400 by A). A explained:

> I knew B was a crook, and I did not want to deal with him any more. But one's most valuable asset is one's reputation. C bought from me the flat land, and I sold him the flat land. I have a responsibility to see to it that he gets it or gets his money back. I incurred significant cost and headache through this ordeal, but I kept my reputation.

I asked A whether he at any point considered taking B to court. He said he had done so when negotiations through the tribal elder broke down. He consulted a lawyer who, after some investigation into B's finances, told him that most of B's property was in Yajouz, and that none of it could be confiscated by court as B had no title to it. The lawyer warned A that the most he could get out of a state ruling was to require B to return the money to A in instalments. A quickly rejected this alternative.

It is not clear from this case whether it was B who tried to cheat A or A who tried to cheat C. The case nevertheless clearly shows the extent of the involvement of A, who was extremely concerned about his reputation as an honest land dealer. The case also shows how gossip, character assassination and personal threats in a close-knit community could contribute to a resolution of the conflict. Finally, recourse to court seemed to come at a later stage in the dispute, and the decision on the appropriateness of such a forum depended on whether the court was perceived to be able to deliver the outcome desired by at least one of the parties to the dispute.

CASE NO. 4   A sold a 1.7 *dunum* plot (1,700 m²) to B. Some time later, B sold one *dunum* out of that plot to C. After C built his house and wall surrounding his plot, B measured the remaining area and found it to be only 0.6 instead of 0.7 *dunums*. When C's plot was measured, it was found to be 1,100 m². B demanded the price of the 100 m² difference, but C insisted that the demarcation lines he followed were those made by B himself, and that B should therefore bear the cost of his own mistake. After long negotiation, they reached a settlement whereby C would pay for only half the price of 100 m² and B would give him a new *hujja* with the area adjusted to 1,100 m².

This case is an example of well-contained disputes, in which errors of measurement are almost always blamed and no premeditated or malicious intentions are usually implied. Such an approach limits the liability to that of redressing the harm and avoids questioning the disputants' motives, which could lead to protracted disputes as issues of reputation become involved. These disputes are resolved through the vendor fulfilling his obligation in the *hujja*: stepping in to protect the buyer from claims made by others. Nevertheless, as will be seen in later cases, the vendor's decision is not always accepted, and there are some disputes in which the vendor has no influence. A disgruntled party to a dispute processed within the community has other alternatives.

Invoking state power   There are instances of dispute when one or both disputants are not satisfied by either the process or the outcome. There are other instances when the dispute involves a state agency, either as a party to the dispute or as the only possible mediator. In any of these cases, state power can be invoked.

CASE NO. 5   Two neighbours, B and C, approached the original owner of the land, A, to settle their dispute over the boundary dividing their respective plots. In the *hujjas*, the area of B's plot was recorded as 700 m², and C's plot as 500 m². B claimed that once C fenced his plot, B was left with less than 500 m². When the original owner A came to establish the boundary, he supported B's claim and demanded that C move his fence back, but C insisted that the area of his plot was only 500 m² and that moving back the fence would mean the area would become less than that recorded in the *hujja*.

Several neighbours interfered to try to 'split the difference', but C adamantly refused to negotiate. Finally, C offered to pay the municipal surveyor to come and measure the plots and establish the boundary. A and B accepted. The surveyor found C's plot to be just about 500 m² but found B's plot to be about 550 m², much less than the 700 m² recorded in his *hujja*. The municipal surveyor announced that the total area of the plots was less than that recorded in both *hujjas*. He said: 'A sold B the plot thinking that it was 750 m² when it was only 550 m².'

A did not challenge the findings of the surveyor, but challenged instead the practicality of such an exercise. He told the surveyor: 'Measurements have always been approximate between vendors and buyers. We never even used measuring tape. If everyone was to go back and measure his plot in centimetres, we would see fights and feuds breaking all over the area.'[13] The surveyor responded: 'I agree, but discrepancies are usually about 50 m² or less. In your case, there is more than a 150 m² difference. It is significant.'

Armed with the surveyor's statement, B demanded that A pay him back JD 450. A at first refused, but the surveyor said: 'If this case reaches the governor's office, they will probably come down hard on both of you.

Why don't you avoid the insult and affront and settle it between you?'
After some bargaining, B agreed to settle for JD 300 which A paid in
cash. A new *hujja* between A and B was written, specifying the area as
550 m².

This case demonstrates the curious role of the state agent, the surveyor,
in the dispute. Although the surveyor was not acting in his official capacity
(as a public employee he is not supposed to provide private services or
earn outside money), the aura of officialdom was obvious in his attitude.
An implicit threat to report the case to the governor's office induced A
and B to reach a settlement. In that sense, the surveyor's role was more
akin to the fluid yet influential role of the 'cultural broker' described by
Antoun (1980).

Resorting to court How can a court of law be involved in a land
dispute between two parties, neither of whom has ownership rights to the
land? The answer is it can and does happen because of the indeterminacy
of law and procedural loopholes.[14]

***Abrogating the* hujja** The courts argue that *hujjas* used in Yajouz are
void because the vendor does not legally *own* the object of transaction –
'state' land – and because all legal land transactions have to take place and
be recorded in the Land Registry. In 1975, however, a Supreme Court
ruling stated that 'an unofficial land sale contract has no legal relevance.
However, the buyer has the limited right of demanding the return to the
status-quo-ante, and to recover the price he paid to the vendor.' This latter
part of the ruling became an opening for dissatisfied buyers to abrogate
hujjas as the following case shows.

CASE NO. 6 B purchased a 3.5 *dunum* plot from tribal member A in
1981. Several months later, B discovered that the plot was designated by
the municipality for a school. This meant that the municipality would
eventually take the land without paying any compensation (as the land
legally did not belong to B but to the state). B accused A of selling the
land in bad faith, knowing that it had been designated for a school. A
denied any knowledge of the designation and refused to return B's money.
B approached friends who were relatives of A to try to persuade A to
negotiate a settlement. A, however, rejected their efforts to mediate, telling
the group he had no compromises to offer and that if B did not like it,
he could take A to court. If B did not have enough money to hire a
lawyer, A would even lend him some.

A's suggestion to lend B money to enable B to sue him was taken by
the group as an insult to their attempts to intervene. They left A's house
and pledged not to enter it again. When B learned what had happened,
he commented: 'I told [A]'s relatives: now that your good-will mediation

efforts have failed, can I take [A] to court? They answered: you have the freedom now to grab him by the neck and bring him to his knees.'

B consulted a lawyer. The lawyer was sure he could obtain a court ruling for B to recover the money he paid for the plot. What the lawyer was not sure about, however, was whether or not A had any property registered officially in his name for the court to confiscate in case A claimed that he had no money and had to pay back in small instalments (a lengthy process, often very hard to enforce). After some investigation, the lawyer found out that A had grain silos and warehouses officially registered in his name. He immediately initiated a case in the court of first instance, and agreed with B on fees of 10 per cent of the recovered money.

When A was informed of the case, he offered to return half of the money to B, but B refused and insisted that unless A paid back the full amount, the court action would proceed. Later, A's business partner came to B and offered to swap the plot for another one in the same area. By that time, however, B's lawyer had advised him not to settle for anything short of the full amount he paid for the land, so B refused to negotiate.

The case was introduced in the court of first instance in mid-1989. By May 1990, the case was decided:

> The court found that the plaintiff had purchased a plot of land from the defendant ... through a *hujja*, and that the defendant had received ... [a total of JD 3,500] whereas the sale [of land] outside the Land Registry Department [that is, without recording the transaction] is a void sale with no legal consequences; and whereas the vendor in such a case has to return the amount paid, the court resolves to commit the defendant ... to return the amount of JD 3,500 to the plaintiff ... in addition to the lawyers' and court fees.

The courts' willingness to abrogate the *hujja* and return the buyer's payment greatly improved the bargaining position of buyers in the area. Dissatisfied buyers none the less went to court only as a last resort.

The court provides injunctive relief If evidence of possession and permanent land improvement are present (construction, agriculture or other investments), the law protects the first possessor against a more recent possessor, even though the first possessor is not the legal owner. Such a case is referred to in court as 'enjoining someone from interrupting possession rights'.

In a landmark decision by the Supreme Court in 1979, the court treated the plaintiff, a holder of state land in the Yajouz area, as a possessor rather than a usurper, thus awarding him the protection due to a prescription by law. The court's decision stated:

> The mere act by the plaintiff of prescription of 'state land' does not accord

him ownership rights to that land. What it does accord him, though, is the position to request the government to grant it to him for an 'equivalent' payment. It is his right, as well, to request [the court] to enjoin the defendant from interrupting his right of possession, but not that of ownership.[15]

This decision, several lawyers maintained, has significantly encouraged aggrieved residents in Yajouz to take their disputes to court.

In an interview with a legal scholar, I asked him how A could sue B for interrupting his right of possession if A's right to possession was itself challenged by the state. He said:

> The court, as a matter of principle, only looks at the case at hand, on the claims brought forward by the plaintiff and the defendant. When the state brings a case against A, the court would adjudicate based on balancing the state's right versus A's rights. But when A brings a case against B [a more recent possessor], then the court would adjudicate based on balancing A's rights versus B's rights. In the latter scenario, the state is not a contender.[16]

Focusing on the case at hand to the exclusion of other, related, issues is a typical characteristic in legal processes. Santos points out that '[t]o fix the object of a dispute is to narrow it … The evaluation of those issues selected is accompanied by an implicit and parallel evaluation of those that are excluded' (Santos 1977: 18).

As will be seen below, cases where family members or neighbours are in dispute over possession, taking the case to court can significantly change the outcome of the dispute.

CASE NO. 7 A, an older woman and mother to three adult sons, got a separation from her husband when he decided to remarry. Her brothers and sons helped her acquire a plot of land in Yajouz and build a two-room house. Later that year, two more rooms with a separate entrance were added, and her eldest son and his wife moved in. The relationship between the mother and the daughter in-law quickly deteriorated. In a bitter feud between the two, the son interfered and battered his mother. Once the other relatives learned of the incident, they reprimanded the son and asked him to move out, but he refused, claiming that he had at least as much right to the property as his mother did. Relatives then attempted to reconcile the mother with the son and his family, trying to persuade her to put up with the situation. The mother tried to do so, but matters seemed only to get worse. After all attempts at reconciliation failed, the mother resorted to court. She asked a lawyer to help her evict her son. The lawyer formulated the case 'facts' as follows: (a) the plaintiff possessed a plot of land and building in [location], and (b) the defendant was contesting the plaintiff's right of possession. The case was litigated in the Magistrate Court.

The defendant (the son) denied that his mother was the sole possessor of the plot and house. He maintained that '[he] was the one who purchased the plot, while [his] mother only helped [him] finance the construction. Whereas the right of possession belongs to both. Therefore, [he] requests that her case against [him] be dismissed.'

The first exhibit the plaintiff's lawyer used was a letter from the officer of the Department of Lands and Surveys which named the mother as the first illegal possessor of the land. The original owner (Bani Hasan tribal member) was then called to testify. He testified that the plaintiff's brother negotiated with him and said that he was buying the land for his sister (the plaintiff). The plaintiff's lawyer then produced the *hujja* which had the plaintiff's name as the buyer.

The lawyer also brought the contractor who built the first part of the house to testify: he said that it was the plaintiff who hired him and she who paid him when he finished building. The plaintiff's nephew (the son of her brother, who had purchased the plot but was now deceased), testified that his father had bought the plot for his sister but paid for the plot with his own money. The nephew also maintained that the defendant 'was never good at saving money' and was therefore unlikely to have paid for either the plot or the house. Several other witnesses supported the mother's claim to possession. The son could muster little support for his claims other than some old receipts for building materials in his name, and a witness who testified that he had seen the defendant participate in the building of the house.

The court found the defendant's claims to be insufficient to establish his claim of possession of plot and house, ruling that:

> Since the plot has been demarcated and the name of the plaintiff appears on official records as the invader, and since it has been proven that she financed the building of the units, the plaintiff is now in a position that enables her to request the government to grant her the land in return for paying the equivalent value. With such a position secured, the plaintiff is now able to demand that the defendant be enjoined from interrupting her possession of the property ... Therefore the court issues an injunction against the defendant, as well as requiring him to pay litigation fees and expenses.[17]

I asked the lawyer representing the mother how the outcome of this case would have changed if the mother had ownership rights to her house instead of possession. He said:

> If the mother had been a legal owner, then the case would be one of tenant eviction. From a procedural point of view, tenant eviction is much harder to obtain. The case could have taken two to three years in court. See, in one case the law protects the tenant from the landlord; in the other, it protects the investor/possessor from a later usurper/intruder.

This case raises the following issues.

First, it is inaccurate to say that '[l]aw is inactive among intimates, increasing as the distance between people increases' (Black 1976: 41). The 'embedded forum' of relatives to whom the mother appealed failed to address her grievances. While customs and the traditional family forum contribute significantly to dispute processing, outcomes are not always perceived as fair, and even when they are, they are not easily enforceable. As Yngvesson (1985: 638) argues: 'less powerful parties may appeal to more distant – and presumably less embedded – fora staffed by officials whose social ties and cultural orientation separate them from local interests.'

Second, taking the dispute to court involved a transformation of the dispute from one of 'family feud' to one of 'enjoining the defendant from interrupting rights of possession'. As far as the mother was concerned, this was simply a way to evict her son and his family. For the court, however, the case was one of property rights.

Third, this case portrays how the plaintiff's position (the mother) *vis-à-vis* the defendant is in fact better served by the law when she enjoys prescription rights than in the hypothetical case of her being a legal owner. Thus, although a legal owner might have more substantive rights in general, a possessor of state land is better served by the law when trying to evict a relative than is a legal owner. This case suggests that it is not *a priori* clear how legality or illegality strengthens or weakens the positions of disputing parties.

Conclusions

Through examining land disputes in Yajouz, I have attempted to show the complex set of norms, rules, roles and networks which are invoked. An approach that could be described as legal centralism, which assumes that having no legal rights means having no rights at all, would fail miserably to explain how land is transacted and disputes resolved in Yajouz. By the same token, however, a dualistic approach, assuming that 'informal' or 'illegal' settlements somehow operate in isolation from the law and bureaucratic agencies is equally misguided. What is needed instead is a nuanced approach which recognizes the ability of legal and bureaucratic institutions to shape the context of rights entitlements, but also treats groups and individuals not as passive recipients of laws and regulations, but rather as active participants who are capable of invoking alternative norms of justice, social networks of kinship and neighbourhood, and generating new market rules and market roles which meet their needs.

First, in an area referred to as an 'illegal', 'squatter', or 'informal' settlement governmental law plays a major role in formulating peoples' claims and bargaining strategies as well as their expectations, even when disputants do not resort to it directly. Governmental law should not, however, be seen as an undifferentiated mass of consistent rules. The fact that governmental law resides in different institutions with different agendas, addressing different constituencies at different times, makes it a plural order in itself, allowing for different interpretations and for ways to manipulate and undermine it. The plurality demonstrated in governmental rules and regulations in this case study has been observed in other cases, where some institutions are 'organized around community justice, others around rule of law standards, and others around cultural predispositions of particular groups in power' (Merry 1988: 890).

Second, the cases demonstrate how the application of governmental law does not always produce the intended results (see Moore 1978: 7). In the case of Yajouz, the court's active move to abrogate *hujja* agreements and force vendors to compensate buyers has reduced uncertainty for buyers. By the same token, it has created significant disincentives to vendors to renege on their undertakings or to cheat purchasers. Thus, while the court deems land sales through a *hujja* to be invalid, it helps validate the system in which the *hujja* operates.

Finally, disputants' choice of forum for processing their dispute is not necessarily constrained by the 'legality' or 'formality' of their dispute, nor is it constrained by issues of accessibility and local control (Yngvesson and Mather 1983). Disputants are increasingly able to exhibit the flexibility of 'forum shoppers' (Benda-Beckman 1981), with a number of alternative fora from which to choose, rather than being the captives of closed systems of dispute processing.

Notes

1. Fieldwork for this chapter was carried out from 1988 to 1991. It included structured surveys, interviews, documentation of land sale contracts, and documentation of a number of land disputes.

2. This 'confidence-building' approach is not significantly different from those used in highly developed markets: the 'satisfaction guaranteed or your money back' slogan aims to allay buyers' fears.

3. A *hujja* (proof) is, however, a legally adequate means of transferring ownership in areas where rights to land have not been settled and registered by the Department of Lands and Surveys. By contrast, for land that has been settled, land transactions require the transaction to be registered at the Land Registry Department and a title deed to be obtained. Yajouz is registered as state property. The *hujja* is therefore null from a legal point of view.

4. Examining the terms of contract in *hujjas* dating between 1970 and 1988, I found that none of the *hujjas* written before 1977 had a provision for the case of state intervention, be it demolition, fines, eviction or appropriation. The first *hujja* I examined with an explicit provision absolving the vendor from any responsibility towards the buyer in case of state intervention was dated 1977. About 60 per cent of *hujjas* dated between 1977 and 1983 had an explicit provision absolving the vendor from responsibility in case of state intervention, and almost all *hujjas* dated after 1983 had such a provision. In all, I reviewed ninety-three *hujjas*.

5. In his brilliant study of a squatter settlement in Rio de Janeiro, Santos (1977) examines the role of the typed document, witnesses, stamps and so on. Describing the role of the typed document, he states: '[t]he keyboard of the typewriter extracts from the white paper a legal fetish in much the same way that the chisel extracts a statue from stone' (Santos 1977: 47).

6. For an in-depth examination of dispute processing, disputing fora and the involvement of the state in processing private disputes in Yajouz, see Razzaz (1991a).

7. The most common problem during the early stages was that of tribal members repeatedly selling the same plot of land to more than one person.

8. The Department of Lands and Surveys used periodically to publish messages in the daily newspaper warning citizens of the risk of buying land without obtaining a proper title through the Department.

9. The names of disputants have been suppressed at their request.

10. One Jordanian Dinar equals US$ 1.4.

11. One *dunum* is equal to 1,000 m².

12. See Yngvesson and Mather (1983) on transformation of disputes within 'tribal' and 'modern' settings.

13. This is true: measurement problems are endemic in the area. One of the most frequent sources of error is that people measure distances along slopes instead of horizontally. This invariably leads to overestimation of distances and therefore area. Also, a rope is often used for measurement instead of a measuring tape. Finally, plot area is obtained by multiplying the average length (the average of opposite sides of the plot) by average width. Where plots are irregular this also causes significant errors.

14. The law in Jordan identifies three types of rights to land: rights to registered privately owned land, to unregistered privately owned land, and to state land. Rights to registered and privately owned land are final. They cannot be adversely possessed and land cannot be illegally occupied. Rights to unregistered privately-owned land are also protected by law, but the door is left open for recognizing rights of adverse possessors whose possession of land is uninterrupted for fifteen years, overt and peaceful (Zu'bi 1987). Rights to state land are not protected to the same degree as registered private rights as courts question whether the registration of public lands meets the elaborate adjudication required by law. As for transferring land, all registered land can be transferred only through the office of land registry. Unregistered land can be transferred through a *hujja* from the owner of the land.

15. Supreme Court decision no. 26, 1979.

16. Interview with Dr Muhammad Yussuf Zu'bi, 10 July 1990.

17. The court referred to Law no. 15 of the Magistrate Court which stipulates: 'If a person imposes his possession over a non-movable good possessed by another, and if the dispossessed party litigates and presents written documentation that he is the *original* possessor of the disputed property, then the ruling would be to enjoin the recent possessor and the property is returned to the original possessor.'

References

Antoun, R. T. (1980) 'The Islamic court, the Islamic judge, and the accommodation of traditions: a Jordanian case study', *International Journal of Middle East Studies*, Vol. 12, no. 4, 455–67.

Azuela, A. (1987) 'Low income settlements and the law in Mexico City', *International Journal of Urban and Regional Research*, Vol. 11, no. 4, 522–42.

Benda-Beckmann, K. V. (1981) 'Forum shopping and shopping forums: dispute processing in a Minangkabau village in West Sumatra', *Journal of Legal Pluralism and Unofficial Law*, no. 19, 117–59.

Black, D. J. (1976) *The Behavior of Law*, Academic Press, London.

Ellickson, R. C. (1991) *Order without Law: How Neighbors Settle Disputes*, Harvard University Press, Cambridge, MA.

Hardoy, J. E. and D. Satterthwaite (1989) *Squatter Citizen: Life in the Urban Third World*, Earthscan, London.

Holston, J. (1991) 'The misrule of law: land and usurpation in Brazil', *Comparative Studies in Society and History: An International Quarterly*, Vol. 33, no. 4, 695–725.

Merry, S. E. (1988) 'Legal pluralism', *Law and Society Review*, Vol. 22, no. 5, 869–96.

Moore, S. F. (1978) *Law as Process: An Anthropological Approach*, Routledge and Kegan Paul, Boston.

Razzaz, O. (1991a) 'Group non-compliance, a strategy for transforming property relations: the case of Jordan', *International Journal of Urban and Regional Research*, Vol. 16, no. 3, 408–19.

— (1991b) 'Law, urban land tenure, and property disputes in contested settlements: the case of Jordan', Unpublished PhD thesis, Harvard University.

— (1992) 'Contested space: urban settlement around Amman', *Middle East Report*, Vol. 23, no. 2, 10–14.

— (1993) 'Examining property rights and investment in informal settlements: the case of Jordan', *Land Economics*, Vol. 69, no. 4, 341–55.

— (1994) 'Contestation and mutual adjustment: the process of controlling land in Yajouz, Jordan', *Law and Society Review*, Vol. 28, no. 1, 7–39.

Santos, B. de S. (1977) 'The law of the oppressed: the construction and reproduction of legality in Pasargada', *Law and Society Review*, Vol. 12, no. 1, 5–126.

— (1987) 'Law: a map of misreading: toward a postmodern conception of law', *Journal of Law and Society*, Vol. 14, no. 3, 279–302.

Yngvesson, B. (1985) 'Re-examining continuing relations and the law', *Wisconsin Law Review*, no. 3, 623–46.

Yngvesson, B. and L. Mather (1983) 'Courts, moots, and the disputing process', in K. Boyum and L. Mather (eds), *Empirical Theories About Courts*, Longman, New York, 51–83.

Zu'bi, M. Y. (1987) 'Quyud sijil al-aradi al-urduni natijat al-taswiah', *Majallat Nagabat al-Muhameen*, Vols 9 and 10, 1419–60.

CHAPTER 5

Law and Urban Change in an Indian City

Amanda Perry

This chapter will examine the role of the law in the process of urban change in the city of Bangalore. The city is the capital of the south Indian state of Karnataka and a major commercial, military, research and industrial centre. Bangalore is rapidly expanding both in terms of population density and geographic size (Suresh et al. 1992: 89). In this city, as in many others, the twin goals of economic success and social welfare are as often mutually beneficial as mutually exclusive. As the population in the city increases, exorbitant pressures are being placed upon its natural resources and infrastructure. Of particular concern to the city are the problems of providing housing, controlling land use, the regulation of planning, the protection of the environment, and the maintenance of an adequate level of infrastructure and civic amenities.[1]

While it is not feasible to address the full range of Bangalore's concerns in this chapter, it is possible to provide an impression of those problems by examining the area of residential land use. This chapter will first outline the legal framework relating to the provision of official and unofficial housing in Bangalore, and then use a case study to illustrate the interface between urban change and the law.

Residential Land Use and the Law

Bangalore has traditionally been a low-rise city of bungalows, with high-rise accommodation arriving only in the 1980s (Suresh et al. 1992: 93). The rapid expansion of the city's population has led to a current trend of multi-storey construction. While new buildings place undesirable strains on infrastructure, it remains true that buildings, at least for the purpose of housing, are a necessary evil. Housing in Bangalore is sparse, inadequate in quality, and unaffordable to many. There are three types of housing in Bangalore: official public, official private and unofficial private. The legal framework surrounding each of these types of accommodation will be examined in turn.

Official public residential developments The 1991 census found that the population density of the city is 2,203 persons per square kilometre. According to one analyst, the city requires at least eight to ten new housing units per thousand persons, per year, but at most three or four are in fact built (Suresh et al. 1992: 93). Part of the reason for this shortfall in accommodation is the high cost of land in the region, which has prevented both private and public residential developments. It is reported that a state government official announced in 1995 that the government needed Rs 300 crore to build 1.5 lakh homes for the poor in the state but could find only Rs 100 crore (*Deccan Herald*, 25 January 1995).[2] The draft annual plan for the Karnataka state government in 1995 showed that the government planned to spend 15,583 lakh rupees in 1994–95 and 13,578 lakh rupees in 1995–96 on housing (Karnataka State Government 1995). The preferred method for providing land, especially to the poor, has traditionally been for public institutions to acquire it by compulsory purchase under the Land Acquisition Act (1894). After the 1984 amendments to the Act, public institutions are now required to buy land at a higher rate and with greater speed than before. This has worsened the existing financial difficulties experienced by public institutions in acquiring land (Banerjee 1996: 7).

The Bangalore Development Authority, a state-appointed body, and the Bangalore City Corporation, an elected body, are primarily responsible for creating and maintaining a suitable living environment for Bangaloreans. While the Development Authority is responsible for developing new areas, the City Corporation is primarily responsible for maintaining existing developments. The Karnataka Housing Board and the Bangalore Development Authority are the two agencies with powers to provide housing in Bangalore. The Housing Board was established by the Karnataka Housing Board Act (1962), and is obliged to act within the constraints of the plans of the Development Authority.[3]

The function of the Development Authority is to 'promote and secure the development of the metropolitan area through building, engineering and other operations'.[4] The procedure by which such developments are to be implemented will be examined in some detail. Any plans for development schemes must provide for the acquisition of the necessary land, the laying of streets, and drainage, water supply and electricity.[6] Plans may, but need not, provide for:

a) raising any land which the Authority may consider expedient to raise to facilitate better drainage;
b) forming open spaces for the better ventilation of the area comprised in the scheme or any adjoining area; the sanitary arrangements required;
c) establishment or construction of markets and other public requirements or conveniences.[6]

Plans may also 'provide for the construction of houses'.[7]

The Development Authority is obliged to notify the public and the Bangalore City Corporation of any scheme that it has prepared.[8] Any comments made by the Corporation and/or members of the public are considered by the Authority before it submits the plan (including comments) to the state government for approval.[9] If the government sees fit to sanction the scheme, then notice to that effect is published in the Official Gazette.[10]

Once the state government is satisfied that development of the land is complete, it declares the land to be vested or re-vested in the Bangalore City Corporation which is generally responsible for running the city.[11] Until the land is handed over to the Corporation the Development Authority takes over the Corporation's functions in those areas under its control.[12] The functions and powers of the Corporation are outlined in the Karnataka Municipal Corporations Act (1976), and relate to the provision and maintenance of infrastructure, sanitation and abatement of nuisances.[13]

Land and buildings developed by the Development Authority must be allocated to members of the public or public purpose institutions such as temples and schools. Where the Authority has implemented a development plan including the building of houses (known as a Self-Financing Housing Scheme), then the allocation of the sites is governed by Bangalore Development Authority (Allotment of Buildings under Self-Financing Housing Scheme) Rules (1982). In these situations, the housing is divided into categories of high-income group, middle-income group, and lower-income group. Under the Rules, 50 per cent of the houses will be allocated by drawing lots, and the remaining 50 per cent will be allocated according to the principles and social reservations identified in the Bangalore Development Authority (Allotment of Sites) Rules (1982) discussed below.[14]

It is noteworthy that the Development Authority has been the subject of a significant degree of public criticism regarding its role in urban development. In 1994, Dr Samuel Paul of the Public Affairs Centre in Bangalore conducted a survey of middle- and high-income group attitudes to local authorities and public service providers in Bangalore, Ahmedabad and Pune. According to the survey, the Development Authority is the most disliked of all the public institutions in Bangalore. Of the 807 respondents in Bangalore, only 1 per cent declared themselves to be 'satisfied' or 'very satisfied' with the Development Authority, while 65 per cent said that they were 'dissatisfied' or 'very dissatisfied' (Paul 1994a: 15–16). It is reported that delays in sales, corruption, the constant regularization of illegal land grabbing and utility connections, and the Authority's failure to supply basic amenities like roads, have caused a good deal of anger to Bangaloreans (*Deccan Herald*, 29 April 1995). It has been shown that slum dwellers experience at least as much dissatisfaction with the municipal institutions of Bangalore as middle- and high-income groups do. In a second survey conducted by Dr Paul in 1994, it was found that only 22 per cent of the sample of slum dwellers in Bangalore had any contact with public agencies. The report suggested that this was due to a lack of confidence in the fairness and effectiveness of the institutions. In particular, Dr Paul's slum-dweller survey found that a disturbing 32 per cent of the respondents having contact with the city's public agencies had to pay 'speed money' to get satisfaction. This was by far the worst record of the three cities surveyed (Paul 1994b: 3133). While 76 per cent of the Bangalore respondents to Dr Paul's study claimed that street lights were available in their area, only 56 per cent of those people found the facility of any use, probably because the fixtures were there, but they rarely worked. Similar responses were made in relation to water and sanitation services (Paul 1994b: 3132).

Official private residential developments   The private rental market in Bangalore is said to be significantly hampered by legislation. According to a study conducted by Professor Tewari of the Indian Institute of Management, rent control laws are particularly to blame in this regard, because they limit the amount of rent which can be charged to a level which makes it unattractive to build properties for rental. The result is that properties are either not built or left vacant, instead of being rented out to a public in desperate need of accommodation (Suresh et al. 1992: 93). There are two remaining 'official' options open to the people of Bangalore: to build accommodation on privately acquired land, or to build accommodation on Bangalore Development Authority-developed land.

Any person wishing to develop land in Bangalore must first get the 'express sanction in writing' of the Development Authority.[15] According to the Karnataka Town and Country Planning Act (1961), the Authority is the planning authority for the city.[16] This Act provides that 'every land use, every change in land use, and every development' shall conform to the provisions of the Act and the Comprehensive Development Plan relating to the area.[17] While the Development Authority's role as the general planning authority in Bangalore will be examined in more depth in the next section, it is important to note here that no development or change in land use can be effected in Bangalore without its approval. The procedure for gaining the Authority's written approval is outlined in the Karnataka Town and Country Planning Act. Any alteration in land use or development of land can be made only after a commencement certificate has been issued in writing by the Authority in response to a written application containing a plan of proposed developments.[18]

Once sanctioned, any private development must also comply with all provisions of the Bangalore Development Authority Act, as well as any rules issued under it.[19] Such developments are subject to the Authority's control in so far as it may order work to be carried out to ensure that the streets in the area are paved and provided with drainage facilities.[20] The Authority has the power to direct persons who have begun work without the requisite permission to cease the work, to pull down any illegal constructions, and to charge the costs of restoring the land to its original state to the wrongdoer.[21] Of course, once a building is constructed, it becomes difficult to remove it, especially if third-party rights have been created. It is therefore often the case that the government will regularize unauthorized constructions instead, in pursuance of the twin goals of vote winning and convenience. For example, on 2 June 1995, the Governor of Karnataka extended the categories of eligible buildings and time limits for regularization of unauthorized constructions in the green-belt area (*Times of India*, 3 June 1995).

Alternatively, members of the public may wish to acquire land developed by the Development Authority and build upon it. Where the Authority develops land without any buildings, allocations are governed by the Bangalore Development Authority (Allotment of Sites) Rules (1982). The intention to allot sites must be publicized in local newspapers.[22] The Authority is empowered, with the sanction of the state government, to set apart 30 per cent of a development to be allotted to 'economically weaker' persons and sold at 50 per cent of the value of the land under section 4 of the Rules. Economically weaker persons are defined as having an income of up to 4,800 rupees.[23] In all developments (including Self-Financing Housing Schemes), the Authority 'shall consider the case of each applicant on its merits' and take into account the following in respect of the applicant: number of children, income, capacity to purchase a site and build a house (except where the applicant is a member of a disadvantaged group such as the scheduled castes and tribes), and the number of years waited for a site.[24] The Rules specify the percentage of site allocations to go to each section of society. For example, 13 per cent are to go to scheduled castes, 3 per cent to scheduled tribes, 12 per cent to state government servants, and 2 per cent to physically handicapped persons. The general public are allotted 49 per cent of the sites.[25]

Unofficial private residential developments   It has been noted that the provision of both official public and official private accommodation is hampered by legislation. Those situations in which Bangaloreans attempt to provide accommodation for themselves, outside the legal framework, remain to be discussed.

Unsurprisingly, the most badly affected members of the public with regard to housing are the poor. The observation of one author that in India 'owing to income inequalities the rich may be able to afford apartments comparable to those in New York or London, but the poor cannot afford the equivalent of London's council housing' is certainly true of Bangalore's population (Crook 1993: 146). While this section will concentrate on low-income-group unofficial developments in Bangalore, it should be noted that it is not only slum areas that are created unofficially or illegally. Many middle- and high-income group residential developments are also made without following the proper planning procedures. As will be seen, however, these constructions are often subsequently regularized by the government.

In 1993 there were approximately 400 slums in Bangalore. Slum dwellers comprised about 13–14 per cent of the population, and about 60 per cent of the slum dwellers were migrants. A 1989 survey showed that 96 per cent of slum households had no water supply and 92 per cent, no sanitation, and that 80 per cent went without electricity (Sluaramakrishnan 1993: 137).

As Crook (1993) observes, several studies have indicated that slum dwellers in India know that they are unable to afford official housing and therefore build slum housing that they intend to be permanent. It is the intention of Indian slum dwellers to stay in and upgrade the accommodation that they provide for themselves, rather than moving on, which distinguishes them from their peers in some other countries (Crook 1993). Indeed, it has been acknowledged by Indian government publications that informal or unofficial development of accommodation 'have performed far better than legal supply systems' (Verma 1996: 4). This realization has led to a new policy, instigated by the National Commission on Urbanization of 1988 and implemented in the National Housing Policy of 1994 and the Seventh National Five-year Plan (1992–97), of encouraging the upgrading of slum accommodation and the extension of security of tenure to slum dwellers (Bhatnagar 1996: 2–3).

In 1995, the Minister of State for Bangalore City Development announced the government's intention to 'take stringent measures to clear all slums in the city'. He hoped to get voluntary agencies to assist in providing drainage facilities to the areas and declared a need for multi-storey accommodation for the poor (*Deccan Herald*, 22 June 1995). The Karnataka Slum Clearance Board is intended to 'eliminate congestion, provide basic needs such as streets, water supply and drainage and to clear the slums'. Former residents of a cleared slum should be provided with new accommodation by the Karnataka Housing Board under the Karnataka Housing Board Act (1962). While the Slum Clearance Board has notified certain areas as slums, however, it has been said that little progress has been made in providing accommodation for the inhabitants, because the land on which they have been living is not of an adequate size to permit construction of the homes required. The authorities have therefore been forced to find extra land on which to build. That task requires a degree of co-ordination and resources which the various authorities are, it is alleged, incapable of providing (Karnataka United Urban Citizens Federation 1989: 8–9).

The result is that slum dwellers are often left to fend for themselves in a real estate market which is unaffordable even for the well-off. It is alleged that developers on occasion set fire to slums in order to frighten the residents into leaving, and then claim that the slum dwellers have started the fires in order to get government compensation for fire damage.[26] This type of incident, if true, illustrates the extent to which the value of land in Bangalore is dictating the city's future, and provides a backdrop for the following case study.

Case Study: the National Games Housing Complex

Having outlined the major problems associated with urban change in the field of residential land use in Bangalore, it remains to examine a case in which these problems were manifested. This section deals with a legal challenge to a proposed official residential development in the city that clearly indicates the clashes that can occur between public official, private official and private unofficial residential developments in Bangalore.

In September of 1994, the government of Karnataka ordered that a major new housing complex should be built in an area known as Koramangala, in order to house the athletes and officials of the forthcoming National Games.[27] The proposed site for the complex was on 47 acres of land owned by the Public Works Department of the Bangalore City Corporation. The land in question was the *atchkat* (irrigated land surrounding a tank) left by the old Shinivagalu water tank and was categorized in the 1984 Comprehensive Development Plan as 'parks and open spaces'. Furthermore, the *atchkat* in question and the nearby Belandur tank have long been used by various species of bird as a breeding ground, and both are considered to be ecologically sensitive areas. The forest department has itself classified the land and Belandur tank as 'wetlands' to be preserved under the Ramsar Conventions.

The government order implementing the scheme explained that:

> the Government of Karnataka has decided to link the requirement for the accommodation of National Games to the proposed project for construction of multi storied flats for Government employees at Koramangala, keeping into account the possibility of utilization of the constructed space after the National Games and since the requirement for the Games is only for a period of 11 days.

The complex is to include 5,000 flats, as well as 'various medical and other services, post offices, shopping complex, telecommunications centres, caterers, and office accommodation'. The order further specified that only builders having 'international experience with prefabricated construction of houses' would be considered for the tender.[28]

The scheme was to be financed by loans from the national Housing and Urban Development Corporation and other financial institutions, and the government order in question authorized the Housing and Urban Development Department to negotiate 'for securing most favourable terms and conditions for the loan'. The land required was ordered to be transferred, free of charge, from the Public Works Department to the Karnataka Housing Board 'in return for the transfer of 1,200 constructed flats by KHB to PWD in 1996 after the National Games are over'. Of those 1,200 flats, 232 were to be set aside for judicial officers and their design was to be specified by the Public Works Department. Rules requiring that Karnataka Housing Board accommodation is allotted on a first-come first-served basis were relaxed in order to allow the flats to be sold to predetermined customers, such as the Public Works Department. Furthermore, the Housing Board was authorized to sell the remaining 3,800 flats at a price 'inclusive of the cost of construction of all the 5,000 flats' rather than simply including the cost of the 3,800 flats themselves.[29] The order empowered the Karnataka Housing Board to be approved as the agency for the building, and specified that the project was to be a 'special project' for the building of MIG (middle-income group) and HIG (high-income group) flats. The government went on to set aside the requirements that would under normal circumstances force the Housing Board to provide LIG (lower-income group) or EWS (economically weaker section) houses as a matter of course when building any housing complex. The clearance and initial construction phases of the project were passed in a record-breaking three months.[30]

In April 1995, a group called CIVIC and five other Bangalore-based non-government organizations challenged the legality of the 400 crore rupee project by filing a public interest petition in the High Court of Karnataka. Their aims were, first, to obtain an interim stay order to prevent further work on the project, and, second, to force the land to be returned to its original status of parks and open spaces.

The petition against the project is based on four major grounds: land acquisition, land reclassification, publicity of the scheme and housing legislation.

First, the legality of the acquisition of the land for residential purposes and the procedures by which the scheme was passed are in question. In particular, it is said that rules concerning the conversion of public parks to other uses, and the proper procedures for public consultation under the Karnataka Town and Country Planning Act have been violated.

Any developments in Bangalore are to be subject to the existing Comprehensive Development Plan for the area, which details 'the manner in which the development and improvement of the entire planning area ... are to be carried out and regulated'. The Comprehensive Development Plan should:

Include proposals for ... comprehensive zoning of land use ... complete street pattern ... areas reserved for agriculture, parks, playgrounds and other recreational uses, public open spaces, public buildings and institutions and areas reserved for such other purposes as may be expedient for new civic development ... areas for new housing [and] new areas earmarked for future development and expansion.[31]

The Development Authority is obliged to submit the proposed Development Plan for approval by the state government. Following provisional state-level approval, the report is to be notified and published for public comments. Comments are accepted over a three-month period, after which the Authority is to resubmit the plan to the state, including such recommendations as it sees fit in order to take into account the comments of the public. The plan must then be finally approved by the state (with or without its own alterations) and made available to the public.[32] The plan may (and, if required by the state government, shall) be revised at least every five years, following the same procedure laid out for the original plan.[33]

Of particular interest in the context of the National Games Complex case is section 24, which states that any existing Comprehensive Development Plans must be followed. This would normally prevent the building of the National Games housing project in Koramangala, as the area concerned was classified under the 1984 Comprehensive Development Plan as 'park' and 'open spaces'. When the Development Plan was revised in 1994, the land continued to be so classified and the plan proceeded through the proper stages of consultation and publicity, until suddenly the land was transferred to the 'residential' category, just before final state government approval was given to the new plan. No notification was given to the public of the change. The petitioners in this case claim that this rendered the procedure for the conversion of the category illegal.[34] If this is the case then any permission for building in the area would be in contravention of the Comprehensive Development Plan and therefore illegal under the Karnataka Town and Country Planning Act.

It is also of interest to note that section 38 of the Bangalore Development Authority Act gives the Authority the power to: 'Lease, sell or otherwise transfer any movable or immovable property that belongs to it, and to appropriate or apply any land vested in or acquired by it for the formation of open spaces or for building purposes or in any other manner for the purpose of any development scheme.'[35] In 1991, however, the Act was amended to include the restriction that the Development Authority 'shall not sell or otherwise dispose of any area reserved for public parks and playgrounds and civic amenities for any other purpose and any disposition so made shall be null and void'.[36] According to the petitioners, the Authority claims that the disposition of the Koramangala land was not subject to section 33A of the Bangalore Development Authority Act, because the Act does not concern itself with the Karnataka Housing Board, to whom the land was transferred by the Public Works Department, and which would be responsible for the sale of the flats.[37] While this contention is probably correct, to allow the conversion of the Koramangala land to a residential classification could be seen as a violation of the spirit of section 33A of the Bangalore Development Authority Act and section 24 of the Karnataka Town and Country Planning Act.

It is reported that the Secretary to the Department of Housing and Urban Development claims that under sections 25 and 22(3) of the Town and Country Planning Act the government has 'inherent powers' to make whatever last-minute alterations it deems necessary before giving its final consent to Comprehensive Development Plans (*Deccan Herald*, 25 February 1995). These sections, discussed above, govern the creation and revisions of such plans in the city. Section 22(3) states that the state government shall 'give its final approval to the plan and the report *with such modifications as it deems fit*', and section 25 makes the same applicable to any revisions of the Comprehensive Development Plan (emphasis added). If this interpretation of the Act is found to be correct then the public consultation procedures required during the initial stages of passing a Comprehensive Development Plan are for all practical purposes rendered useless.

The second ground for the petition is that the project was not properly publicized. The petitioners claim that the Koramangala development constitutes a 'scheme' within the meaning of section 2(12) of the Karnataka Town and Country Planning Act and that therefore, under sections 28 to 34, the Development Authority is bound to undertake a publication and consultation procedure. Sections 28 to 34 of the Town and Country Planning Act require the Authority to follow a publication and consultation procedure which is similar to that outlined in sections 15 to 19 of the Bangalore Development Authority Act in relation to 'development schemes'.

Under the Town and Country Planning Act, the Development Authority must publish its declaration of intention to make a town planning scheme within twenty-one days of making the declaration and make the plan of the area available to the public. Within twelve months of the declaration, the Authority must publish the details of the draft scheme. If it fails to publish the scheme then the state government may do so instead. If the state government fails to publish the scheme, then the declaration of intention to make a scheme is no longer valid and no further such declarations may be made in respect of that area for three years.[38]

Under the Bangalore Development Authority Act, no public declaration of intention to create a plan need be given. A development scheme need not be made public until after the scheme has been prepared, at which point it must be published, a copy must be put on display, and individuals owning land to be acquired under the scheme must be notified.[39] Publication is again required when the state government sanctions the scheme.[40]

It is not clear why the petitioners have chosen to challenge the project using sections 28 to 34 of the Karnataka Town and Country Planning Act rather than sections 15 to 19 of the Bangalore Development Authority Act. It appears that 'town planning schemes' in the former Act are indistinguishable from 'development schemes' in the latter. Moreover, section 73 of the Development Authority Act states that it shall override other existing laws, and section 74M of the Town and Country Planning Act states that a development shall not be considered to be illegal where it does not comply with the Act but does comply with other legislation. It therefore seems both appropriate and logical to attack the Koramangala scheme using the provisions of the Development Authority Act which is the most recent piece of legislation on the subject. It is, however, possible that the petitioners see more opportunities for challenging the scheme through the Town and Country Planning Act under which publication of the scheme is required at the earlier stage of declaration of intent, and under which the declaration becomes invalid if the plan is not published in time. It remains to be seen what the courts will make of this decision.

A further obstacle to this ground of challenge is that the land concerned was transferred by the state to the Karnataka Housing Board to build the flats, and the relevant provisions of the Bangalore Development Authority Act and the Karnataka Town and Country Planning Act do not apply to the plans of bodies other than the Development Authority. The court may find difficulty in accepting this technical evasion of planning procedures. It is likely that it will prefer to take the view that it is unjust and illogical to allow the Authority to transfer development activities to other bodies thus avoiding consultation procedures with impunity.

The third ground for challenge of the Koramangala project is that the scheme itself violates certain principles of the law relating to housing in Bangalore. The 2,800 flats are being built by the Karnataka Housing Board using money lent by the Housing and Urban Development Corporation, an autonomous body created by the central government. The flats are to be used by athletes and Games officials for just eleven days. After the Games, half of the flats are to be used to house government officials and the other half are to be sold off to high-income buyers for a profit. Under section 32(2) of the Karnataka Housing Board Act (1962) the Board is expressly not allowed to make a profit from its activities. The Board claims that it is merely generating resources for its own use, rather than making a profit. Also, the spirit of the Housing Act does not allow for developments set aside for expressly high-income use.[41] The project has, however, been 'termed a special project' in order to relax the Housing Board rules and allowing it to provide high-income housing only. Not even a small amount of funds was set aside for the rehousing of the slum dwellers living in the area. The three or four hundred families have been relocated on a refuse dump. Ironically, the slum dwellers had applied to have a section of the land allocated to them, so that they could build proper housing, but their request was refused because the area was categorized under the Comprehensive Development Plan as park and open space. Before work began on the National Games Housing Complex, there were ten suspicious slum fires in the area, and three people were killed. It is alleged that these fires were started by the company responsible for building the Complex.[42] An activist who works with slum dwellers claimed that the failure of the government to investigate these incidents or to give the dwellers legal rights to the land that they inhabited 'makes one believe that the private builders are being supported and encouraged by the government to harass the poor, in view of the proposed National Games Complex' (*The Hindu*, 19 April 1995).

Outside the courtroom, it has been suggested that the Karnataka Housing Board could easily have built housing for the Games on the land that it already owns in Kengeri satellite town, instead of adding to the congestion of Bangalore. Alternatively, it could have used the 2,500 flats that are built and empty, and the 8,000 other flats that are nearing completion in the city (*Deccan Herald*, 25 January 1995).

The fourth ground of challenge is that there was no environmental impact assessment carried out on the project, as required under the Environment (Protection) Act (1986). The purpose of this Act is to provide a general framework for the protection of the environment in India.[43] The central government has issued a notification under the Act that requires that any proposal for expansion and/or modernization of an existing project, or for the creation of a new project where that project falls within schedule one of the notification, shall not be undertaken unless it has been given environmental clearance.[44] An application for such clearance shall include an Environmental Impact Assessment Report/Environment Action Plan.[45] Schedule one of the notification lists the types of projects for which clearance must be obtained. It is difficult to see how the National Games Complex fits into any of the categories, which are concerned primarily with large-scale industrial or irrigation projects. The most closely conforming category is that of 'tourism projects'. To construe the National Games Complex as a tourism project would require an untenable degree of interpretative elasticity. It is doubtful that this ground of the petition will succeed.

The petitioners in the case are demanding that the land be returned to being parks and open space and that trees be planted on it.[46] It is difficult to see how this can be done when, by March 1996, the vast majority of the construction had been completed. The court has yet to pass judgment on this case, but the political effect of the legal challenge is already wide-reaching. Whether the High Court of Karnataka finds in favour of the government or the petitioners, and whether or not it is possible in the latter case to reverse the effect of the completed project, the National Games case has performed the important function of stirring a significant degree of debate among public officials and residents of Bangalore. Opposition party members have taken an interest in the affair and accused the government of irregularities in the awarding of contracts and the Estimates Committee of the Karnataka legislature is investigating the financial aspects of the project (*The Hindu*, 18 April 1995). In addition, board members of the national Housing and Urban Development Corporation are also questioning the propriety of the scheme.[47]

Conclusion

It is clear that the law cannot rationally be excluded from a consideration of urban change. It controls the ways in which urban change can legally occur, which in turn dictates the methods by which people are forced to evade rules in order to survive. Furthermore, it provides, at least in India's legal system, a means by which the public can control the destiny of their surroundings. As the mirror, the protector, and the weapon of social goals, the law is central to the process of urban change.

Notes

Amanda Perry wishes to thank the Ford Foundation and the Economic and Social Research Council (ESRC) for financial assistance during the field work on which this chapter is based.

1. See Anderson and Perry (1996) for a detailed description of the status of Bangalore.

2. One lakh is 100,000. One crore is ten million, or 100 lakhs.

3. Section 68, Bangalore Development Authority Act (1976).

4. Section 14, Bangalore Development Authority Act (1976).

5. Section 16(1), Bangalore Development Authority Act (1976).

6. Direct quotation from section 16(2), Bangalore Development Authority Act (1976).

7. Section 16(3), Bangalore Development Authority Act (1976).

8. Section 17, Bangalore Development Authority Act (1976).

9. Section 18, Bangalore Development Authority Act (1976).

10. Section 19, Bangalore Development Authority Act (1976).

11. Section 30(1), Bangalore Development Authority Act (1976).

12. Sections 28–29, Bangalore Development Authority Act (1976).

13. Section 58, Karnataka Municipal Corporations Act (1976).

14. Sections 7–8, Bangalore Development Authority (Allotment of Buildings under Self-Financing Housing Scheme) Rules (1982).

15. Section 32, Bangalore Development Authority Act (1976).

16. Section 81B, Karnataka Town and Country Planning Act (1961).

17. Sections 24 and 14(1), Karnataka Town and Country Planning Act (1961).

18. Section 14(2) and 14(3), Karnataka Town and Country Planning Act (1961).

19. Section 32, Bangalore Development Authority Act (1976).
20. Section 34, Bangalore Development Authority Act (1976).
21. Section 15(4), Karnataka Town and Country Planning Act (1961).
22. Section 3(2), Bangalore Development Authority (Allotment of Sites) Rules (1982).
23. Section 2, Bangalore Development Authority (Allotment of Sites) Rules (1982).
24. Section 11(1), Bangalore Development Authority (Allotment of Sites) Rules (1982).
25. Section 11(4), Bangalore Development Authority (Allotment of Sites) Rules (1982).
26. Interview with Bangalore civil rights activist, Bangalore, 6 May 1995.
27. Government of Karnataka Order no. HUD 161 KHB 94, Bangalore, 2 September 1994.
28. Ibid.
29. Ibid.
30. Interview with Bangalore civil rights activist, Bangalore, 6 May 1995.
31. Section 21(1), Karnataka Town and Country Planning Act (1961).
32. Section 22, Karnataka Town and Country Planning Act (1961).
33. Section 25, Karnataka Town and Country Planning Act (1961).
34. Interview with Bangalore civil rights activist, Bangalore, 6 May 1995.
35. Section 38, Bangalore Development Authority Act (1976).
36. Section 38A, Bangalore Development Authority Act (1976).
37. Interview with Bangalore civil rights activist, Bangalore, 6 May 1995.
38. Sections 29 and 30, Karnataka Town and Country Planning Act (1961).
39. Section 17, Bangalore Development Authority Act (1976).
40. Section 19, Bangalore Development Authority Act (1976).
41. Interview with Bangalore civil rights activist, Bangalore, 6 May 1995.
42. Ibid.
43. Statement of Objects and Reasons, Environment (Protection) Act (1986).
44. Section 1, S.O. 60 (E) 27 January 1994 as amended by S.O. 230 (E) 17 March 1994.
45. Section 2(1), S.O. 60 (E) 27 January 1994 as amended by S.O. 230 (E) 17 March 1994.
46. Interview with Bangalore civil rights activist, Bangalore, 6 May 1995.
47. Ibid.

References

Anderson, M. A. and A. J. Perry (1996) *Access to Environmental Justice in Bangalore*, School of Oriental and African Studies Working Paper no. 8, University of London, London.

Banerjee, B. (1996) 'Where are we?', *Shelter: Special Edition on Land*, January, 7.

Bhatnagar, K. K. (1996) 'Extension of security of tenure to urban slum population in India: status and trends', *Shelter: Special Edition on Land*, January, 2–3.

Crook, N. (1993) *India's Industrial Cities: Essays in Economy and Demography*, School of Oriental and African Studies Studies on South Asia, Oxford University Press, New Delhi.

Karnataka State Government (1995) *Draft Annual Plan 1995–1996, Karnataka State*

Government. Vol. II, Planning Institutional Finance and Statistics and Science and Technology Department, Bangalore.

Karnataka United Urban Citizens Federation (1989) *Save Bangalore*, KUUCF, Bangalore.

Paul, S. (1994a) *A Report Card on Public Services in Indian Cities: A View from Below*, Public Affairs Centre Research Paper no. 4, Bangalore.

— (1994b) 'Public services for the urban poor: report card on three Indian cities', *Economic and Political Weekly*, Vol. XXIX, no. 50, 3131–3.

Sluaramakrishnan, K. C. (1993) *Managing Urban Environment in India. Vol. 2*, Times Research Foundation, Calcutta.

Suresh, V., D. Nagasaila and D. Geetha (eds) (1992) *The Hindu: Survey of the Environment*, Sri S Rangaraja, Madras.

Verma, G. D. (1996) 'Land for the urban poor: the path where we stand', *Shelter: Special Edition on Land*, January, 4–5.

CHAPTER 6

Law and Urban Change: Illegal Settlements in the Philippines

Asteya M. Santiago

The Philippines' experience in the formulation and implementation of laws which influence urban development, and specifically those affecting illegal settlements, is a long and continuing story within the broader legal, political and socio-economic changes affecting the country. It reflects the vision and the formal and informal agenda of the decision-makers and other stakeholders, and the countless forms taken by the exercise of political will.

The two most important factors influencing the outcome of legislation on urban development have been policy-makers' perceptions of the significance and priority to be accorded this area of concern, and the way in which these perceptions have been translated into legislation and implemented by government agencies.

In the Philippines, the term 'illegal settlements' refers primarily to settlements on government and/or private properties to which the occupants, generally the urban poor, have no title or any semblance of one, or which they occupy without the knowledge or against the express wishes of the lawful owners. The term may also apply to areas whose residents knowingly or unknowingly break the planning regulations. Non-compliance with the legal requirements for housing development and/or the introduction of urban services often accompanies unlawful occupation of the land. It might appear almost natural that when a settlement is founded outside the law, a failure to comply with the rules on building construction and land development should follow. This is not to say that such an outcome has been deliberately planned, in flagrant violation of the laws in question. Violations generally arise out of ignorance of legal requirements or residents' inability to comply with the high standards imposed.

Illegal settlements have been part of the country's urban landscape for more than half a century. They are known by a variety of names such as 'squatter and slum areas' or (following international usage) 'uncontrolled', 'informal' or 'invasion' settlements. The political, legal and administrative response to illegal settlement has also varied, with different consequences for the pattern, quality and direction of urban development.

The situation has been complicated by the fact that the prospects for these types of area are affected, not only by the legal measures directly concerning them, but also by legislation and policy directives on matters which may at first appear to be of only peripheral significance to the status and conditions of their occupants. These include property law amendments affecting the rights and obligations associated with land ownership, and a wide range of economic and fiscal measures seeking to promote the economic stability and self-sufficiency of the country's citizens. They also include reforms affecting land use plan implementation. For example, the provision of 'socialized housing' (including slum clearance and the relocation and resettlement of squatters and slum dwellers) has been recognized as meeting the 'public interest' requirement for expropriation on the grounds of eminent domain. Other laws of relevance to our discussion are those establishing new strategies for rural development, such as agrarian reform and land conversion laws, and measures seeking to provide better protection for human rights, particularly those of the poor urban residents of illegal settlements.

In short, other legal measures have influenced the way decision-makers deal with illegal settlement, and some of these – such as human rights policies – have made illegal settlement a more controversial and often an emotionally charged issue.

The Philippines: Location and Socio-economic Characteristics

History and demography The Philippines has a land area of some 115,600 square miles (300,000 km²). An archipelago, it consists of more than 7,000 islands, only 800 of which are permanently settled. The exact number of islands has varied over the years as some become submerged to re-emerge later (Roland 1967). The biggest of the islands are Luzon (where Metro Manila is located), Visayas and Mindanao.

The country's most significant cultural imports from its curious mix of colonizers (the Spaniards for 400 years, the British for two, the Japanese for four and the Americans for forty years) are generally acknowledged to be Christianity from Spain and republican democracy from the United States. Hispanic Christianity and American democracy have, however, been fundamentally reshaped to fit pre-Western spiritual notions and social processes (Corpuz 1970).

The population of the Philippines had reached 66 million by the mid-1990s and is growing at 2.2 per cent each year. The urban population rose from 24 per cent in 1948 to 42 per cent in 1989, and is expected to reach 48 per cent of the total by the year 2000 (Nuqui 1991).

Socio-economic characteristics In the past three decades the country has emerged from its unique pre-1960s dual economy. This featured, on the one hand, a large agricultural sector supporting a population living at or near subsistence level who maintained a traditional way of life amid the onset of modernization; and, on the other, small towns which were fairly prosperous and more receptive to modern techniques and new ideas (Corpuz 1970).

From its primary reliance on agriculture, the Philippines has become more economically diversified. The employment share of the agricultural sector declined from 58 per cent in 1958 to 46 per cent in 1989, while the manufacturing and service sector's share rose from 26 per cent to 35 per cent over the same period (Nuqui 1991). By the late 1980s the Philippine economy had registered some economic gains, although their distribution had been highly unequal. Thus, rural incomes amounted to only 40.5 per cent, 48.0 per cent, and 47.4 per cent of urban incomes in 1961, 1971, and 1985 respectively. In 1985, the top 20 per cent of all families controlled 51.1 per cent of total income, while the bottom 30 per cent, the poorest of the poor, received only 9.9 per cent (University of Santo Tomas Research Center 1992).

Since the dismantling of martial rule in 1986, the Philippines has launched an aggressive economic recovery programme, leading to what the administration of President Fidel V. Ramos calls 'the Philippines 2000'. Its basic thrust is to put the country back to the economically competitive position which it enjoyed during the late 1960s, with a view to achieving, by the turn of the century, the status of a Newly Industrialized Country (Ramos 1997). The present government's Social Reform Agenda addresses the following objectives: poverty alleviation, social justice, sustained economic growth and the generation of productive employment (MMDA-JICA 1996).

Urban poverty In 1985, the number of Filipino families living below the poverty line (those deemed unable to meet their basic needs) was estimated to be 5.67 million or 59.3 per cent of all families. The number of people living in poverty had leapt from 20.5 million in 1971, to 30.6 million in 1985. By 1988, it was 35 million, 30 million of whom were reported to be living in absolute poverty, deprived of basic needs such as food, shelter, health services and education (University of Santo Tomas Research Center 1992).

Most of the poor urban families are in the Metropolitan Manila Area (which consists of seventeen local government units), and in the other highly urbanized areas. About 1.5 million families display the universal characteristics of the urban poor in third world countries: they are engaged in informal service sector activities; their average income is half that of other urban families; and they dwell in substandard homes located in densely occupied areas (University of Santo Tomas Research Center 1992).

The most visible manifestation of urban poverty is the increasing number of squatter settlements. It has been reported that in major cities nation-wide there are over 10 million dwellers in slum and squatter settlements. They are mostly found in Metro Manila and the cities of Davao, Cebu and Bacolod in Visayas and Mindanao (Nuqui 1991).

The Political and Legal Environment

Structure of government The Philippines gained independence in 1946; it was the first of the new nations to achieve full political freedom after World War II (Kuhn and Kuhn 1966). It is now a democratic and republican state with three equal branches of government: the legislative, executive and judicial branches. Legislative power is vested in a two-chamber Congress consisting of a twenty-four-person Senate and a House of Representatives with not more than two hundred members. Executive power is vested in the President of the Philippines, while judicial power is exercised by one Supreme Court and such lower courts as may be created by law.[1]

The relationships between the three branches of government are defined by the principle of checks and balances such that each branch is given certain powers with which to check the exercise by the others of their constitutional functions (De Leon 1994). The power of judicial review which authorizes the judiciary to declare any legislative or executive act invalid is not seen as undermining the equal status of these branches. The Supreme Court merely enforces and upholds the supremacy of the Constitution as the highest law of the land, against which the acts of the legislative and executive branches are measured (De Leon 1994).

The country's government is unitary in form, with the President exercising general supervision over the territorial and political subdivisions of local government units (LGUs) consisting of the provinces, cities, municipalities and *barangays*. These LGUs are assured their local autonomy by the Constitution and the 1991 Local Government Code.[2]

Legal structure The Philippines is a highly legalistic society, where there is practically no aspect of socio-economic and cultural life that is not governed by statutes or other forms of regulation. The source of all legal directives is the Constitution, the highest law of the land. Below the Constitution are the other legal measures, namely national statutes (called 'Republic Acts'); executive and administrative orders (the two most common legal measures of the President); and memorandum orders or circulars emanating from more than a dozen departments of the bureaucracy. There are also local ordinances issued by the LGUs, and by the Metropolitan Manila Development Authority (MMDA), the agency responsible for the seventeen local government units constituting the metropolitan area.

According to the Philippines' revised Civil Code, judicial decisions interpreting the laws or the Constitution form part of the country's legal system. The Court's interpretation of a statute thus constitutes part of the law as of the date it was originally passed, because it is held to establish contemporaneous legislative intent that the interpreted law carries into effect (Tolentino 1990).

The Constitutional Framework for Urban Settlements Legislation

There are a number of broad constitutional provisions which provide the basis for legislating on the various aspects of low-income urban settlements. One is the principle which seeks to free the people from poverty through policies that provide adequate social services and promote full employment, a rising standard of living and an improved quality of life for all.[3] Another is that which prioritizes the enactment of legislation 'that protects and enhances the right of all the people to human dignity, reduces social, economic and political inequalities and removes cultural inequities'. For this purpose, the state is authorized, in the common interest, to regulate the acquisition, ownership, use and disposal of property and its increments.[4]

Another provision of the Constitution with a significant impact on these communities is that which empowers the Commission of Human Rights[5] to provide assistance and legal aid to the underprivileged whose human rights might have been violated or need protection.[6] The relevance of this provision becomes obvious when it is considered that in various parts of Asia, including the Philippines, the ways in which poor families have been evicted from their settlements have been criticized as bordering on a violation of their human rights (*Manila Chronicle*, 26 January 1994).

For the first time in the country's history, the Philippine Constitution of 1987 established a legal framework for the enactment of laws to rationalize urban development, and, more specifically, to improve the conditions of low-income urban settlements and safeguard the rights of their occupants. While earlier constitutions contained provisions with implications for urban land, it was the 1987 Constitution which explicitly provided comprehensive mandates for land reform in urban areas. The relevant provisions are contained in the article on Social Justice and Human Rights (Article XIII); 'social justice' here includes 'the commitment to create economic opportunities based on the freedom of initiative and self reliance'.[7]

Within this framework are specific sections directly affecting low-income urban settlements.[8] These are the provisions dealing with urban land and housing. They cover the following:

a) the legal authority for the state to co-operate with the private sector in a continuing programme of urban land reform and housing to make decent housing and basic services available at affordable prices to underprivileged and homeless citizens
b) respect for the rights of small property owners in the implementation of this programme
c) non-eviction of urban and rural dwellers and the non-demolition of their dwellings except in accordance with law and in a just and humane manner
d) adequate consultation with urban and rural dwellers and with the communities where they are to be relocated, before they are resettled.

These broad mandates have recently been translated into specific functions, tasks and activities for both national agencies and LGUs by the Urban Development and Housing Act of 1992 which now governs urban planning and development in the country.[9]

The Formulation and Implementation of Laws Affecting Illegal Settlements

The legislative record   By the early 1990s, the Philippines had accumulated extensive experience in the provision of land for housing and urban development purposes. Their statutory basis lies in the legal measures issued by the legislative and executive branches of government. A review of the plethora of legislation on the subject shows that these laws can be divided into the following categories (PLANADES 1988). Examples of the most important legislation in each category are included.

1. *Land documentation and registration*   This category includes laws to streamline and regulate the titling and registration of land. Among them are laws which:

a) facilitate the registration of land
b) order the compulsory survey and registration of all lands within cities and municipalities
c) require the registration of instruments or transactions involving unregistered private lands
d) provide a special procedure for the judicial and/or administrative reconstruction of lost or destroyed certificates of title.

2. *Land acquisition*   This category of legislation aims to promote the expansion of the pool of government or private lands which can be devoted to housing and other social services, facilities and amenities. Examples include those laws which have:

a) modified the area of public lands that may be acquired under various forms of concession
b) regulated the sale or lease of government lands
c) authorized the acquisition at public auction of public lands, by sale or lease, for residential, commercial, industrial or other productive purposes
d) granted municipalities and cities the authority to reclaim foreshore areas, at their own expense, by dredging, filling or other means.

3. *Land development* The objective of legislation in this category is to regulate the development of public and private lands; to provide lands for housing the poor and disadvantaged groups; and to explore other land tenure systems as alternatives to ownership. Among the more important measures under this heading are:

a) the empowerment of the Human Settlements Commission to formulate an integrated national plan on policies, standards and guidelines for the development of human settlements
b) the formulation of rules governing land subdivision and condominium development
c) the application of innovative land use and land tenure schemes to help solve the housing problems of low-income groups
d) the declaration of urban land reform zones and of areas for priority development to increase low-income families' access to housing
e) the regulation of land conversion from agricultural to urban uses.

4. *Land alienation and provision* These laws aim to regulate the alienation of land for specific purposes, with the aim of making more lands available for public use, particularly for housing. They include laws authorizing or regulating the following:

(a) land subdivision for urban development and its sale at public auction
(b) the alienation of friar lands[10] to qualified Filipino citizens
(c) the area of public lands that may be acquired under government concessions
(d) the sale or lease of lands from the private domain of the government
(e) the subdivision and sale of government lands in military reservations no longer needed for military purposes
(f) the purchase and/or expropriation by cities and municipalities of vacant properties and estates, and their subdivision for resale at cost price
(g) the sale of certain foreshore lands to lessees or their existing occupants.

Implementation

The post-war years The list of legislation influencing the extent to which the urban poor can avail themselves of land for housing undoubtedly appears impressive at first sight. The implementation of these laws, and the extent to which they have actually solved the housing problems of the poor and reduced the growth of illegal settlement is, however, a different story. There are no comprehensive studies of this subject, but a study by Richard Poethig on the implementation of policies affecting squatting in Metropolitan Manila from the 1940s to the 1960s showed how legislators and the executive had dealt with these issues (*Solidarity*, 4 November 1969).[11] The major findings of this study are discussed in the following paragraphs. In conjunction with an update on developments in recent decades, it provides valuable insights into the present status and possible future experience of illegal settlement in the Philippines.

The twenty-year postwar period analysed by Poethig was characterized by a constant stream of migrants from the rural hinterlands which caused rapid urban growth and put pressure on the infrastructure and amenities of all the major cities. The period also saw the proliferation of the squatter settlements which had begun to present problems for government officials and landowners since the end of World War II, and which, almost thirty years later, remains one of the most intractable problems facing most cities in the country.

Poethig's major findings are dwelt on at length because they remain as relevant and instructive as they were in the 1960s. They even read like a commentary on illegal settlement in the Philippines in the 1990s.

First, Poethig found that squatting had been treated as a local problem rather than a priority issue affecting national development. This short-sighted approach was aggravated by the government's response to squatting being confined to Metropolitan Manila, with little attention given to other urban areas. The LGUs in these areas were unable to respond effectively to the problem because of a lack of financial resources with which to provide the facilities and services needed for the rational expansion of their cities.

Second, the government's approach to solving the problem suffered from rural bias. It viewed migration to the urban areas as a rural problem to be addressed by means of an appropriate rural solution. Policies such as the relocation and retraining of illegal settlers had, according to Poethig, 'miscalculated their aspirations', operating on a 'let us return him to his rural roots' basis. This approach ignored the reality: that the exodus of rural dwellers to Manila had been motivated by a desire to get away from the land and take advantage of the opportunities on offer in the city. An obvious demonstration of the urban character of the squatter problem was provided by the return to the city of the great majority of families resettled in rural areas.

Third, policies towards squatting were both inconsistent and ambivalent, alternating between permissiveness and harsh treatment. They also suffered from political opportunism and clientilism: for example, where protection from eviction was provided in exchange for votes; where long-drawn-out legal procedures provided opportunities for politicians to intercede on behalf of illegal settlers; and where low-income housing units were allocated to people who did not meet the selection criteria, but who had political connections to help them gain their ends.

On the basis of these findings, the Poethig study put forward a comprehensive set of recommendations which remain as relevant to the illegal settlements of the 1990s as they were to their late 1960s' counterparts. The most basic of these was the recommendation that the search for a solution to the problem of illegal settlement should focus on the issue of land and the settlers' need to secure a foothold in the city. Land ownership, according to the author, should be viewed not from a rural perspective emphasizing productivity, but an urban perspective acknowledging social mobility. Without an assurance of eventual ownership of the land on which they were squatting, or of an acceptable (urban) alternative, squatters would have little interest in improving conditions in their community.

Since squatting was a national problem, Poethig argued, responses to the squatter problem should be built into national urban and regional planning efforts making allowance for rural–urban migration patterns. The squatting problem was (and remains) most serious in Metro Manila as a result of its historic primacy. The concentration of economic, political and cultural activities in Manila had held back the development of the other regions, and an integrated urban and regional development strategy was required to address this problem. Such a strategy would include the designation of urban growth poles to provide a focus for the development of their respective regions. These growth poles would act as counter-magnets to migration to Manila and stimulate economic activity in their regions. A livelihood component would be essential for this development strategy, enabling low-income people to live near their source of income. Where resettlement was necessary, the areas selected to house relocated squatters should preferably be government-owned properties near the city. Resettlement areas should be located close to actual or planned industrial growth centres and be provided with infrastructure such as roads and an adequate supply of water and electricity.

Poethig's study also emphasized the provision of social infrastructure to provide the skills necessary for settlers to find employment on the urban labour market and enable them to adapt to an urban way of life as quickly as possible. Any policy affecting squatters should be directly related to human capital development plans, one component of which were skills training programmes to integrate the squatter population into the industrial and service sectors of the economy.

The 1970s and 1980s Many of the recommendations of the Poethig study influenced government policy during the 1970s and 1980s, a period which saw the creation of the Ministry of Human Settlements and the

National Housing Authority. These agencies went beyond the concerns of the existing planning authorities and the conventional housing strategies of previous decades, which had consisted primarily of relocation and resettlement. In many cases, these had proved unacceptable to the intended beneficiaries.

The earliest post-war central planning agencies, such as the National Urban Planning Commission, the Capital City Planning Commission and the National Planning Commission[12] had, understandably, focused on the rehabilitation of urban areas destroyed during the war. Physical planning had taken a back seat to the overall economic development effort as economic policies sought to provide for the masses of unemployed people displaced by the war and the waves of rural migrants drawn to the urban areas in search of a better life or seeking to escape the worsening law and order situation in some rural areas. Manila and its suburbs had received most of these settlers – hence the tolerance which local and national government officials had displayed towards the illegal settlements that proliferated during this period.

The postwar legislation had created the first policies seeking to provide for the planned development of the country's urban areas. They were complemented by a handful of legislative and presidential orders designed to decentralize power to the LGUs and promote local autonomy, and sought to co-ordinate the reconstruction and development of urban areas. Apart from the hundreds of city and municipal land use plans produced over the years – most of which were never implemented – there is, however, no evidence to suggest that these legal measures had effectively shaped urban development.

Several factors had militated against the government's pursuit of planned development. The basic problem was the inherent weakness of the legal measures adopted. The National Urban Planning Commission and its successor, the National Planning Commission, had been created not by law but by presidential orders. Agencies created by executive orders have little security because, unlike organizations established by statute, they can easily be abolished by subsequent presidential orders or by laws passed by Congress. In this case, moreover, the executive orders had made no provision for the agencies' funding. This had made them entirely beholden to the Office of the President which had direct control of them.

In brief, the factors which had prevented the urban planning agencies from attaining their objectives were the government's preoccupation with economic development, their lack of adequate political, financial and human resources, and the weaknesses and limitations of the organizational structure for urban planning and development. Responsive low-income housing programmes and projects were lost in the maze of planning activities of these national agencies and of local city governments.

The period of martial law (1972–86) is credited with having generated more legal measures affecting human settlements than any other period in the country's history. In addition to his presidential decrees, President Ferdinand Marcos (who had abolished Congress and was now the country's sole law-maker) also promulgated other legal measures: executive orders, administrative orders, letters of instruction, letters of implementation, memorandum circulars and proclamations.

The Marcos administration placed human settlements second only to agrarian reform at the centre of its policies. This could be attributed to the keen interest shown in planning by First Lady Imelda Marcos who, as Minister of Human Settlements and Governor of the Metropolitan Manila Commission, headed two very influential organizations during the martial law period. Her interest gained much-needed support from President Marcos who guaranteed that his wife's concerns were translated into law and administrative orders.

These presidential directives covered a wide range of government concerns from land use planning to housing provision and finance and environmental management, with the prime responsibility for their implementation falling on the shoulders of officials in the Ministry of Human Settlements complex. This included the National Housing Authority, the National Environmental Protection Council, the National Pollution Control Commission and the Human Settlements Regulatory Commission.

The verbal and written policies seeking to address the problems brought about by rapid urbanization during this period encountered many difficulties. These may be attributed to the lack of research before the policies were enacted. Some of the policies – particularly those announced verbally – were therefore abandoned before they could be implemented. In other cases, it became obvious during implementation that policy amendments would have to be introduced immediately. Examples include the shift from outright sale to leasehold of public lands (announced in President Marcos's speech on Independence Day, 12 June 1974, but subsequently shelved because of the complex problems encountered), a policy to rationalize the use of urban lands by recognizing only their legitimate tenants (Presidential Decree 1517, 1978) and proposals to penalize squatting in urban areas (Presidential Decree 772, 1975). These last two decrees were for many years the object of much criticism, leading to calls for their amendment or repeal. Presidential Decree 1517 was superseded by the Urban Development and Housing Act of 1992, and Decree 772 may soon be repealed, judging from the results of deliberations in the legislature and of nation-wide consultations with the urban poor and their supporters.

Another reason for the failure to improve living conditions in urban areas was that some measures were contradicted by subsequent legislation. An illustration of this is provided by a conflict that emerged between two apparently unrelated legal measures. Presidential Decree 1259 (1977) declared that the provision of social housing via the expropriation of lands needed for slum clearance and the relocation and resettlement of squatters and slum dwellers met the 'public interest' requirement for the valid exercise of the government's expropriation powers. Thus, while Presidential Decree 772 had penalized squatting, Decree 1259 authorized the use of expropriation to acquire lands for use by squatters, thus benefiting those who had been declared guilty of a punishable act.

This example provides a clear illustration of inconsistent and contradictory policy directives from the martial law government. It also confirms my earlier observation that some policies (such as the decree extending the government's powers of expropriation), which may not initially appear to concern the urban poor, may have positive or negative effects on them.

In response to accumulated experience with the enforcement of 1960s and 1970s legislation, the statutory directives of the 1980s leaned towards more innovative but realistic land and housing strategies. Policy-makers had realized the difficulties of achieving the ambitious targets set by earlier legislation, such as the provision of a detached home for each family (early housing projects had consisted of this type of housing) or the outright sale of the land on which these homes were constructed. This led to the exploration of other forms of land tenure in order to place housing within reach of the majority of the homeless. For it soon became obvious that detached houses and freehold plots could not be made affordable to those who were in dire need of them.

Experiments have been carried out, therefore, with medium-rise housing, alternative types of housing finance, extension of credit provision and a community mortgage programme. The mortgage programme deserves special mention as it is emerging as one of the most promising programmes for the urban poor. It was launched to provide the financial means for members of organized low-income communities to buy the plots they occupy, should the landowner agree to sell the property (*Manila Bulletin*, 20 December 1989). The policy-makers and implementors have also drawn into their originally closely-knit decision-making circle other participants, such as private sector representatives, non-government organizations and community members.

A battlecry of the Marcos regime helped pave the way towards these more innovative approaches to housing the urban poor and rationalizing urban development. It was that 'No Filipino shall be a squatter in his own land'. Although mistakenly construed by many as de-criminalizing squatting,[13] this slogan was actually intended to ensure that no Filipino should occupy any land or house illegally while living in his/her own country. This imposed a responsibility on the government to provide squatters with both the opportunity (through forms of land tenure other than ownership) and the wherewithal (through easier access to housing loans or credit) to house themselves without the constant threat of eviction.

The threat of eviction arose from the squatters' inability to demonstrate any right or title, or even any semblance of a title, to the land and/or the house they occupied.

This philosophy, seeking to give the urban poor the dignity of being law-abiding citizens and security of tenure, served as a precursor to the urban land reform introduced by the Marcos administration. The Urban Land Reform Act of 1978 (Presidential Decree 1517) consolidated existing provisions and practices promoting the planned development and up-grading of urban communities and the optimum use of land as a limited resource. In practical terms, it aimed to provide for the housing needs of those who would be unable to meet them without government assistance. The Act was supported by companion legislation controlling land values and rents so as not to exclude the urban poor from the land and rental housing markets.

The Urban Land Reform Act guaranteed equitable access to the use and enjoyment of land through various forms of tenure other than ownership. Housing agencies and LGUs were encouraged to devise in-novative land acquisition and alienation techniques to provide the urban poor with greater access to land for housing. Widely regarded as a landmark law, the Act generated undue optimism that the housing problems of the urban poor would finally find a satisfactory solution. It failed, however, to live up to expectations (PLANADES 1988). For one thing, it was targeted not at the homeless and 'legitimate' (as opposed to illegitimate or 'pro-fessional') squatters but at 'legitimate tenants'. This category was restricted to the legal occupants of land and its associated structures, excluding those whose presence was merely tolerated rather than guaranteed by contract, those who had gained access to land by force or deceit, and those whose possession was the subject of litigation.

Thus, the target beneficiaries of the Act were not the most desperate among the homeless or those who, unable to find accommodation on the open market or with government assistance, had assumed the status of illegal settlers. For although legitimate tenants are homeless in so far as they do not *own* the structures they occupy, they are not necessarily financially unable to purchase or mortgage a home. They may be capable of obtaining housing with some assistance from friends, private organiza-tions and/or lending institutions and could well be living in entirely acceptable accommodation (PLANADES 1988).

Apart from this basic deficiency, the law also had other weaknesses preventing it from fulfilling the hopes of the great many aspirants to home ownership. It made no provision for the operationalization of other forms of land tenure such as leasehold. Furthermore, the law insisted that before tenants could avail themselves of its benefits (namely, eventually to own the land or house they had been occupying for a prescribed period), they should first be able to present an existing contract with the owner of the land or house. This effectively excluded the many tenants who could not demonstrate that they had a contract with the owner.

Even assuming that the tenant could indeed present an existing contract with the owner, there were other obstacles to be overcome. Before tenants could exercise the right of first refusal on the land they were occupying, the owner would first have to decide to sell. Thus, even if tenants had been occupying the house for more than ten years – the qualification period prescribed by law – there was no way they could acquire the property if the owner refused to sell (PLANADES 1988).

Although the Urban Land Reform Act has since been amended by the 1992 Urban Development and Housing Act, these criticisms have been cited to underline the difficulty of translating what appear to be clear policy intentions (in this case, the provision of homes for the homeless) into workable legislation. It is not easy to tell whether or not such ambiguities were deliberately intended to give those responsible for implementing the policy more discretion in exercising their powers. The question of whether the deficiencies of such legislation reflect a lack of legislative ability or poor legal draughtsmanship, on the one hand, or the existence of a covert agenda, on the other, never fails to arouse debate. It may also be that the problem is one of those which simply defy solution.

The 1990s In addition to the 1987 constitutional mandate on urban land reform and housing, the Philippine Development Plan of the National Economic and Development Authority (NEDA, the country's central economic planning body) prescribes broad policies and strategies for promoting access to land and housing. Most of these appear to have been derived from the lessons learned in the implementation of earlier legislation.

NEDA policies concerning land include the promotion of a balance between population, resources and environment. The objectives are to ensure sustainable development, rationalize land use and create regional growth centres to address such concerns as land conversion and population pressure on land and other resources (NEDA 1993). As regards housing, the objectives include the identification of government lands as re-settlement sites for squatter families occupying unsafe locations or areas intended for infrastructure projects; the encouragement of private sector and NGO/government participation in the provision of low-income housing; and the implementation of a comprehensive preventive and remedial programme on squatting (NEDA 1993).

Within the framework of the 1987 Constitution and the Philippine Development Plan, other legal directives[14] intended to promote urban and regional development have become part of the country's legal system. They incorporate provisions for the planned development of cities and municipalities; the delivery of basic community services, facilities and amenities ranging from livelihood and skills training to roads, water and electricity;

the promotion of environmental management and sustainable development; and popular empowerment.

Amendments have also been introduced to existing laws and regulations such as those which guarantee local autonomy,[15] relax some standards and technical requirements for low-cost and social housing,[16] and devolve more planning functions to LGUs.[17]

Only a critical examination of the provisions of this legislation and the way it has been implemented could reveal the impact these policies have had on the housing situation to date. The policies in question involve finding ways of increasing access to land, expanding the range of tenure alternatives and regularizing illegal occupancy of government and private lands. The following section offers some observations and conclusions about the existing legislation, with a focus on illegal settlement, that could serve as the starting point for such a critical examination.

Conclusions

Urban change in the Philippines has taken place in the context of a plethora of laws and executive and administrative orders dealing with land use planning and development, housing finance and construction and the provision of urban services and amenities; all of this within a broader context of rural–urban interaction. This appears to be a promising approach, given that the housing problems of third world countries are widely regarded as revolving around land use and resource planning (Abrams and Koenigsberger 1959; McAuslan 1985; Payne 1976; Rama-chandran 1985).

In the case of the Philippines, certain observations and conclusions may be made concerning legislation affecting urban change; from these may be gleaned the nature and direction of the changes that need to be effected in this area.

There is obviously no shortage of legislation intended to address the problems of the homeless and the deprived, via, for example, the provision of easier access to land for housing and greater security of tenure. The past half-century has seen voluminous legislation issued in this area by the different administrations (including the martial law government). The reasons why these efforts have not brought about the intended results are weak and unresponsive legislation, poor or inadequate implementation, the absence of sustained political will to carry out the programmes in question, and inadequate human and financial resources to support them.

These problems are not unique to legislation on housing and urban development, and recommendations to improve the situation abound. In this case, however, the subject matter is much more complex and multi-dimensional, involving not only socio-economic but also political and human rights issues. It also affects a large proportion of the population and traces its roots to the most basic problem afflicting third world countries: poverty. Its eventual, if not necessarily permanent, solution lies in the overall economic development of the country.

Past experience has revealed an urgent need for a shift in direction from an inordinate preoccupation with law-making to stricter law enforcement and better programme implementation. In this respect, it is essential that the obstacles to effective implementation, long identified but still not acted upon, be overcome. One of these is the lack of responsive legislation. This may be partly due to the fact that, until recently, most proposed legislation has not been based on thorough research and adequate consultation with the target beneficiaries and other groups likely to be affected by it. Complex as the numerous issues involved may be, they require action research with contributions not only from the law-makers but from the intended beneficiaries.

Reforms to both the formulation and implementation of laws to reduce homelessness and improve access to land through a variety of tenure arrangements should go hand in hand with reforms in the general laws on property rights and on obligations and contract. After all, the specific laws on land and housing derive their authority from and have their legal basis in these general statutes. Legal changes of this nature are not, however, easy to bring about and generally require longer than more specific legislation. This should not prevent the law-makers from launching the studies and consultations needed to support such reforms.

Turning to another aspect of law reform, there has been a lopsided focus on the procedural aspects of safeguarding squatters' rights when evicting them or demolishing their houses. Among the measures involved are the provision of financial and other forms of assistance during the squatters' voluntary or involuntary relocation; efforts to ensure the availability of resettlement areas; and precautionary measures to avoid violence during the eviction. These constitute part of a 'post hoc' approach which has sometimes added to rather than mitigated the problems of uncontrolled settlement. It is suggested that there is an equal or even more serious need for decision-makers to address the substantive problems of reducing the growth in the numbers and area of illegal settlements and to introduce preventive and remedial measures to bring their occupants within the law. These could include more realistic health and safety standards in housing and a relaxation of those which have only aesthetic implications. Adequate protection for the rights of the deserving poor should be initiated at the earliest possible opportunity rather than deferring them to form part of a package of remedial measures.

While squatting is primarily an economic issue with socio-cultural and legal implications, attempts to solve the problem have addressed the issues in the reverse order. The government has approached the phenomenon of illegal settlement from a predominantly legal perspective, regarding its socio-economic causes and effects as tangential. This is reflected in the changing legal definition of who should or should not benefit from the government's land and housing programmes. The terminology has changed from the 'urban poor', to the 'homeless and disadvantaged',[18] to 'professional' and 'non-professional' squatters.[19]

There is, therefore, an urgent need to reassess and modify the approach employed. A multi-disciplinary approach to economic or urban planning should be adopted in the formulation of the laws which serve as instruments for the implementation of these plans. A comprehensive approach to legislation should be considered: one which includes in the legal drafting team not just the law-makers and their legal staff but also a multi-disciplinary group conversant with the socio-cultural and economic characteristics of the urban poor.

There has been, in the recent past, an increasing sensitivity to the gender component not only of the housing problem but of many other significant national issues. This is demonstrated by the enactment of a law for the protection of women's rights and the formulation of a national development plan for the enhancement of the status and condition of women in Philippine society. It is, however, too early to be overly optimistic about the impact of these measures on the conditions of women in the Philippines. As with other government policies, gender awareness is likely to take time to evolve and to find a secure niche in the field of such basic services as land and housing. If, however, legislation on urban change is supposed to promote social justice, as mandated by the Constitution, it must cease to treat gender issues as a marginal consideration.

Together, these observations lead to the conclusion that, as in other policy areas, it is not enough to translate good intentions into statutes and other legal measures. The effective *implementation* of these measures is equally, if not more, critical. It is highly dependent on competent and committed civil servants and well-crafted statutes. This, in turn, will require meaningful research to be conducted into the socio-economic and cultural aspects of urban change and how these can be taken into account in more responsive legislation. It would also be extremely useful if some time and attention could be devoted to reviewing and learning from the lessons to be gained from the country's experience in implementing urban legislation over the past half-century.

Notes

1. Philippine Constitution 1987, Articles VI, VII and VIII.
2. Ibid., Article X, Section 2. Republic Act no. 7160 (1991), Section 2.
3. Philippine Constitution 1987, Article II, Section 9.
4. Ibid., Article XIII, Section 1.
5. Created under the 1987 Constitution, Article XIII, Section 17 (1).

6. Philippine Constitution 1987, Article XIII, Section 18 (3).

7. Ibid., Article XIII, Section 2.

8. Ibid., Article XIII, Sections 9, 10 and 17.

9. Republic Act 7279.

10. Lands acquired through donation, sale or auction by the religious orders which were the main landowners during the Spanish period (Kiunisala 1985; McAndrew 1994).

11. Richard Poethig's study was published under the heading 'An urban squatters policy for metropolitan Manila' on pages 20–32 of the 4 November 1969 issue of *Solidarity*.

12. The legal measures creating these bodies included Executive Order no. 98 (1946), Republic Act no. 333 (1948) and Executive Order no. 367 (1950).

13. To counter the declaration of squatting as a punishable offence in Presidential Decree 772 (1975).

14. Republic Acts of the Philippine Congress and executive and administrative orders issued by the President.

15. 1991 Local Government Code.

16. Batas Pambansa Blg. 220 (1982). Batas Pambansa were the national laws enacted by the Batasang Pambansa, the legislative body created by President Marcos in 1978.

17. Executive Orders nos 71 and 72 of 1993.

18. 1987 Constitution.

19. Republic Act 7279 (1992).

References

Abrams, C. and O. Koenigsberger (1959) *Report of Housing in the Philippine Islands*, Report submitted to the Government of the Philippine Islands, United Nations Development Program (UNDP), Manila.

Corpuz O. D. (1970) *The Philippines*, Prentice-Hall, Englewood Cliffs.

De Leon, H. (1994) *Textbook on the Philippine Constitution*, Rex, Manila.

Kiunisala, E. R. (1985) *The Quiet Revolution: Agrarian Reform in the Philippines*, Newtime, Quezon City.

Kuhn, D. and F. Kuhn (1966) *The Philippines, Yesterday and Today*, Holt, Rinehart and Winston, New York.

McAndrew, J. P. (1994) *Urban Usurpation: From Friar Estates to Industrial Estates in a Philippine Hinterland*, Ateneo de Manila University Press, Quezon City.

McAuslan, P. (1985) *Urban Land and Shelter for the Poor*, Earthscan, London.

MMDA–JICA (Metropolitan Manila Development Authority and Japan International Cooperation Agency) (1996) *Urban Planning and Development in Metro Manila*, MMDA, Makati City.

NEDA (National Economic and Development Authority) (1993) *Medium-Term Philippine Development Plan: 1993–1998*, NEDA, Manila.

Nuqui, W. G. (1991) *Country Paper on the Philippines*, Paper presented to Regional Seminar on the Urban Poor and Basic Infrastructure Services in Asia and the Pacific, Manila.

Payne, G. K. (1976) *Urban Housing in the Third World*, Leonard Hill, London.

PLANADES (University of the Philippines Planning and Development Research Foundation) (1988) *Access to Land for Housing Project: Final Report*, Report submitted to the Housing and Urban Development Coordinating Council (HUDCC), PLANADES, Makati City.

Ramachandran, A. (1985) 'Foreword', in P. McAuslan, *Urban Land and Shelter for the Poor*, Earthscan, London, 9–10.

Ramos, F. V. (1997) 'Ulat sa Bayan' (A Report to the Nation), in Fookien Times (ed.), *The Philippine Yearbook*, Fookien Times, Manila, 35–40.

Roland, A. (1967) *The Philippines*, Macmillan, New York.

Tolentino, A. M. (1990) *Commentaries and Jurisprudence on the Civil Code of the Philippines*, Central Professional Books, Quezon City.

University of Santo Tomas Research Center (1992) *Urban Poverty: the Case of the Railway Squatters*, Occasional Paper no. 6, University of Santo Tomas Press, Manila.

CHAPTER 7

Legal Pluralism in Caracas, Venezuela

Rogelio Pérez Perdomo and
Teolinda Bolívar

In Venezuela the term '*barrio*' is used to describe an area of self-built housing occupying land which belongs to someone other than the occupiers, and in which the residents are mostly low-income families.[1] The *barrios* frequently fail to respect either the 'official' land use assigned to the area or other urban planning regulations. As this form of housing has been given different names in different countries, social scientists have sought a generic term for it. The term 'marginal' settlements was rejected in the 1970s as inappropriate; these areas and their residents are neither geographically nor economically marginal. The terms now in favour generally refer to the legal status of such areas: we speak of unregulated, uncontrolled areas, of informal housing and also, directly, of illegal areas.[2] The advantage of these terms is their evocation of the common character-istic shared by such settlements: their failure to respect urban planning regulations and also, frequently, formal property rights.

Although planning specialists took the lead in analysing this type of housing, given its high visibility, social scientists rapidly realized that questions of illegality or informality were by no means confined to housing issues.[3] There is also illegal manufacturing, illegal commerce, illegal trans-port, and in general any activity can be termed legal or illegal, although there are no 'informal people', if by this term we mean people who undertake every single one of their activities in the informal sector. In fact, it is not uncommon to find police officers or formally licensed taxi drivers living in illegal housing areas. Conversely, many people who live in legal housing may be illegal taxi drivers or illegal traders. They may also be involved in organized crime.

In this chapter we explore what is meant when we say that a housing area is illegal or informal or that it fails to respect planning regulations. We try to take into account the point of view both of legal practitioners and of the people who build illegal houses, live in them, and necessarily undertake a variety of 'legal' acts with them: buying or selling them, bequeathing them, letting them. In other words, what are the theoretical and practical implications of illegality or informality in urban housing?

Before we turn to the specific question of informality or illegality it is worth reviewing some of the main themes underlying discussion of legal theory. Legal regulations undoubtedly have a technical dimension but this does not make them either politically or morally 'neutral'. The parliaments that make laws and the governments that draw up administrative regulations, as well as local authorities and judges, are all organs of the state and as such exercise political power. Legal studies have a long tradition of exploring this political aspect of law-as-domination. Merely by reading the newspapers we can soon see that political changes lead those who have the power to define what is legal or illegal at one moment being considered villains or criminals as soon as they fall from power. Others, considered rebels or delinquents, become heroes and the fount of legitimacy as soon as they assume political power. Hoenecker, Mandela and Karadzic will serve as good examples for those with a short memory. The classification of particular types of housing area as illegal or informal thus has an ideological component which we would be wise always to bear in mind.

The Meaning of Illegality

The first thing we must stress is that people are not converted into criminals by the fact that they happen to live in a *barrio*. There is nothing about building or inhabiting a house which fails to comply with planning regulations to turn the builder into a criminal. Nor is it a criminal act to sell or let such a house. This may seem obvious, but it is none the less worth making the point because certain types of settlement are often the subject of processes of stigmatization and even 'criminalization'. It is neither wholesome nor fashionable to live in an area which the residents of the 'legal city' consider dangerous, alienated or socially polluted.[4] The residents of such areas are often already criminalized for other reasons, also associated with their poverty. For example, in Caracas, to ride a motorbike, have dark skin and wear poor-quality clothing is tantamount to an invitation to the police to detain you and check your identity cards and business. If this occurs after 9 p.m., this encounter will probably lead to your arrest and a visit to a police station for more detailed questioning and a bit of rough treatment. The police themselves enter the *barrios* only with the greatest reluctance. The *barrios* are enemy territory, even though many police officers were born and continue to live in such areas. It is important, however, to note that the police are even-handed in this respect: it is not only the *barrios* that are criminalized in this fashion, but also other low-income neighbourhoods.[5]

It is none the less true that the *barrios* are the product of an illegal action: the unauthorized occupation of unserviced plots of land for which the occupier has neither a property title nor a construction permit.[6] The legal consequences of this settlement process are extremely complex. In the first place, ownership of the building cannot be formally registered until the landowner's authorization has been obtained (Pérez Perdomo and Nikken 1979). In the second place, the municipal surveyor can order the demolition of the house because it fails to respect planning regulations and lacks the certificate of habitability which this official is supposed to issue once a variety of exacting legal requirements have been fulfilled. The surveyor can even order the eviction of an entire area because no urban services have been installed prior to its development. Finally, if the house can be described as a *rancho* (shack), or fails to meet certain standards of sanitation or safety, the owner is expressly forbidden to let it to tenants (Pérez Perdomo and Nikken 1979).[7]

We have described, very briefly, the relation between the *barrios* and their inhabitants on the one hand and the formal legal system on the other, rather than seeking to provide an historical or political overview of the development of *barrios* in Caracas. It is estimated that 40 per cent of the city's population live in the *barrios* – that is, approximately 1.2 million people (Villanueva and Baldó 1995). It is clearly impossible to evict such a large number of residents from their housing areas. Indeed, the major urban renewal schemes undertaken in Caracas during the last fifty years have led to the eviction of only a small number of people (Bolívar et al. 1993). How has this seemingly paradoxical situation come about?

We can identify three periods in the construction of the *barrios*. The first, prior to 1958, was basically a period of progressive development, on an individual or small-group basis. The municipal and national authorities implicitly sanctioned squatting in certain areas (but not others). As the city as a whole was undergoing rapid growth at this time, the area of illegal settlement remained small in relative terms and the government hoped in time to be able to deal with the problem of the *ranchos*. The second period can be characterized by the development of clientelistic politics in which the authorities' role *vis-à-vis* the *barrios* changed from one of tolerance to something quite different, as the settlement and subsequent servicing of *barrios* acquired political significance via the opportunities they offered for politicians to build up a following of loyal 'clients'. The *barrios* therefore grew faster than the city as a whole, at a time of explosive overall urban growth and economic difficulties. The third period can be approximately dated to what Venezuelans usually call 'the crisis', starting in 1982. This period of economic recession has seen a decline in the rate of growth of urban expansion, especially in the formal sector, and has thus increased the *barrios*' share of the built-up area. Caracas has acquired a number of 'satellite' cities, which also have their own *barrios*. Together with the other major cities, Caracas now contains the lion's share of the population living in poverty or extreme poverty, as the rural areas have fared rather better. This has led to a down-turn in rural–urban migration.

The loss of legitimacy of the political parties has meant that land invasions are no longer politically motivated; instead, individual enterprise plays a greater role, as in the earlier period, or invasions may be organized by small, informal entrepreneurs who continue to seek political support in the long run but whose primary concern is commercial rather than political. The situation has become very fluid and cases of multiple invasion (i.e. squatting on land that has already been squatted) have emerged, as well as some other types of conflict which we will discuss below.

The second period to which we have referred is the best documented (see, for example, Ray 1969). In this period, the foundation of a *barrio* was a political action. With the support of a municipal politician, a large group of people would make plans to occupy a given area at a pre-determined time. There was thus a system of social agents underwriting the establishment of the *barrios* (Bolívar 1989). Areas were chosen for invasion because the squatters were thought unlikely to encounter much resistance, as the land belonged to the state or was abandoned or its owner had died intestate. Other characteristics of interest included the area's proximity to major roads or the existing built-up area. The choice of an area to be occupied and the preparations for the invasion were the responsibility of a group of leaders, who could count on the support of municipal officials and of the authorities in general. Invasions organized by opposition parties could expect a rapid response from the police or national guard, who would evict the squatters, since their action was deemed a violent and subversive one which had to be repressed. An invasion organized by those with the appropriate contacts would be unlikely to meet the same fate.

Since 1982 the areas offering the best opportunity for illegal settlement are areas of 'in-fill' between existing *barrios* or those situated on their more remote fringes, further and further away from the main access roads. The degree of resistance likely to be encountered by the settlers is more unpredictable. Officialdom is to a large extent indifferent to their fate. It is not that clientilism is no longer at work in the *barrios*, but the decline of the political parties and their lack of both legitimacy and resources have substantially reduced the parties' ability to continue doing business as usual. This leaves the way open for private interests seeking modest profits from organizing an invasion or, in the case of the initial occupants, from selling on their 'right' to build to new purchasers.

It is important to understand the role of the legal system in all this. In research conducted in 1975 by Pérez Perdomo and Nikken (1979), it was found that the courts had played no role in deterring invasions or evicting the squatters. Collusion between politicians and lawyers is one possible explanation for the absence of judicial intervention, but the legal system's difficulty in addressing *collective* actions is a more likely explanation. In effect, legal intervention would require squatters to be identified and prosecuted individually, which would be virtually impossible in an invasion settlement. The legal authorities, including the police, would be unwilling to get involved in trying to evict the residents of densely settled *barrios*. Instead, the municipality created a Legal Aid Department supporting the peaceful occupation of housing in invaded areas. More recently, the municipal authorities have shown no interest in protecting *barrio* residents and we have come across cases of landowners bringing strong pressure to bear on residents to get them to buy the area they have occupied.

In summary, to maintain a rigid distinction between the two elements of the legality/illegality dualism presupposes the existence of an ordered society in which the rule of law prevails and in which both citizens and government acknowledge their responsibility to observe or to ensure the observance of legal norms. Venezuela does not fit this description, although there is a greater tendency to accept the rule of law in certain social sectors than in others. Our political system can be characterized as both democratic and clientilistic. Public policy in housing matters has been to observe a tacit distinction between 'formal' housing areas and *barrios*, and to be particularly permissive in its approach to the latter. But this practice serves to subvert the boundary between the legal and the illegal. In global terms, the residents of the *barrios* have managed to secure for themselves a space in the city: collective eviction is impossible and individual eviction requires negotiation or a *sui generis* process of expropriation, generally accompanied by compensation or relocation, even though from the formal point of view an administrative order by the municipal surveyor can evict squatters and require the demolition of their homes without compensation (Pérez Perdomo and Nikken 1979).

From an urban planning perspective, it is not strictly true to say that the *barrios* are located in open spaces, areas with no officially designated land use or areas unsuitable for low-income housing development of the 'social interest' type (Bolívar et al. 1991; 1993). It is true that city plans have traditionally failed to record the existence of the *barrios*. The area in question would appear as vacant land. More recently, the existence of these areas has started to be acknowledged. Moreover, not all the *barrios* infringe the land use zoning of the area. Some of them fall in the same land use category as adjacent, 'legal' areas. In other cases, they have been granted special zoning status permitting the area's use as housing for low-income families (the terminology used to describe these areas varies from one part of the city to another). Although there is no reliable estimate of the total area of *barrios* falling into these categories, Bolívar et al. (1991; 1993) suggest that approximately one-third of the area of Caracas' *barrios* falls within this 'legal' category. Forty per cent of the area occupied by *barrios* is outside the city limits, but we must bear in mind a large part of the built-up area in general also falls outside the official urban boundary. About one-quarter of the area occupied by the *barrios* clearly fails to comply with zoning regulations – for the most part, those *barrios* which occupy what should be open spaces.

Failure to comply with predetermined land uses is not a problem for the *barrios* alone. The municipal authorities have in general been very permissive in this respect. Given the situation prevailing *de facto*, the most logical solution is a change of official zoning, bringing the situation on paper in line with that on the ground. A river cannot be made to flow under a bridge. The adjustment of legal norms to match existing practice has come to characterize a substantial part of the supposedly 'legal' city, in which a change of zoning has proved necessary. In the *barrios*, the changes which are needed go beyond the scope of a mere change of land use zoning. Many urban planners would argue that it is necessary to rethink the whole idea of prescriptive planning, since it makes no sense if the plans fail to match the situation on the ground. They would argue that we should step up efforts to 'regularize' and upgrade the *barrios*, a task which has been accepted in principle but which has seen very little real progress to date (Fundación de la Vivienda Popular 1991).

The existence of the *barrios* and the need for regularization has led to different forms of legal recognition of these areas and to efforts to ensure a better match between planning norms and what happens on the ground. The 1987 Urban Planning Act (Ley Orgánica de Ordenación Urbanística) allows special plans to be created for certain parts of the city requiring particular attention. These may be areas of special historic or tourist interest, but they also include 'uncontrolled settlements' (Article 49). The Act also allows for progressive urban development projects offering housing solutions to the low-income population (Article 70 ff.). These measures may be applied either to existing *barrios* or to areas which have yet to be developed. In other words, the Urban Planning Act recognizes self-help housing development as a legitimate strategy for urban development and supports it by establishing less rigid regulation of self-help areas (Garrido Rovira 1988). In practice it is the municipal authorities who are responsible for taking the necessary initiatives, and unfortunately they have to date taken little advantage of the new possibilities offered by the Act.

The fact that the *barrio* residents have secured a place for themselves in the city does not solve all their problems. There remains the possibility of internal conflicts within the *barrio* or of conflicts with a range of different government agencies. At present there is also a greater probability of successful intervention by the owners of the invaded land, especially when they focus their efforts not so much on eviction but on getting the residents to pay them for the land. In the latter case the owner often threatens to use the judicial system to advance their ends, although they very rarely, in practice, do so. In conflicts between residents, on the other hand, there tends to be little recourse to the legal system as such. It is for this reason that we may argue that legal pluralism characterizes not only the city of Caracas as a whole but also the *barrios* themselves. To support our use of this term to describe the situation within the *barrios* we must, however, turn to the question of what it means, from the residents' point of view, to live in such an area.

The Swings and Roundabouts of Illegality

The physical characteristics of the *barrios* are determined by their origins as areas of uncontrolled settlement. There is no planning of the area prior to its occupation, and in consequence the plots are all different shapes and sizes, the line of the streets, irregular, and the streets, paths and steps of dramatically varying width. The largest *barrios*, built on steeply inclined hillsides, are like enormous labyrinths of houses piled up one above the over with only minimal provision for pedestrian access. The average, for all of the *barrios* of Caracas, is a level of access of 5.7 per cent, when according to planning regulations it should be 15 per cent or more.

Most of the *barrios* were built without any allowance for vehicular access. Streets wide enough to permit the passage of a car are few and far between. Given the steepness of the hillsides on which the *barrios* are built, the only types of motor vehicle which can be used are in any case very expensive four-wheel-drive vehicles. The emphasis is therefore on journeys by foot, with construction on steep slopes meaning that the average vertical distance covered is equivalent to twenty floors, without the benefit of a lift (Bolívar et al. 1993). Of course, this is only an average: some *barrio* residents have a bus or metro station relatively close to their homes, or may live on a street which can take cars, while others have to go up or down the equivalent of forty to fifty floors without a lift.

The growth of the *barrios* is the product of a myriad individual efforts, with no one providing any guidance on the way in which the houses should be built. Next door to a house built of solid, lasting materials, with a construction quality similar to that found in legal housing areas, we can find another house with poor-quality, provisional or unfinished construction, with earth floors and walls of adobe or cardboard. Even though each building is likely to be irregular in plan, the urban landscape may curiously possess a certain harmony and regularity (Figures 7.1 and 7.2). The streets, alleys, steps, squares and other open spaces vary in form in a way which is not easy to predict. Geometry is certainly not the weak point of the *barrios'* builder-architects (Bolívar et al. 1994).

There is relatively little semi-public space (educational, sporting, cultural or welfare facilities) in the *barrios*, amounting to only 1.4 per cent of the total area occupied by this type of housing area in Caracas (Bolívar et al.

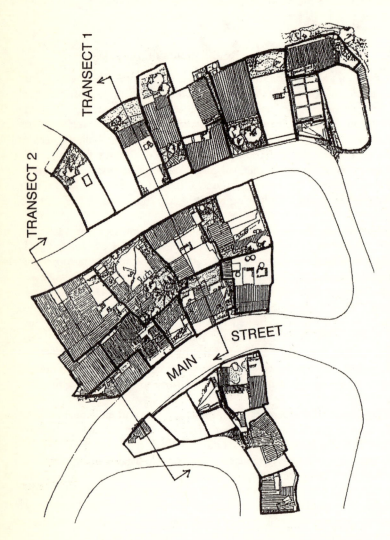

Figure 7.1 Plot layout in the *barrio* of Carpintero-Valle, Caracas

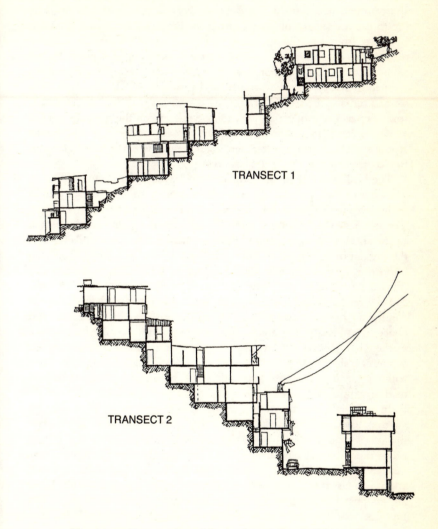

Figure 7.2 Cross-section of *barrio* of Carpintero-Valle, Caracas

1991). Imagination or the tendency to 'just see how things turn out' (*'arreglarselas como se pueda'*) has led to a variety of practical solutions to this lack of amenities. A street and a wall with a basket-ball net create a sportsground where none was foreseen. Forgotten corners can easily be put to use for a game of bowls. Given the height of the *barrios*, kites can be flown from virtually any small patch of ground on one of Caracas' many windy days. Informal crèches (*hogares de cuidado diario*) appeared when women started to look after their neighbours' children. The government stepped in to regulate the practice, and provide a small subsidy for the woman running the crèche. Private schools, with highly dedicated teachers, sprang up as the product of joint initiatives between the teachers and the *barrio* residents, in response to the lamentable condition of the public school system. In some *barrios* there are libraries and small cultural centres, funded from a great variety of sources.

The quality of life in the *barrio* nevertheless leaves a lot to be desired. The houses lack privacy: there is no possibility of getting away from prying eyes for a spot of quiet relaxation on one's own or with the family. The area is inevitably noisy, and the buildings are all tightly packed together. In the absence of intervention by the municipal surveyor, ventilation and the amount of light received by each house may be affected by the building next door. Even safety may be endangered by a higher adjacent property (Figure 7.2). The growing densification and consolidation of *barrio* areas and the tendency to build high, without adequate knowledge of sub-soil conditions or the necessary anti-seismic measures, give rise to great concern, especially as Caracas suffers from a considerable number of earthquakes (Bolívar et al. 1994). The problem of landslides affecting the *barrios* can also be attributed in part to the activities of people building without adequate technical knowledge of the potential problems or how to deal with them (Jiménez Díaz 1994).

In a city in which the deficiencies of public services are a problem for all the residents, the situation is naturally even worse in the *barrios*: municipal rubbish collection services do not serve the *barrios* and getting rid of domestic waste is no easy task. Cleanliness is not one of the *barrios'* outstanding properties. Less than half of the houses have running water, and it is unusual to find a *barrio* with a good water-supply network. There are no postal services in the less accessible *barrios*. Personal safety is a problem, not only because of the activities of petty criminals but also because of abuses by the police. It must, however, be said that there is no great difference between the *barrios* and other poor neighbourhoods in this respect (Ontiveros 1995).

There are, however, certain aspects of life in the *barrios* which are indeed different from what happens elsewhere in the city: the residents of the *barrios* have a much stronger sense of community, especially when faced with death, illness or extreme economic distress. The man next door who works in the construction industry can still lend a hand when his neighbours are building their home, although he will naturally expect to be offered some small thanks, such as an invitation to share a beer. He will also expect the woman two doors away, who is a teacher, to show her thanks for services rendered by helping his children with their homework. The electrician down the street will also help neighbours with the wiring, or in repairing a liquidizer or a radio, although he too will expect payment in kind. The basis on which these services is exchanged is not one of financial self-interest, and it is no coincidence that parties in the *barrio* are never short of guests.

Our subject is not, however, the anthropology of the *barrios* but the residents' relationship with the law, and in this context we must turn to the question of violence and criminality (Ugalde et al. 1994). The inhabitants of 'the other Caracas' have the idea that the *barrios* are violent places because they are illegal places. As a general rule, this is a mistaken perception. Clear rules of social interaction are followed by the majority of inhabitants and social stratification within the *barrio* population is reflected in an elaborate system of social etiquette involving the expression of respect for others (Pedrazzini and Sánchez 1992). Violence may occur but it is not the norm. It is, sadly, true that the presence of drugs dealers has led to an increase in violence. The dealers each have their own patch and any intrusion by the competition or failure to pay monies owed leads to murder and vendettas. In some cases children or innocent bystanders get killed in shoot-outs between the dealers. In addition, some addicts have started to rob the neighbours in their own *barrio* or the one next door to support their habit, breaking a long-established tradition of respect for one's own 'backyard' (Trigo 1992; Ugalde et al. 1994). In the absence of adequate policing, several of the perpetrators of these crimes have paid for their actions with their lives. These cases receive wide coverage in the press and create a great public outcry. We estimate, however, that approximately a dozen delinquents have been murdered in this fashion in the last six months – not many when compared with the number of people killed by the police or by citizens acting in self-defence elsewhere in the city. In short, although life in the *barrios* is indeed more violent than any sane person would wish, this is inevitable, since Caracas is, in general, a violent city. The authorities' failure to police the *barrios* leaves the door open to all kinds of violent acts; above all, it encourages the belief that it is criminals who live in the *barrios*. This generalization is doubly misguided: not all the city's criminals live in the *barrios* and not all *barrio* residents are criminals. There is no objective evidence to support the belief that the *barrios* are inherently criminal places. In saying this we are not trying to become involved in the wider polemic about whether or not, on the one hand, the poor are more likely to turn to crime (regardless of where they live) than other members of society or whether, on the other hand, they are more likely to suffer from a process of 'criminalization'. What we are trying to say is that the social stigma accompanying life in the *barrios* means that the police venture into these areas only rarely, in short and violent incursions, only to get out quickly and leave the residents to their fate (Navarro and Pérez Perdomo 1991; Pérez Perdomo 1991).

It is interesting to note that the very size of the *barrio* population and the special nature of legal needs in these areas have produced a response in the shape of lawyers who specialize in providing legal services to this population. They are drawn from the lowest levels of the profession, and their legal expertise is, to say the least, questionable, but their approach to dealing with problems is pragmatic and perhaps more appropriate than a more formalistic approach would be, given the somewhat symbolic role that tends to be attributed to legal documentation by *barrio* residents. A recent case serves to illustrate this.

María Miranda bought a house in a *barrio* of Petare. The vendor was a Guyanese woman who migrated to the United States and left her sister in charge of collecting the remaining part of the payment on the house. When María Miranda finished paying for her house, María came to see one of us and showed me her papers, including the private sale contract under which the Guyanese woman had acquired the property from a vendor recorded as the owner of both land and building. The other document was the private contract by which María bought the house. I consulted a lawyer from a practice with plenty of experience in property transactions in the formal sector, and asked him what could be done in this case. The lawyer confirmed that the original vendor was indeed still the owner of the land and suggested that the Guyanese woman should go to a Venezuelan consulate in the United States in order to give someone in Venezuela power of attorney to formalize the sale on her behalf. Then all the documents could be formally recorded in the Property Register. The problem with this proposal was that it was rather complex and costly, because drawing up the power of attorney and inscription in the Property Register would both be expensive. María went to see a lawyer who was used to handling legal business in the *barrios*, who suggested that the easiest solution would be to draw up a 'provisional title' (*título supletorio*)[8] in which it would be stated that María Miranda built the house at her own expense on land which was her own property, without getting involved in the business of formal registration. I suspect that María will prefer this less expensive solution because in this way her house will 'have papers', increasing its value should she wish to sell it, and she can rest safe in the knowledge that no one is likely to challenge her ownership of the property.

From a formal point of view, the 'provisional title' solution is worthless, because such a document has no legal value and does not protect María's property rights. The Guyanese woman could in theory find another purchaser willing to buy the property in the way recommended by the first lawyer and this purchaser would then be able to take María Miranda to court to claim title to the property. María would almost certainly lose her home. This is not, however, likely to occur because it is probable that all involved have acted in good faith and without a scrap of knowledge of the formal legal situation. The '*barrio*' lawyer is very unlikely to know much about official property law. In other words, collective ignorance of the law and the assumption that everyone is acting in good faith, as well as the high cost of formal legal services, are what underpin these trans-actions and give some measure of security to the parties in question. The '*barrio*' lawyer provides documents with only a symbolic value.

In contrast to what the people of the other Caracas believe, life in the *barrios* is not in fact particularly conflict-ridden. For example, Camacho and Tarhan (1991) noted that conflict over house rentals is very rare. The explanation for this is the scrupulous attention paid by landlords to selecting the right tenant. Relatives or friends are preferred, to ensure a degree of extra personal commitment to meeting one's responsibilities as a tenant. This practice has advantages for both parties, since if the tenant gets into financial difficulties, the owner is likely to know the whys and wherefores of the situation and therefore to be prepared to wait a little longer for the rent. In recent years, however, a more commercial logic has been at work in landlord–tenant relations, with the emergence of a number of specialized property companies letting housing in the *barrios*. In this case, personal trust is replaced by more formal means of ensuring appro-priate behaviour, such as deposits, or the practice of getting tenants to sign IOUs. The situation in the *barrios* is not unusual in this respect: Venezuela is very far from being a highly litigious society. This is normally explained in terms of a lack of confidence in the judicial system. For this reason, even in the formal business sector, conflict prevention is preferred to conflict resolution, and when conflicts do emerge, negotiation is seen as the key to a solution, rather than having recourse to judicial arbitration (Pérez Perdomo 1996).

It is important to understand how potentially conflictive situations are resolved, as in the case, for example, of noisy neighbours or noxious smells affecting someone's home. The absence of police intervention clearly rules out one possibility for solving the conflict, but this situation is by no means confined to the *barrios*. The denizens of the 'legal city' also try to avoid seeking police help to deal with these kinds of problems. In general, the way in which people go about dealing with them is either simply to put up with the nuisance or to raise objections, but in a manner which is likely to promote greater co-operation between neighbours (prompting, for example, an invitation to a party). As a rule, people do not stand on their dignity in terms of seeing themselves as having a natural right to absolute privacy and tranquillity, or to the exclusive enjoyment of their property; instead, they believe that it is important to

take into account the needs and preferences of their neighbours. This
generates an atmosphere of tolerance and co-operation. It is rare for a
conflict or a potentially conflictive situation between neighbours to escalate
into violence.

The usual means of resolving a conflict is negotiation between the
parties concerned. To give one example: a neighbour is putting up a
building that looks likely to affect either my means of gaining access to
my home or the amount of light my property receives. My first response
is to try to get him or her to change the design of the building, so that
my property will not be affected. If this attempt at negotiation and co-
operation does not yield results, I may seek help from people who are
well respected in the community, who will act as (entirely untrained)
mediators in the dispute. A relatively small number of conflicts are taken
to the authorities, such as an office of the municipal government, where
the staff will try to find a mutually acceptable solution to the problem.
The status of the municipal official, conveyed by their possession of a
number of key symbols (a security officer at the door, the national flag
and a portrait of Bolívar in the office itself), lends an extraordinary degree
of persuasiveness to what they have to say. Pérez Perdomo and Nikken
(1979) studied one municipal office (the Legal Aid Department of the
Federal District Municipal Recorder's Office), in which the staff had got
the art of mediation off to a tee. There were even some officials whose
role it was to visit the site of the conflict and take photographs and
measurements in order to help the mediator put forward alternative
solutions. Heredia and Lugo (1987) later confirmed these findings.

Conclusion

From the point of view of a lawyer who has been properly trained in the
formal legal system, the *barrios* are lawless places and their residents have
not a shred of legal security. It then goes almost without saying that the
barrios must be subject to the rule of violence. We hope that we have
been able to show, that this is an inaccurate impression of life in the
barrios. The residents have managed to create not only a place for themselves in the city (however precarious), but also an efficient system for
dealing with the conflicts that may arise in their neighbourhood. To people
who have been brought up to see the law as the guarantor of individual
rights, these means of resolving conflicts appear to be insubstantial and
unreliable, since they do not provide any legal security concerning, for
example, the use and enjoyment of one's property. We can perhaps all
learn something from the way in which life in the *barrio* leads to a vision
of everyday life and conflict resolution which is less individualistic and
more co-operative. As we have seen, there is an impressive degree of
community solidarity among *barrio* residents. For this reason it is possible

to talk of another type of urban law, the law of the *barrios*, and to see Caracas as characterized by legal pluralism.

We also hope to have been able to demonstrate that life in the *barrios* is far from idyllic. Serious problems confront the residents as a result of the origins and nature of this type of housing. Perhaps the worst of their problems, however, arise from our own lack of understanding and the way in which we stigmatize life in the *barrio*. In particular, the 'criminalization' of these areas by the police and the entire legal system is without doubt a critical element in this process of stigmatization – even if it is an experience shared by other low-income areas. It is for this reason that we have deliberately set out to avoid reinforcing this process of stigmatization by discussing only the negative aspects, of illegality and violence, of the life of the *barrio*.

Notes

Translated from Spanish by Ann Varley.

1. The residents of the *barrios* are generally people who live in poverty or even extreme poverty, but there are exceptions. It is not unusual to find residents in professional occupations or middle management. The quality of construction also varies considerably.

2. For examples, see Turner 1969; Hernández 1972; Hardoy and Satterthwaite 1989.

3. See, for example, Lomnitz 1977; Bolívar and Rosas 1994; De Soto et al. 1989.

4. 'Areas without order, without legality, without sanitation, whose residents suffer an unnatural and destructive degree of overcrowding, enduring a mixture of perpetual defensiveness and aggression, weighed down by need, ruled by instinct, deprived in many cases of family life, abandoned by their parents ... hundreds of thousands of Venezuelans find themselves excluded from the most elementary benefits of urban society' (A. Uslar Prieti: '*O ranchos o desarrollo*' ['Either shacks or development'], *El Nacional*, 7 January 1974, cited in Brewer Carias 1975: 603).

5. We refer to the major public housing projects, such as the '*23 de enero*' estate.

6. Approximately one-half of the *barrios* are built on private property; 38 per cent occupy land in the public domain or which is the property of public agencies; and 12 per cent are located on municipal property (Bolívar 1987). In a few cases, the owners of the housing also own the land, but these cases are still likely to contravene urban planning regulations.

7. Article 20 of the Rent Act (Ley de Regulación de Alquileres) makes it illegal to let housing which does not meet 'minimum standards of sanitation and habitability'. This includes in particular *ranchos* (shacks) which are 'built of inadequate or perishable materials, such as planks, metal sheets or cardboard, and lack running water and a sewage disposal system'.

8. A *título supletorio* arises from a formal request to a judge to call two or more witnesses who, under oath, respond to a number of questions. In property matters, these usually involve: whether or not they know the person who lives in the house, whether or not that person built it with their own money, and how long that person has been in unchallenged possession of the property. Depending on the

answers to these questions, the judge may declare that the person who inhabits the house, and who has sought the *título*, should be considered the effective owner of the property, so long as no one with a better claim appears.

References

Bolívar, T. (1987) 'La production du cadre bâti dans les barrios à Caracas. Un chantier permanent!', mimeo.

— (1989) 'Los agentes sociales articulados a la producción de los barrios de ranchos', *Coloquio*, Vol. 1, no. 1, 143–61.

Bolívar, T. and I. Rosas (1994) 'Los caminos de la investigación de los asentamientos humanos precarios', in A. Lovera and J. J. Martín Frechilla (eds), *La Ciudad, de la Planificación a la Privatización*, Universidad Central de Venezuela and Fondo Editorial Acta Científica, Caracas, 109–40.

Bolívar, T. with T. Hernández and T. Ontiveros (1991) 'Problemas de densificación de los barrios caraqueños y sus consecuencias I', Research report, mimeo.

Bolívar, T. with T. Ontiveros, A. Monteverde, P. Paez, M. Guerrero, Y. Benmergui and J. De Freitas (1993) 'Problemas de densificación de los barrios caraqueños y sus consecuencias II' Research report, mimeo.

Bolívar, T., M. Guerrero, I. Rosas, J. De Freitas, T. Ontiveros, H. Arnal and R. Sancio (1994) *Densificación y Vivienda en los Barrios Caraqueños: Contribución a la Determinación de Problemas y Soluciones*, Consejo Nacional de la Vivienda, Ministerio de Desarrollo Urbano, Caracas.

Brewer Carias, A. R. (1975) *Cambio Político y Reforma del Estado en Venezuela*, Tecnos, Madrid.

Camacho, O. O. and A. Tarhan (1991) *Alquiler y Propiedad en los Barrios de Caracas*, International Development Research Center, Ottawa, and Universidad Central de Venezuela, Caracas.

De Soto, H. (1989) *The Other Path: The Invisible Revolution in the Third World*, Tauris, London.

Fundación de la Vivienda Popular (FVP) (1991) *Tenencia de la Tierra en los Barrios: Regularización*, FVP, Caracas.

Garrido Rovira, J. (1988) *Ordenación Urbanística*, Editorial Arte, Caracas.

Hardoy J. E. and D. Satterthwaite (1989) *Squatter Citizen: Life in the Urban Third World*, Earthscan, London.

Heredia, M. P. and Y. Lugo (1987) 'Estudio sobre los principales centros de asistencia jurídica para personas de bajos ingresos en Venezuela', in R. Pérez Perdomo (ed.), *Justicia y Pobreza en Venezuela*, Monte Avila, Caracas, 173–98.

Hernández, O. (1972) *La Planificación Urbana y el Desarrollo Urbano no Controlado*, Fondo Editorial Común, Caracas.

Jiménez Díaz, V. (1994) 'The incidence and causes of slope failures in the *barrios* of Caracas, Venezuela', in H. Main and S. W. Williams (eds), *Environment and Housing in Third World Cities*, Wiley, Chichester, 125–32.

Lomnitz, L. A. (1977) *Networks and Marginality: Life in a Mexican Shanty Town*, Academic Press, New York.

Navarro, J. C. and R. Pérez Perdomo (1991) 'Seguridad personal: percepciones y realidades', in J. C. Navarro and R. Pérez Perdomo (eds), *Seguridad Personal: Un*

Asalto al Tema, Instituto de Estudios Superiores de Administración, Caracas, 27–74.

Ontiveros, T. (1995) 'Densificación y memoria espacial en los territorios populares contemporáneos', in E. Amodio and T. Ontiveros (eds), *Historias de Identidad Urbana: Composición y Recomposición de Identidad en los Territorios Populares Urbanos*, Fondo Editorial Tropykos and Universidad Central de Venezuela, Caracas, 31–44.

Pedrazzini, I. and M. Sánchez (1992) *Malandros, Bandas y Niños de la Calle: Cultura de Urgencia en la Metrópolis Latinoamericana*, Vadell, Valencia.

Pérez Perdomo, R. (1991) 'Las instituciones de la seguridad personal', in J.C. Navarro and R. Pérez Perdomo (eds) *Seguridad Personal: Un Asalto al Tema*, Instituto de Estudios Superiores de Administración, Caracas, 75–98.

— (1996) 'De la justicia y otros demonios', in M. E. Boza and R. Pérez Perdomo, (eds), *Seguridad Jurídica y Competitividad*, Instituto de Estudios Superiores de Administración, Caracas, 118–73.

Pérez Perdomo, R. and P. Nikken (1979) *Derecho y Propiedad de la Vivienda en los Barrios de Caracas*, Fondo de Cultura Económica, México, and Universidad Central de Venezuela, Caracas.

Ray, T. (1969) *The Politics of the Barrios of Venezuela*, University of California Press, Berkeley.

Trigo, P. (1992) 'Violencia en los barrios', *SIC*, 541, 26–9.

Turner, J. F. C. (1969) 'Uncontrolled urban settlement: problems and solutions', in G. Breese (ed.), *The City in Newly Developing Countries*, Prentice-Hall, Englewood Cliffs, NJ, 507–34.

Ugalde, L., L. P. España, C. Scotto, A. Castillo, T. Hernández, N. L. Luengo, M. Bisbal, M.G. Ponce (1994) *La Violencia en Venezuela*, Monte Avila and Universidad Católica Andrés Bello, Caracas.

Villanueva, F. and J. Baldó (1995) 'Tendencias de crecimiento en las zonas de barrios del Area Metropolitana de Caracas y Sector Panamericana-Los Teques de la Región Capital', *Urbana*, 16/17, 13–30.

CHAPTER 8

Law and Urban Change in Brazil

Edésio Fernandes and
Raquel Rolnik

The process of industrialization and urbanization that began in Brazil in the 1930s, when less than 30 per cent of the population lived in urban areas, has provoked dramatic changes in the country's socio-economic and spatial order, as well as some serious environmental problems. Since the mid-1950s, most economic activity has taken place in the urban areas, and, in spite of all the country's long-standing financial problems, its impressive industrial growth means that Brazil now has the world's eighth largest Gross National Product. After more than five decades of intense urban growth, about 80 per cent of the Brazilian population (some 150 million people) now live in the cities, while over 40 per cent of the urban population live in metropolitan areas. Although there has been a significant decrease in migration rates over the last decade, Brazil's urban population is still growing at high rates, particularly in metropolitan areas.[1]

A systematic approach to urban planning was not instituted at the national level until the period of military rule in the 1970s, the peak years of the urbanization process. Urban planning during this period was characterized by the subordination of state agencies to private interests, and planning interventions were therefore subordinated to market, and particularly property market, requirements. Depoliticized and technocratic – given the centralized, authoritarian, nature of the state at that time – urban planning subordinated urban development policies to the interests of large companies developing urban infrastructure.

Given the prevailing political conditions and constitutional provisions which silenced civil society, severely restricted local government's financial autonomy and blocked the few existing channels for political representation, local urban policies were also hostages to the strategies adopted by large-scale property developers, who used urban planning models and techniques to 'sell' their projects to local authorities.[2] This was made easier by the fact that, until 1988, and regardless of its direct intervention in almost all sectors of the economy and some attempts to enact urban legislation and implement urban policies at the municipal level in particular, the Brazilian state failed to reform *laissez-faire* legal ideologies regarding the use and development of urban land.

As a result, in the main Brazilian cities modern central areas are surrounded by very poor peripheral, and usually illegal, settlements, where housing is largely self-help housing built by the residents. Even in rich neighbourhoods, state-of-the-art buildings sit side-by-side with precarious shanty towns, the thousands of *favelas* resulting from land invasion. If we consider how people gain access to urban land and housing, we find that about 60 per cent of the population in the major cities live in what may be described as illegal settlements.[3] The spatial coverage of urban services, infrastructure and public amenities is extremely uneven, with the poorer areas lacking almost everything, especially sewerage and drainage, health centres and schools, leisure facilities and open spaces. Public transport is inadequate and expensive. In short, the quality of daily life in the cities is extremely low and unequal.[4]

As a result of intense speculation, the hoarding of land which has been serviced at state expense is responsible for the existence of a large percentage of privately owned vacant plots in metropolitan areas (estimated at up to 40 per cent of all properties in some cases), as well as marked discontinuites in the physical expansion of urban areas. As well as neglecting basic social needs, the nature of urban development has also produced a significant depletion of environmental resources and irreversible environmental damage, the result of low-density expansion of poor settlements over areas endowed with significant natural resources. Even those areas protected by law because of their environmental importance have been subjected to uncontrolled urban development because of the loss of (formal) market value resulting from their protected status. On the other hand, the best-serviced areas, which are scarce and geographically concentrated, have been the subject of very intensive development, both horizontal and vertical, leading to the rapid destruction of much of urban Brazil's cultural and historic heritage. In short, Brazilian cities, and especially the metropolitan areas, are inefficient and costly to manage, socially segregated and environmentally unfriendly.[5]

This situation is the result of several complex factors, but, for the purposes of this chapter, two major, complementary, factors require discussion.

On the one hand, until the 1988 Constitution came into force the legal protection and endorsement of private property rights was virtually absolute, leaving little room for state control of the use and development of urban property. For the same reason, when called to decide on conflicting interests in cases of effective state intervention, the judiciary has long tended to favour individual rights, to the detriment of socially oriented legal restrictions on the use of urban property. It should be stressed that, as an inheritance from the centuries of colonial rule, most Brazilian land is privately owned, which accounts for the existence of few public spaces in the cities and elsewhere.[6] Urban legislation enacted at all levels of government was rarely concerned with democratizing land acquisition by the poor. On the contrary, especially at the local level, urban laws have been one of the main factors reproducing the overall conditions of segregation of economic activities and the denial to much of the urban population of access to the advantages of living in metropolitan areas.[7]

On the other hand, the lack of attention to urban and territorial jurisdiction issues in the Constitution led, in the context of Brazil's contradictory federal system, to endless legal controversies and institutional conflicts between federal, state and local administrations as to which had the power to enact urban legislation and implement urban policies. As mentioned above, given the wider context of a high degree of centralization of power, especially during the years of authoritarian rule between the 1964 military coup and the 1988 Constitution, state intervention in urban areas was largely decided at the federal and state levels, with a corresponding attrition of the autonomy of the more than 5,000 municipalities. Local administrations lacked legal, technical and financial resources and instruments to tackle the problems brought about by urbanization.[8]

Moreover, the urban population was virtually excluded from the process of decision-making on urban questions at all levels, especially in the nine formal Metropolitan Regions, which were administered in a blatantly authoritarian fashion from 1973 to 1988.[9] While the state had little scope for intervention in urban areas, the pattern of such interventions as it did undertake was determined by its elitist, undemocratic nature.

In brief, in the context of such a distorted planning apparatus, the private interests of minority groups have led the process of urban development, towing the state along in their search to facilitate the conditions of capital accumulation in the cities. Most state interventions consisted of sectoral policies, and as such they were capitalized upon by the economic groups which controlled the state. Given official neglect of the needs of the urban poor, and in particular the lack of an effective response to the prevailing unsatisfactory housing conditions, an enormous housing problem developed, along with other serious social and environmental problems. Urban space clearly reflects, and reinforces, the unequal conditions of wealth distribution in the country, which are among the world's worst, as well as its tradition of political exclusion of the less favoured population. This has been a process full of contradictions and conflicts, directly related to the broader process which has recently promoted changes in Brazil's socio-economic and political order. More progressive urban legislation has been enacted by the federal government since the late 1970s, such as the laws governing the subdivision of urban land and the formulation of a national environmental policy. This has come as a response both to increasing social mobilization and to the pressure to create new opportunities for capital investment in urban areas, as important elements of the real estate sector have been adversely affected by the high levels of speculation prevailing in metropolitan areas.

The pace of urban reform has been slow, given the complexity of the conflicting social, political and economic interests involved. Many different versions of a National Urban Reform bill have been inconclusively discussed in the National Congress since 1983, but, on the whole, the scope for municipal action under general national directives has been widened. Of special importance was the promulgation of the 1988 Federal Constitution, which resulted from a process of intensive social mobilization and involved unprecedented popular participation. Over 130,000 people, social movements and non-government organizations signed a 'Popular Amendment on Urban Reform', which was approved in part to form the Constitution's innovative chapter on urban policy.

State Action and Urban Legislation

As has been widely discussed and analysed in the existing literature, the pattern of urban growth in Brazil has largely been due to the nature of state intervention in the process, through its overall economic policies, lack of effective social policies and attempts at urban planning.[10] It must be added that the enactment of legislation has also played important, though to date little-studied, roles in the urban development process.[11] In fact, countless federal, state, metropolitan and local laws and rules concerned in some way with land use control in urban areas have been enacted since the mid-1930s. The basic principle of the social function of property has been declared and repeated by all constitutions since the 1934 Federal Constitution.

Nevertheless, as a whole, the existing body of urban legislation is still far from satisfactory, while the ideology of unconstrained private property rights and their embodiment in law is still very strong and widely diffused throughout Brazilian society. Despite the current evolution in urban legislation and the progressive provisions of the 1988 Federal Constitution, as far as most judicial decisions and administrative measures are concerned the old Civil Law of 1916 still seeks to dictate the ideological framework concerning the question of property rights. Even when they do exist and are considered adequate by planners, urban laws do not work satisfactorily.

The reasons for this phenomenon have not been properly addressed in critical urban research. Researchers, planners and administrators alike have failed to understand properly either the extent of the reactions to the exclusionary and segregated legal order in urban areas or the impact several forms of legal pluralism arising from social practices have had on the formal legal order.

It could be argued that the most important issue concerning urban law in Brazil is a conceptual one. It relates to the 'latent conflict' – to use Patrick McAuslan's (1987: 187) phrase – which has long existed around the conceptualization of property rights and the corresponding issue of state intervention in the field of urban private property, rather than to the merely technical aspects of urban planning and the necessary legal instruments required. Indeed, no matter how important the creation of new legal instruments may be, the main point to be considered is the redefinition of the conceptual framework on the subject, for the use that is given to the contents of whatever progressive legislation may be enacted will always be limited by the survival of archaic principles of judicial interpretation.

The evolution of urban law in Brazil since the 1930s has not been straightforward.[12] In fact, the body of existing legislation seems at first to be a mere collection of fragmented and incomplete rules, which refer to partial and specific aspects of the general process of urban growth. Urban rules are dispersed and asystematic, for there exists in Brazil, as yet, no consolidation of existing rules governed by general principles. Moreover, as was mentioned above, the lack of constitutional attention to urban questions prior to the 1988 Federal Constitution brought about several conflicts between different levels of government over legislative jurisdiction on the subject of urban development, as well as conflicting judicial interpretations of existing legislation.

Nevertheless, the existing laws have not been enacted fortuitously. There has been a process behind their enactment, and there is a logic inherent in such a process.[13] On the whole, the evolution of urban legislation has involved the progressive reform of classical economic and legal liberalism, with three main objectives: the redefinition of the nature and extent of individual rights; the increase of state intervention in the socio-economic relations governing the production of urban space; and the imposition of limits on private property rights, especially through restrictions on the freedom of contract and the redefinition of contractual equality (Pessoa 1982).

In retrospect, the evolution of Brazilian urban law has shown that, while legislation is instrumental in the definition of property relations, which are exclusionary and foster social segregation, the approval of new urban laws only leads to changes in the existing social order when it reflects, and is supported by, a participatory political process.

The fight for a new paradigm   At the time when the first laws of some relevance to urban development were passed, in the mid-1930s, Brazilian industrialization was still in its early stages and consequently the social pressure on urban land was just beginning. Analysis of this legislation reveals the federal government's commitment to modernizing the existing legal and institutional framework for urban growth, to help prepare the cities for the influx of migrants required by the new economic model.[14]

At the same time, the basis for clientilistic practices concerning urban land was established in Brazilian politics. Urban legislation, like the labour laws, was presented as a 'gift' of the state to the urban masses. This placed the urban population in the position of 'debtors' *vis-à-vis* the state. From that point on, the upgrading of low-income settlements became a 'concession' granted to the residents by the government; it could only be undertaken at the discretion of the state.[15]

In this context, and with the same reforming spirit, several laws and judicial decisions partly related to the question of urban development were formulated between 1930 and 1963.[16] Although the motivations behind these legal measures varied, they can be interpreted, collectively, as part of the attempt to construct a systematic legal order to promote public control of urban land use and to lay the foundation for a new understanding of private property rights.

The legal concept of social property appeared for the first time in the 1934 Constitution. Private property rights were henceforth to be recognized only provided that the use to which the property was put fulfilled a social function. This same principle can be traced through all the federal constitutions since 1934 (i.e. 1937, 1946, 1967/69 and 1988), although prior to 1988 it was never made clear what it would mean in practice.

The enactment of more progressive, socially oriented legislation was the means by which the federal government tried to break with the definition of private property rights in urban areas which had been established by the Civil Code of 1916, an unequivocal expression of the liberal ideology which had long determined the country's social and political organization. This Civil Code is still in force. Its definition of private property rights is highly individualistic: the economic uses to which a given property can be put are determined by the individual interests of its owner. There is no obligation for its use to be in the public interest: 'the law guarantees the owner the right to use, to profit from and to dispose of his goods and to get them back from the power of whoever possesses them unjustly'.[17] The only existing restrictions are external to the right and less significant; they concern the rights of the owners of neighbouring properties.[18]

In the period between 1930 and 1963 there was an attempt to redefine private property rights as the *right to private property*, the contents of which would be specified by the state after considering how the public interest could be affected by the use to which the property was put. This gradual but significant process of ideological change was never completed. The conservative provisions of the Civil Code remained in force, and may even have been strengthened, and legal experts could not agree as to the relationship between the new legislation and the Civil Code. Given the vague constitutional definition of the social function of property and the conservative, positivist, training of Brazilian legal experts and judges, the majority of judicial decisions to date have reaffirmed the Civil Code as the prevailing legal paradigm.

In addition, the process of reform was violently interrupted by the legislation approved after the 1964 military take-over. The post-coup legislation adhered to the ideology of the 1916 Civil Code, as was to be expected given the military government's economic policies and political alliances. It was not until the late 1970s that the process of reform was renewed with the enactment of Federal Law no. 6,766 of 1979, in the context of efforts to overcome the anti-national and anti-popular economic development model imposed by the military government in 1964.

More recently, several very important federal laws and thousands of state, metropolitan and local laws and regulations have been passed concerning land use zoning, subdivision of urban land, regularization of *favelas* and the protection of historical buildings and of the environment. All of these have helped to reinforce the concept of the social function of property.[19]

This is a new attempt to reform liberalism, with a major impact on the laws enacted by the military regime and public policies concerning access to urban land. The establishment of the Constitutional Congress in 1986, leading to the 1988 Constitution, was the most important step in this process.

Urban policy in the 1988 Federal Constitution Despite its limited composition and autonomy, the Constitutional Congress of 1986 to 1988 was expected to fill the vacuum left by the lack of political leadership in Brazil since the early 1980s. A new political order had to be established, which would recognize the lively nature of contemporary Brazilian politics.[20]

The strengthening of trade unions and social movements had already forced a partial redefinition of the national political order, since their attempts to participate in decision-making and their identification of some principles of 'popular justice' were leading to a serious crisis of legality. The Constitutional Congress was somehow supposed to face the increasing legal pluralism of Brazilian society, and the main expectations it aroused among the urban poor concerned recognition of the legitimacy of practices and rules they observed that were not based on official legislation.[21]

From the perspective of this chapter, the main demand made on the Constitutional Congress was that the new Constitution should explicitly uphold the notion of social property. Simply repeating the same old tired slogan that had been used in constitution after constitution would not do; the Congress was expected to define the notion in such a way as to establish a new legal paradigm, replacing the one based on the Civil Code.

This claim was advanced in several ways, but the most important one was undoubtedly the remarkable 'Popular Amendment on Urban Reform' which was formulated by various civil organizations, signed by over 100,000 people and presented to the Congressional deputies. The organizations supporting the petition for the Popular Amendment were mostly the urban social movements, and especially housing movements, formed in peripheral areas and *favelas* during the 1970s, with the participation of committed professional advisers from the fields of law and urban planning.[22]

The main claims put forward by the Popular Amendment were for recognition, regularization and upgrading of illegal settlements; democratization of access to urban land and measures to combat property speculation; and the adoption of a democratic and participatory form of urban management. Following intense debate, several compromises were agreed upon and the Constitutional Congress eventually approved a whole chapter dedicated to urban policy in the Constitution promulgated on 5 October 1988.

Three major points about the new Constitution should be emphasized.

First, it conferred on local government the power to enact laws governing the use and development of urban space in order to guarantee the 'full development of the city's social functions' and the 'welfare of its inhabitants'.[23] Moreover, cities with more than 20,000 inhabitants were obliged to pass a Master Plan Law, the 'basic policy instrument for urban expansion and development'.[24]

Second, the right to private property was again recognized as a basic principle of the economic order, provided, however, that it fulfilled a social function according to the 'dictates of social justice'.[25] In a highly significant development it was stipulated that urban property accomplishes its social function only when it attends to the 'fundamental requirements of city planning as expressed in the Master Plan'.[26]

Third, it approved the right to adverse possession (*usucapião* – 'squatters' rights') in private urban landholdings up to a maximum of 250m^2 after only five years of peaceful possession of the property.[27]

These three points constitute a new framework for Brazilian urban law. In particular, the right of *usucapião* is extremely significant, especially with regard to programmes for the regularization of *favelas*, since it probably applies, in theory, to more than half the existing *favelas*. Many legal experts argue that further legal ratification is necessary in order for this principle to be put into practice, but the formal recognition of the rights of millions of *favela* residents to remain on the land they occupy certainly constitutes a remarkable change of outlook: it is the first step towards their recognition as citizens.

With respect to the question of private property rights in urban areas, the Constitution went further than its predecessors in trying to define the notion of the 'social function' of property. Instead of repeating vague rhetorical statements, it identified the principle of a social function with adherence to the precepts of the Master Plan for a given city. In other words, private property rights are to be subjected to local regulations defining permissible types of land use and construction. Thus, the economic potential of individual landholdings in urban areas is to be determined by the state, after it has considered possible conflicts of interest involved. Consequently, the more developed and comprehensive the Master Plan, the more advanced and progressive the notion of social property should be. Private property rights therefore no longer have a pre-determined content, since the new Constitution converts private property rights into a *right to property*, that is, a legal obligation, with a social purpose whose contents will vary according to local circumstances.[28]

From the conservative viewpoint of traditional property development interests, the Constitution's introduction of a compulsory Master Plan could be viewed as a convenient mechanism to restrict recognition of urban social movements' demands and application of the new planning instruments, as it requires further 'technocratic' intervention. The movements in favour of urban reform, however, acknowledged the political impossibility of having their claims fully recognized, and decided, pragmatically, to appropriate the traditional notion of the Master Plan, turning it to their own advantage. A thorough redefinition of its contents, objectives and methodology would enable the Master Plan to become another avenue for popular mobilization, in a wider political arena.

As was to be expected, the new Constitution placed great emphasis on state intervention. There are, however, two significant innovations that may contribute to changing the nature of urban planning. First, the Constitution reserved the most important role in this respect for the municipality.[29] Although federal and state governments also have the power to enact laws and formulate land-use programmes, their powers are limited to very general directives or specific issues that cannot be solved at the local level.[30] Local government is, in practice, the real authority in this area; it has immediate responsibility for urban legislation and the implementation of urban policies.

This is a significant advance: since the municipality is the sphere of government that is closest to the population, it has certain advantages in the effort to solve the problems facing city dwellers. It also has the legal capacity to control urban activities affecting environmental resources. Any activity with land use implications must be approved by the municipality, which is responsible for regulating the actions of private citizens and public agencies.

On its own, however, this is not enough to change the nature of urban planning, since it is clear from past experience that effective management of urban problems presupposes democratization of the decision-making process. Over and above the re-evaluation of particular models and techniques, there is a need to rethink the processes of political adminis-tration and conflict resolution implicit in urban planning, as well as the chosen means of enforcement. In general, favoured approaches to planning have been adopted without significant participation by the different interest groups involved in land use questions.

In this context, the second constitutional innovation was particularly important, for it ensured the possibility of some, albeit still rudimentary, degree of popular participation in decision-making.[31] In addition to its revalidation of the classic principles of representative democracy, the new Constitution accepted the possibility of direct community participation in urban planning at the local level. Non-governmental organizations are now able to formulate bills on some urban questions and submit them to the local parliament.

This principle requires elaboration and adaptation to local circumstances, and it will need to be vigorously defended by progressive forces, but its very existence is an important sign of political change. It co-exists, moreover, with a broader recognition of the 'collective right for diffuse interests',[32] which offers more scope for citizens and NGOs to make use of the courts in seeking to uphold the rights conferred by urban law and to pursue other social and environmental concerns.[33]

To summarize, according to the 1988 Constitution the economic content of urban property rights is to be decided by local governments through a participatory legislative process, and no longer by the exclusive individual interests of the owner. This principle was also expressed in the creation of new legal instruments such as a compulsory building requirement, progressive taxation and flexible expropriation, which, together with the other instruments to be created by local legislation, will place the local state at the forefront of the urban development process.[34] The local population is now entitled to participate in the decision-making process both directly and through their elected representatives.

It is for this reason that it can be said that the 1988 Constitution recognized, above all, that the process of decision-making on urban questions is a *political* process, which defines the options for the economic exploitation of urban property. For the first time, the population can to some extent be considered a political agent, and therefore popular mobilization against dominant economic groups may be expected to take place within legal and institutional spheres. Although the leading role of the state in controlling urban growth was reaffirmed, a new social right was recognized: *the right to urban planning*. Rather than being merely a faculty of the administration, this is one of its main legal obligations and an expression of social citizenship. The main novelty is surely that urban law has been placed where it always belonged: in the political process.

Conclusion: the Prospects for Urban Management

Following the 1988 Federal Constitution, several new state Constitutions and municipal laws have recently reinforced, and extended, the principles described above. Many interesting experiments in urban management have been undertaken, now that municipalities are politically stronger and somewhat richer.[35] Although the prospects for urban planning are better than ever before, the scale of the urban, social and fiscal crisis that has emerged during the past four decades is enormous. Since Brazil is still struggling with a deep economic and financial crisis, the scope of such local experiences has been determined, and constrained, by the broader national context.

The success of local initiatives will depend primarily on the consolidation of Brazil's fledgling democracy, especially as regards the promotion of social justice. The metropolitan areas have been badly affected by the economic crisis since the 1980s, and growing poverty and escalating urban violence have contributed to further deterioration in the already low living standards and social disintegation. In particular, it is necessary to mention the impact of international drug trafficking which has increasingly been organized from the main cities since the late 1980s, provoking serious problems in the relationship between the state and civil society.

Changes in the local political sphere have also been responsible for both the abandonment and/or failure, on the one hand, and the success, on the other, of urban planning experiments. An example of the first type of outcome is provided by São Paulo, where a conservative government elected in 1992 immediately put a stop to the progressive urban policies of the previous government. Consistency in local government planning efforts is exemplified by Curitiba, in the south of Brazil, which has been internationally praised for the success of its planning strategies. It should, however, be stressed that, whatever its merits, the experience of Curitiba is largely restricted to the central area of the city, where a minority of the population live (whereas 20 per cent of the population live in *favelas*). Curitiba may have the most efficient and environmentally balanced city centre in Brazil, but the issues of social segregation and exclusion have never been properly tackled.[36]

For all its limitations and shortcomings, however, urban reform is none the less gradually taking place in Brazil, and it is supported by an increasing social awareness of urban questions. The future of urban planning, and for that matter the fate of Brazilian cities, will depend on how the current political reforms combine income redistribution measures with recognition of the citizenship rights of the urban population. In this context, the renewal of social mobilization in urban areas is of crucial importance.

The new constitutional principles concerning urban property have provided the basis for reform of property rights in Brazil, replacing the liberal paradigm set by the Civil Code. In legal terms, although further federal legislation in this area would be most welcome, the fundamental issue was properly addressed.

Nevertheless, these legal changes will result in a genuine change in urban policies, and therefore in the standard of living of the urban population, only if the political process in the country leads to deeper changes in the nature of the state. The reforms introduced by the 1988 Constitution were certainly not enough to bring about structural change, for much of the existing, exclusionary, system for the distribution and exercise of political power was retained, often accompanied by chronic corruption. The class-bound nature of the state remained essentially unaltered. Major structural changes in urban life will take place only when deeper political changes improve the conditions of *legal or political, as well as socio-economic,* citizenship of the Brazilian people.

It can be argued that greater public participation in the decision-making process is the only way to confront the serious urban problems existing in Brazil, in order to put an end to the existing situation of extreme social injustice. It can no longer be accepted that the majority of the urban population – living in *favelas* or illegal subdivisions, or lacking security of tenure for other reasons – should have to live as second-class citizens in an 'illegal city', where the norms of the 'legal city' do not apply. It can no longer be accepted that millions of city dwellers should be excluded from the running of their cities and from the political process constituting the urban order.[37] The question of access to urban land and housing cannot be left to market forces alone, and the recognition of the long-sought 'right to the city' is the condition for the consolidation of Brazilian democracy.

It is essential to transform these millions of marginalized people into citizens. Urban reform is not, however, conferred by law: it has to be attained through the political process. The 'right to the city' has to be won, as its full recognition is an essential stage in the broader 'struggle for the freedom of the city' (Lefebvre 1971: 205).

Notes

Translated from Portuguese by Edésio Fernandes and Ann Varley.

1. Although this is true for most metropolitan areas, which are growing at rates higher than 2.5 per cent per year, a new phenomenon has been identified in recent years, especially in São Paulo and Rio de Janeiro, the two largest metropolitan areas: a significant decline in population growth (-0.82 per cent in Rio and 1.7 per cent in São Paulo). This phenomenon will certainly change the distribution of urban population in the country as well as influencing the potential for new approaches to urban planning.

2. For an analysis of Brazilian urban development and urban policy, see, among others, Oliveira (1985); Schmidt and Farret (1986); and Rolnik (1994).

3. In São Paulo, Brazil's largest city, 67 per cent of the population is reported to live in illegal and precarious conditions (Somekh 1996).

4. For general economic information on urban Brazil, see, among others, Valladares (1988); Todaro (1989); United Nations (1987); and Ribeiro and Santos Jr

(1994). The low standard of living in urban areas can be seen from the statistics on monthly per capita income, weekly working time, life expectancy at birth, mortality rates, food consumption, levels of education and of access to urban services and amenities and so on; for detailed data, see Valladares (1988); World Bank (1993).

5. The process of urban growth 'through the expansion of peripheral areas' was analysed by Santos, showing how new urban areas for poor people were created on the outskirts of cities at a 'zero' economic cost, having, however, an 'infinite' social cost because of the lack of infrastructure, the responsibility for the provision of which was transferred to the state. This pattern of development kept the speculative process going since there were large stocks of vacant land between the peripheral areas and the central, well-serviced, ones (C. Santos 1980); see also Kowarick (1979).

6. The structure of land ownership was already well established before rapid urban growth began. The domination of the economy by export agriculture had led to a highly concentrated pattern of landholding with many large estates. During more than four centuries of colonization (1500–1822), imperial rule (1822–1889) and republican government (from 1889), Brazil had experienced an intense process of privatization of land use, which was officially endorsed by imperial legislation in 1850. An historical analysis of this process, which has also heavily influenced the pattern of urban landownership in Brazil, can be found in Marx (1991).

7. See Rolnik (1997) on São Paulo; for a general analysis, see Fernandes (1995a).

8. For an analysis of the political and financial realities of local government during the military regime and following re-democratization, see Sousa (1997).

9. A critique of the legal and institutional aspects of the authoritarian nature of metropolitan government in Brazil from 1973 to 1988 is provided by Fernandes (1992b).

10. The vast literature on urban development in Brazil has been summarized by Valladares (1986; 1988). She identifies the main research themes as urban poverty, government policies, concerning in particular housing and urban planning, and studies on urban social movements. Kowarick (1994) provides a collection of articles on the social and political aspects of urban development in São Paulo, while Ribeiro and Santos Jr (1994) have edited an innovative study of the impact of economic globalization on Brazilian cities. More recently, Ribeiro and Azevedo (1996) have edited a major study of the complex questions surrounding access to housing and the process of urban reform in Brazil.

11. For an overview of the legal and socio-legal literature on Brazilian urban development, see Fernandes (1996c).

12. A description of the evolution of Brazilian urban law and of the roles played by legislation in the urban development process, can be found in Fernandes (1995a); for an account of the role of illegality in urban growth, see Fernandes (1993) and Maricato (1996).

13. Torn between the pressure to stimulate new opportunities for capital accumulation in cities and the need to neutralize growing social mobilization, urban legislation has aimed to confer a 'new ethic' on Brazilian capitalism (Herkenhoff Filho 1981: 76); for an historical analysis of the conflicts within real estate capital, see Ribeiro (1982; 1993) and Campos Filho (1983). For a more detailed analysis of the conflicts inherent to the enactment of urban legislation, see Fernandes (1995a).

14. An interesting analysis of the legislation enacted in the 1930s is provided by Pessoa (1982; 1984).

15. Clientelism in Brazilian urban politics is discussed by Rolnik (1994; 1997).

16. Some laws worth mentioning are: Decreto-Lei no. 25 (1937), establishing the legal basis for protection of the cultural and historical heritage (and still in force); Decreto-Lei no. 58 (1937), which originally established rules for the subdivision of urban land; Decreto-Lei no. 3,665 (1941), which permitted land expropriation for reasons of 'public utility'; and Federal Law no. 4,132 (1962), which allows land expropriation for reasons of 'social interest'. There are many other federal rules, judicial decisions and administrative acts related to the subject, not to mention state and municipal building regulations.

17. Civil Code, Article 524.

18. The nature of property rights as defined in the Civil Code was such that the state had little ability to control the use and development of urban land, and that land and other natural resources were viewed basically in terms of their exchange value, as mere commodities. As a result, access to land and housing was to be determined by market forces alone. For a more detailed analysis, see Fernandes (1995a).

19. Some laws worth mentioning are: Federal Law no. 6,766 (1979), which governs the subdivision of urban land; Federal Law no. 6,803 (1980), which deals with industrial zoning in polluted areas; Federal Law no. 6,931 (1981), which formulated the National Environment Policy. In different versions, the National Urban Development bill has been waiting to be discussed by the National Congress since 1983. For an analysis of the evolution of environmental legislation in Brazil, see Fernandes (1992a; 1996a).

20. The process of writing the new Constitution has already been discussed by many authors; see, among others, Lamounier (1987); Reis and O'Donnell (1988); and Faria (1989).

21. The phenomenon of 'informal justice' and the development of an 'internal legal system' in illegal settlements has formed the subject of important studies by Santos, showing how a variety of 'intra-class' disputes among residents are settled through unofficial 'legal' processes (B. Santos 1977; 1992).

22. After an initial period of euphoria, deeply influenced by the theoretical paradigm set by Manuel Castells in the early 1980s, according to which social movements were considered by many to be the most lively and innovative manifestation of and seedbed for revolutionary ideals, more recent research has looked at the phenomenon of social mobilization in a more sober way. In spite of all the difficulties of considering Brazilian social movements as independent political agents, many analysts nevertheless still believe in their fundamental importance in this context; see Kowarick (1994).

23. 1988 Federal Constitution, Article 182.

24. 1988 Federal Constitution, Article 182, paragraph 1.

25. 1988 Federal Constitution, Article 5, XXII, XXIII; Article 170, II, III.

26. 1988 Federal Constitution, Article 182, paragraph 2.

27. 1988 Federal Constitution, Article 183.

28. A thorough analysis of the constitutional requirement for the approval of Master Plans is provided by Saule Jr (1997).

29. 1988 Federal Constitution, Article 27, XVIII, XIX.

30. 1988 Federal Constitution, Article 21, XX; Article 23, III, IV, IX; Article 24, VI, VII, VIII.

31. 1988 Federal Constitution, Article 1; Article 29, X, XI.

32. 1988 Federal Constitution, Article 5, LXXIII.

33. For an evaluation of the concept of a 'civil public action' on which this type of judicial review is founded, see Fernandes 1994; 1995c.

34. The new constitutional instruments are discussed in detail by Aguiar (1996).

35. A general overview of the recent, successful experiences of local government in cities such as Belo Horizonte, Campinas, Joinville and Osasco is provided by Figueiredo and Lamounier (1996).

36. Fernandes (1995b) provides a general discussion of the internationally renowned experience of Curitiba.

37. An important step in the right direction is provided by the 'participatory budgets' implemented by Workers' Party administrations in cities such as Porto Alegre, Belo Horizonte and Diadema over the course of the last ten years. These grant residents' associations some participation in the process of setting the local investment budget; see Fernandes (1996b).

References

Aguiar, J. C. (1996) *Direito da Cidade*, Renovar, Rio de Janeiro.

Campos Filho, C. M. (1983) 'A terra no desenvolvimento urbano – o caso do Brasil', *Revista Brasileira de Planejamento*, Vol. 13, 24–72.

Faria, J. E. (1989) *O Brasil Pós-Constituinte*, Graal, Rio de Janeiro.

Fernandes, E. (1992a) 'Law, politics and environmental protection in Brazil', *Journal of Environmental Law*, Vol. 4, no. 1, 41–56.

— (1992b) 'Juridico-institutional aspects of metropolitan administration in Brazil', *Third World Planning Review*, Vol. 14, no. 3, 227–44.

— (1993) 'The legal regularisation of favelas in Brazil: the case of Belo Horizonte', *Social and Legal Studies*, Vol. 2, no. 2, 211–36.

— (1994) 'Defending collective interests in Brazilian environmental law: an assessment of the civil public action, *RECIEL – Review of European Community and International Environmental Law*, Vol. 3, no. 4, 253–8.

— (1995a) *Law and Urban Change in Brazil*, Avebury, Aldershot.

— (1995b) 'Curitiba, Brazil: successfully integrating land use and transport policies', *Report*, Vol. 5, 6–8.

— (1995c) 'Collective interests in Brazilian environmental law', in D. Robinson and J. Dunkley (eds), *Public Interest Perspectives in Environmental Law*, Wiley, Chichester, 117–34.

— (1996a) 'Constitutional environmental rights in Brazil', in M. R. Anderson and A. E. Boyle (eds), *Human Rights Approaches to Environmental Protection*, Oxford University Press, Oxford, 265–84.

— (1996b) 'Participatory budget: a new experience of democratic administration in Belo Horizonte, Brazil', *Report*, Vol. 11, 23–4.

— (1996c) 'Agenda de investigación para una sociología del derecho urbanístico en Brasil', *Enlace*, Vol. 1, no. 1, 27–36.

Figueiredo, R. and B. Lamounier (eds) (1996) *As Cidades que Dão Certo*, MH Comunicação, Brasilia.

Herkenhoff Filho, P. E. (1981) 'Questões anteriores ao direito urbano', in A. Pessoa (ed.), *Direito do Urbanismo – Uma Visão Sócio-Juridica*, Instituto Brasileiro de Administração Municipal/Livros Técnicos e Científicos, Rio de Janeiro, 73–90.

Kowarick, L. (1979) *A Espoliação Urbana*, Paz e Terra, Rio de Janeiro.

— (ed.) (1994) *Social Struggles and the City*, Monthly Review Press, New York.

Lamounier, B. (1987) *Perspectives on Democratic Consolidation: The Brazilian Case*, Instituto de Estudos Sociais e Políticos, São Paulo.

Lefebvre, H. (1971) *Everyday Life in the Modern World*, Allen Lane, London.

McAuslan, P. (1987) 'Land policy: a framework for analysis and action' *Journal of African Law*, Vol. 31, 185–206.

Maricato, E. (1996) *Metrópole na Periferia do Capitalismo*, HUCITEC, São Paulo.

Marx, M. (1991) *Cidade no Brasil, Terra de Quem?*, Nobel/Editora da Universidade de São Paulo, São Paulo.

Oliveira, F. (1985) 'A critique of dualist reason: the Brazilian economy since 1930', in R. Bromley (ed.), *Planning for Small Enterprises in Third World Cities*, Pergamon, Oxford, 65–95.

Pessoa, A. (1982) 'O uso do solo em conflito', in L. A. M. da Silva (ed.), *Solo Urbano – Tópicos Sobre o Uso da Terra*, Zahar, Rio de Janeiro, 79–95.

— (1984) 'O uso do solo em conflito', in J. A. Falcão (ed.), *Conflito de Direito de Propriedade – Invasões Urbanas*, Forense, Rio de Janeiro, 185–216.

Reis, F. W. and G. O'Donnell (1988) (eds), *A Democracia no Brasil – Dilemas e Perspectivas*, Vértice, São Paulo.

Ribeiro, L. C. de Q. (1982) 'Espaço urbano, mercado de terras e produção da habitacão', in L. A. M. da Silva (ed.), *Solo Urbano – Tópicos Sobre o Uso da Terra*, Zahar, Rio de Janeiro, 34–44.

— (1993) 'The formation of development capital: a historical overview of housing in Rio de Janeiro', *International Journal of Urban and Regional Research*, Vol. 17, 547–58.

Ribeiro, L. C. de Q. and S. de Azevedo (eds) (1996) *A Crise da Moradia nas Grandes Cidades: Da Questão da Habitação à Reforma Urbana*, Editora da Universidade Federal do Rio de Janeiro, Rio de Janeiro.

Ribeiro, L. C. de Q. and O. A. dos Santos Jr (eds) (1994) *Globalização, Fragmentação e Reforma Urbana*, Civilização Brasileira, Rio de Janeiro.

Rolnik, R. (1994) 'Planejamento urbano nos anos 90: novas perspectivas para velhos temas', in L. C. de Q. Ribeiro and O. A. dos Santos Jr (eds), *Globalização, Fragmentação e Reforma Urbana*, Civilização Brasileira, Rio de Janeiro, 351–60.

— (1997) *A Cidade e a Lei*, Studio Nobel, São Paulo.

Santos, B. de S. (1977) 'The law of the oppressed: the construction and reproduction of legality in Pasargada', *Law and Society Review*, Vol. 12, no. 1, 5–126.

— (1992) 'Law, state and urban struggles in Recife, Brazil', *Social and Legal Studies*, Vol. 1, 235–55.

Santos, C. N. F. dos (1980) 'Velhas novidades nos modos de urbanização brasileiros', in L. Valladares (ed.), *Habitação em Questão*, Zahar, Rio de Janeiro, 17–48.

Saule Jr, N. (1997) *Novas Perspectivas do Direito Urbanístico Brasileiro*, Sergio Antonio Fabris Editor, Porto Alegre.

Schmidt, B. and R. Farret (1986) *A Questão Urbana*, Jorge Zahar, Rio de Janeiro.

Somekh, N. (1996) 'Plano Diretor de São Paulo: uma aplicação das propostas de solo criado', in L. C. de Q. Ribeiro and S. de Azevedo (eds), (1996) *A Crise da Moradia nas Grandes Cidades*, Editora da Universidade Federal do Rio de Janeiro, Rio de Janeiro, 257–66.

Sousa, C. (1997) *Constitutional Engineering in Brazil: The Politics of Federalism and Decentralization*, Macmillan, London.

Todaro, M. (1989) *Economic Development and the Third World*, Longman, New York.

United Nations (1987) *The Prospects of World Urbanization*, United Nations, New York.

Valladares, L. (1986) *La Recherche Urbaine au Brésil: Bref Aperçu de Son Évaluation*, Centre de Recherche sur le Brésil Contemporain, École des Hautes Etudes en Sciences Sociales, Paris.

— (1988) 'Urban sociology in Brazil: a research report', *International Journal of Urban and Regional Research*, Vol. 12, 285–302.

World Bank (1993) *Poverty and Income Distribution in Latin America*, World Bank, Washington, DC.

CHAPTER 9

Tenure Regularization, Private Property and Public Order in Mexico

Antonio Azuela and
Emilio Duhau

Mexico, like most developing countries, is undergoing rapid urbanization. As in other countries, much of the urban population lives in illegal housing areas in conditions of great poverty. Mexico has, however, one of the most – if not the most – ambitious and long-established land tenure regularization programmes in the world. Analysis of the Mexican experience of tenure regularization may therefore contribute significantly to our understanding of this process.

In this chapter, we explore the role regularization plays in two central aspects of urban development: the creation of private property and the consolidation of public order (the rule of law). Regularization is significant in this context because illegality is a basic characteristic of low-income settlements. There can, however, be major differences between settlements and the social meaning of illegal land tenure varies accordingly. When, for example, settlers occupy land by squatting, without the owner's consent, they are usually breaking the law and can therefore find themselves liable to prosecution and legal sanctions, including eviction. By contrast, when people buy housing plots from a landowner who has not complied with planning regulations, it is the owner who has broken the law. The legal implications of these two situations are therefore very different, even if both types of settlement are described as 'squatter settlements' in common international parlance.

Leaving aside such differences between illegal settlements, the very fact that a city is divided into 'legal' and 'illegal' areas has profound implications for society as a whole, since a truly *public* order, in the sense of social norms to which all members of society must adhere, does not exist. As long as a substantial part of the population gains access to land by a different set of processes from the rest of society, it is clear that not all individuals are subject to the same rules, regardless of whether or not those rules can be formally classified as 'law'. It is hard to think of cases where this does not entail the existence of profound social inequalities.

As we shall see, urban researchers have shared the general assumption that such inequalities are a 'natural' or inevitable feature of urban society.

The Evolution of Tenure Regularization Policies in Mexico

The institutionalization of regularization policies took place in Mexico during the 1970s. Previously, the government had dealt with illegal settlements in a more *ad hoc* fashion. The Mexican Revolution caused a wave of migration to the capital city, giving rise to new low-income settlements in the 1920s. A new figure – the resident of illegal settlements – had arrived on the urban scene. What made this figure different from the poor urban resident of previous centuries was that the settlers organized themselves to make demands on the government. Since post-Revolution governments' alliance with peasant and labour organizations meant that they were committed to social reform, they could not afford to ignore the demands of the urban poor. Governments therefore had to provide some sort of policy response, however limited the results (Córdoba 1980). In addition, the emerging political elite could not afford to ignore the opportunity to manipulate the settlers' demands in order to gain their political support. During the 1930s, the government therefore started to recognize the existence of low-income settlements described as 'proletarian settlements' (*colonias proletarias*); in the following decade, the mayor of Mexico City expropriated private land to create more than 120 such settlements. Such measures could not, however, keep up with the scale of demand for urban land, and other settlements were created by invasion or by illegal subdivision. In 1946, government reports began to make explicit reference to tenure regularization in these illegal settlements, depicting it as an official concession to the urban poor, giving them security of tenure.

Subsequent governments were far less tolerant of land invasions, but low-income settlements continued to be accepted where they involved the illegal subdivision of private land or, from the early 1950s, of *ejido* land. It might be useful to offer a few words of explanation on the legal and political characteristics of that most Mexican of institutions, the *ejido*. Legally, the Mexican agrarian reform gave property rights, not to individual peasants, but to rural communities (*núcleos agrarios*). The word *ejido* thus refers to both the community and the land itself. The community owns the land, but in almost all *ejidos* each member (*ejidatario*) has the exclusive right to work an area of land called a 'parcel' (*parcela*). In the context of this chapter, the most important point about the agrarian reform is that, until 1992, neither *ejido* communities nor individual *ejidatarios* could sell or in any other way dispose of their land. Land sales were considered legally 'non-existent'.

Politically, the *ejido* was, and still is, the basis of the corporatist 'alliance' between the Mexican government and the peasantry. From organizing elections to conveying rural demands to those in power, the *ejido* is the foundation on which, since the 1930s, the complex web of relations between peasants and government has been built.

In the early 1970s, a series of scandals drew attention to the illegal urban development that had been taking place on *ejido* land, at a time when dealing with urban poverty was being given a more prominent place on the government agenda. A question arose as to which branch of government should take responsibility for the *ejidos* on which urban development had taken place. In 1973, President Luís Echeverría created a Committee for the Regularization of Land Tenure, as well as a variety of other agencies intended to address a range of urban problems. Urban planners working in these agencies tried to take the lead in government intervention in illegal settlements on *ejido* land, but they were unsuccessful. It was the 'agrarian sector' agencies – those with responsibility for rural affairs – that gained control of what, in 1974, became the Commission for the Regularization of Land Tenure (CORETT).

Although urban planning agencies became important at both federal and state (provincial) level during the 1970s, the planners were never able to control the development of *ejido* land. To do so, they would have had to embark on cumbersome expropriation procedures, which would have made the *ejido* communities deprived of their land look like the victims of the 'technocrats'. For those who controlled the land within the *ejidos*, it was, and still is, more profitable to sell the land, even if that was expressly forbidden by law. By the early 1980s, then, the development of *ejido* land had become the subject of a competition between the urban planners and the agrarian sector. The planners tried to create land reserves to provide a supply of cheap land for legal, adequately serviced, urban development. To succeed, they had to overcome the difficulties presented by expropriation and gain the support of the state governments who would be the immediate beneficiaries of the expropriations. The former had a great advantage over the urban planners, in that they had the political connections needed to enable them to protect (and therefore enjoy the support of) those responsible for the illegal sale of *ejido* land. Moreover, regularization became an increasingly important political asset for the government, as land titles could be used as official largesse to secure the loyalty of the urban poor.

For these reasons, tenure regularization on *ejido* land follows the logic of agrarian law (Azuela 1989). Although most settlers acquire their plots not by squatting but by buying land from the *ejidatarios*, the law declares these sales 'non-existent'. Therefore, the only way to give title to settlers is to obtain a presidential decree expropriating land from the *ejido* in favour of CORETT, which then sells the land to residents on an individual basis. A legal fiction, the 'non-existence' of the original land sales, becomes reality when settlers have to buy from the government what they have already bought from the *ejidatarios*. Even if, as we shall see later, the price they pay for regularization is generally affordable, they are dependent on the good-will of the government, since the law concerning *ejido* land allows the state to depict regularization as an act of charity towards the poor.[1]

Nevertheless, it must be stressed that not all low-income settlements – not even the majority of them – are founded on *ejido* land. Private land has also been subdivided illegally and regularization programmes established for these areas. The main difference between these programmes and those of CORETT is that, in Mexico, private property is regulated by state law. The tendency has been for individual regularization agencies to be created in each state, as part of the state government. Thus, in the Federal District, the agency that regularizes settlements on private or government property, the General Directorate for Territorial Regularization (DGRT), is part of the Department of the Federal District (DDF). In the State of Mexico, the Commission for Land Regularization in the State of Mexico (CRESEM), part of the state government, is in charge of the process.

The regularization of settlements on private property thus offers limited opportunities for direct intervention by the federal government. Regularization in *ejido* areas, by contrast, is based on expropriation procedures laid down by federal law and therefore always follows the same pattern. No matter what the local circumstances and complications, the focus is always on the property rights of the *ejido* community, whereas the regularization procedures of agencies like the DGRT and CRESEM respond to a variety of situations. In many cases, disputes between landowners and residents over settlements on private property can be settled only by the courts, and regularization often entails isolated, one-off, interventions.

The Major Characteristics of Mexican Regularization Policies

In Mexico, regularization of low-income settlements generally involves the delivery of property titles to residents. There are two elements to the process: formal transmission of ownership to the settlers and formal recognition of the settlement by the urban authorities. Although local governments often claim that settlement illegality prevents the introduction of urban services, the truth is that there is no formal connection between regularization and servicing. Legalization is neither a necessary nor a sufficient condition for the introduction of services. Many settlements receive services before they are legalized and not all legalized settlements necessarily receive services as a result of regularization. There is no formal obligation for local governments to service regularized settlements.

Thus, although regularization has in recent years been accompanied by the provision of urban services via the National Solidarity Programme (PRONASOL; the best-known example being the Chalco Valley),[2] it has generally been a form of state intervention in low-income neighbourhoods that depends on the degree of social and political priority given to the policy at higher levels of government, rather than the financial resources available.

In order, however, for political decisions to lead to the delivery of property titles, appropriate administrative procedures and agencies are needed, and these must necessarily operate in terms of the legal regulation of property rights. Although the laws defining property rights can be changed, as in the 1992 reforms to *ejido* property, they have a much greater permanency than the policies associated with each presidential administration. The enormous boost given to the regularization effort by President Carlos Salinas de Gortari in the early 1990s – apparently the result of his decision to convert PRONASOL into the flagship of his government's social policy – thus relied on the existence of government agencies that already had what we may call a tried and tested 'technology' of regularization. The normative and procedural framework for regularization has been based less on recognition by the courts of tenure rights acquired by dint of possession than on government initiatives creating effective administrative institutions and procedures for tenure regularization. In spite of the role that administrative procedures have played in creating what De Soto (1989) has called 'expectative' property rights (i.e. the anticipation by residents of regularization), the initiative still lies in the hands of the executive.

Rather than dwelling on the complex procedures entailed in regularization,[3] we wish to emphasize the major characteristics of tenure regularization as a form of state intervention in low-income settlements in urban Mexico.

First, this is a form of intervention requiring minimal assignment of budgetary resources, since regularization agencies, and particularly COR-ETT, are supposed to be self-financing, meeting their costs from the charges levied on beneficiaries (Azuela 1994).

Second, although regularization programmes cost the state very little, they have major social and political implications (although some of these are subject to debate, as we shall show).

Third, over the past two decades, regularization has been the one urban policy to have been applied consistently by the Mexican government, particularly in Mexico City; as a result, it has made the informal land market the preferred route by which the urban poor gain access to housing.

Fourth, regularization of *ejido* land entails direct and centralized intervention by federal government agencies acting with relative autonomy in relation to local conditions or authorities.

Fifth, with some exceptions, the residents of low-income settlements in Mexico City generally welcome regularization, since they believe that it is both necessary and in their interests.

By the early 1980s, the most conservative of official estimates showed that regularization in Mexico City had reached enormous proportions, involving an area of more than 9,000 hectares, 220,000 plots and 1,300,000 residents in the Federal District and seventeen metropolitan municipalities of the State of Mexico (Iracheta 1989).[4] For the period 1989–94, when regularization became a central element of the federal government's social policy in PRONASOL, it was stated that at least 300,000 plots were to be regularized in Mexico City by CORETT, the DGRT and CRESEM. Official estimates at the beginning of this period reported 500,000 irregular plots in the Federal District: 180,000 on communal and *ejido* property and 320,000 on private property. By mid-1994, 125,000 titles had been issued for housing plots on private or government land (DGRT 1994a: 78–9); approximately 55,000 had been issued for settlements on communal or *ejido* land. In the peripheral municipalities belonging to the State of Mexico, there were, by 1992, about 93,000 plots to be regularized on communal or *ejido* property and another 15,000 on private property.[5]

What matters here is not so much the accuracy of specific figures as the orders of magnitude involved. A significant proportion of the Mexico City population has benefited from regularization in the past fifteen years. Given the continuous expansion of illegal settlement, regularization has clearly become a routine form of state intervention in low-income housing in Mexico City. There can be no doubt that it delivers a loud and clear message about the government's attitude to informal urban development to all involved in the process.

Regularization and the Creation of Private Property

What are the social and political consequences of tenure regularization in urban Mexico? Before exploring these questions, we must make a general point about the apparently contradictory effects of regularization on such a scale: that it promotes further illegal settlement at the same time as it removes the illegality which is one of the main causes of the urban poor's dependence on the state.

Regularization is regarded as a positive measure by international agencies such as the World Bank (see World Bank 1994) and a large number of progressive professionals and academics (see, for example, INTERURBA 1995). The arguments in favour of regularization are varied: that it enables the development of the land market, that it encourages housing improvement and settlement consolidation, or that it is only right and proper that the state should acknowledge in this way the time and money invested by the urban poor in building their own homes.

These arguments have not prevented critics from expressing severe doubts about the consequences of regularization – particularly in Mexico:

> The introduction of urban services to illegal settlements ... tends to drive residents out, leading to further illegal urban development elsewhere. This can be explained by rising land values and the high cost of introducing services when these settlements are regularized, leading to the displacement of population to other peripheral areas. (Legorreta 1994: 61)

> Although regularization ... is clearly necessary, the ways in which the process has been designed and the procedures used do not appear to be the most appropriate ones ... the re-establishment of private property in land which was previously social property[6] ... opens the door to increased land price speculation. Although regularization provides tenure security for residents, these speculative pressures threaten the success of the regularization process, since they often undermine residents' ability to keep possession of their plots. (Iracheta 1989: 272)

These quotations illustrate a common criticism of regularization, which can be summarized as follows: when regularization involves the delivery of individual property titles, it produces a series of 'perverse' results that undermine the stated intention of providing security of tenure for the beneficiaries. Speculative rises in the price of land and the costs imposed on residents both directly and indirectly (in the form of service charges and property taxes) lead to the displacement of the original population. Rather than increasing security of tenure, regularization actually diminishes it; but security of tenure is precisely what residents need, not property titles *per se*. In addition, in Mexico, the expropriation of *ejido* and communal land for regularization means the privatization of what was previously 'social' property.

It follows that regularization should provide security of tenure by means other than the recognition of individual private property rights.

In our opinion, this argument disregards the empirical evidence about the consequences of regularization and implies that the beneficiaries need to be 'protected' from the dangers of private property. To 'protect' them against privatization, however, would lead to an institutionalization of class differences that would surely not be welcomed by the critics of regularization – for reasons we shall now explore.

One of the main arguments advanced by proponents of regularization is that giving people security of tenure promotes housing improvements and settlement consolidation. Research has shown, however, that although there is a relationship between tenure security and housing improvement, it does not depend on formal regularization, since other processes (such as the introduction of urban services) produce similar effects (Varley 1987).

Furthermore, the argument that regularization leads to the displacement of the original settlers is not supported by the available research findings for urban Mexico. We have discussed elsewhere (Duhau forthcoming) why the argument that land price increases caused by regularization will lead to the displacement of the original residents by new, higher-income, purchasers does not hold water, and we will not dwell on this point here. It is also argued, however, that the costs of regularization itself, as well as the indirect costs resulting from the formalization of ownership (property taxes, service charges and so on) also lead to the displacement of the original residents, and this point requires further consideration.

As regards the costs of regularization: research carried out in low-income settlements in Mexico City shows that these costs, although significant in relation to prevailing income levels, have not placed an intolerable burden on household finances in the vast majority of cases (Duhau and Schteingart 1996; Varley 1987).

As regards the indirect costs: some of the arguments put forward by the critics of regularization seem to be contradictory. On the one hand, these costs are described as leading to the displacement of the original population (Legorreta 1994: 61); yet, at the same time, evidence is presented to show that the costs of informal services[7] are higher than the charges levied by municipal authorities for formal service provision (Legorreta 1994: 143).

Furthermore, we must remember that the residents of low-income settlements always have to pay (and often provide labour) for the introduction of infrastructure, whether or not settlements have been regularized, and once their houses are connected to the mains they have to pay for the services consumed, whether or not they hold legal title to their property. It is also normal, in the State of Mexico municipalities of Mexico City and elsewhere[8] for residents to pay property taxes before their tenure has been regularized.

In short, all the empirical evidence points to the same conclusion: that regularization *per se* does not place greater demands on household finances than those that have to be met by the residents of illegal settlements. Moreover, even if regularization should lead to higher land and housing prices, this will surely be in the interest of property-owners whose assets will now have a higher value than they would otherwise have done.

Should, then, the poor be 'protected' against the effects of regularization, as many specialists seem to suggest? If the intention is to avoid land price speculation, we need to be clear, at the least, why this should be necessary. Would it be to prevent other low-income households being denied access to home-ownership? If so, it is not clear why, for this reason, the property rights given to the beneficiaries of regularization should be limited in ways that no one would dream of suggesting for other social groups, who generally welcome, and often profit from, rising property values resulting from improvements to the urban environment.

In practice, measures designed to 'protect' low-income home-owners have if anything had the opposite effect. Until the 1970s, the government sometimes made use of a legal device that was supposed to protect home-ownership. This was a type of tenure known as 'family patrimony' (*patrimonio familiar*), which prevented the sale of the properties in question. It was initially used in the Federal District in the *colonias proletarias* described above, in which the government gave residents housing plots on which to build their own homes; it was subsequently used in housing projects built by the Federal District authorities. The idea was, on the one hand, to protect the beneficiaries in a paternalistic fashion, preventing them from engaging in transactions that would lead to the loss of their homes, and, on the other, to prevent people from speculating with assets that had been acquired with government subsidies.

Some political parties put forward similar arguments during the parliamentary debates about the housing provided by the reconstruction programme after the 1985 earthquake. Some argued that the new homes should be allocated under the 'family patrimony' system; others, that beneficiaries should not be allowed to sell their property without the majority approval of the residents' association.[9] These proposals were not accepted, partly because of the firm opposition of the intended beneficiaries of the programme (Duhau 1991).

The Department of the Federal District's use of the 'family patrimony' device has had consequences that are very different from what was intended. According to the DGRT (1994c), it simply promoted illegal transactions in the low-income subdivisions and housing projects in which it was applied. On the one hand, the authorities failed to keep effective records of the payments people made for their property; in some cases they did not register that payment was now complete. On the other hand, in the housing projects in particular:

> the contract of sale limited the property rights of the owners, given that, in an effort to ensure security for the purchaser's family, the property was defined as 'family patrimony', meaning that it could not legally be sold ... This meant that even when the house had been paid for in full, any subsequent transaction concerning the property was technically invalid and, therefore, effectively illegal. (DGRT 1994c: 23)

The result was that, given the large number of sales that did take place, the DGRT has had to include these housing projects in its recent regularization programmes.

But why should these transactions have been prevented in the first place, and how were legal impediments to sale such as the 'family patrimony' device supposed to be able to stop them? Just as restrictions on *ejido* and communal property have been unable to prevent their sale, making property 'family patrimony' could not prevent its sale. It seems as if the authorities believed that giving poor families access to housing in this way would solve their housing problems once and for all, and that they would never, for example, wish to move home.

Finally, it must be pointed out that in the great majority of cases, people who buy land illegally do so by means of a private commercial transaction in which the plot is purchased from someone who acts as though they were a private owner (or their agent), without any sort of subsidy or other government assistance. Even if the vendors are *ejidatarios*, they behave like private landowners rather than individuals whose 'social' property rights are limited to the right to use the land in question. What is more, many researchers have too readily accepted that in Mexico there are three types of property: private (regulated by civil law), public (state-owned) and social (*ejido* and communal property). It can, however, be argued that *ejido* and communal property are a form of collective private property, an institution through which a set of property rights governed by agrarian rather than civil law is granted collectively to a village or *ejido* community (Azuela 1989).[10]

In short, to describe regularization as positive because it provides security of tenure, but negative because it privatizes land tenure and exposes residents to market forces, is to remain trapped in a set of presuppositions that do not stand up to critical scrutiny. Clearly, it is precisely because there is a low-cost, illegal, land market (operating on the same speculative basis as any other urban land market) that the poor have been able to acquire land on which to build their homes in urban Mexico. To suppress market mechanisms by limiting property rights in order to 'protect' the urban poor or to fulfil the social mission of the *ejido* would therefore institutionalize class differences. Self-help housing, after all, is not 'social' or 'public' housing: it is not the existence of progressive social policies, but rather the *absence* of such policies, that accounts for the existence of this type of housing.

Regularization and the Maintenance of Public Order

We turn now to the political consequences of regularization, remembering the general point that at the same time as it promotes further illegal development, regularization removes the illegality that is one of the main causes of the urban poor's dependence on the state.

The acceleration of the regularization programme during the Salinas de Gortari administration was clearly intended to capitalize on the popularity of a policy that required little financial outlay by the authorities. Virtually no attention was paid to its future repercussions or to the need to control the process of urban development. Indeed, like the agrarian reform of 1992, regularization under Salinas can be understood as a form of deregulation of the land market. In Mexico City at least, and particularly in the outlying municipalities, it effectively brought urban planning efforts – including the half-hearted efforts to create land reserves for low-cost urban development – to a standstill.

The opportunist use of regularization can be seen in the role it played in the National Solidarity Programme (PRONASOL), the principal social policy of the Salinas government:

> Property regularization was not one of the priorities of PRONASOL at the beginning of the Salinas administration. It would seem, rather, that those responsible for PRONASOL happened on CORETT almost by accident, and recognized it as an agency that could help them achieve their objectives. PRONASOL was originally defined as a programme to address the needs of the poorest members of society, but it turned out that the largest geographical concentration of poor households occurs in urban areas, in the low-income settlements (*colonias populares*) in which CORETT had been working for years. Amongst the many problems facing the residents of these areas, the lack of property titles is the one that can be satisfied at least expense, since the cost of regularization bears no comparison with the cost of installing services or any but the most minor of material improvements. (Azuela 1994: 85)

CORETT regularization programmes therefore received unprecedented support during the Salinas administration. In the first two years, 14,989 hectares were expropriated for the regularization of low-income settlements on *ejido* land, equivalent to more than 80 per cent of the area expropriated during previous administrations. In Mexico City, 2,442 hectares were expropriated between 1989 and 1990 (Azuela 1994). CORETT was also issuing land titles for plots in the 3,323 hectares expropriated by the previous government. In Mexico City at least, then, the top-down nature of the programme was already apparent before Salinas came to power. During his presidency, however, there was also a change in the Federal District programme for the regularization of private land, as the DGRT also issued titles on an unprecedented scale and with unprecedented speed and efficiency.[11] The agency put enormous effort into gaining public support for its work, after many years of unsuccessful attempts to regularize these settlements had led to general cynicism and unwillingness to co-operate on the residents' part. The intention was clearly expressed in the title of a DGRT report documenting its work during the period from 1989 to 1994: it was to 'consolidate [private] property in the Federal District' (DGRT 1994c).

On the one hand, therefore, this policy was clearly the outcome of a decision to allow the accelerated development of a low-cost land market based on the illegal subdivision of *ejido*, communal and private land. This is the conclusion of both our own research and of other studies which have shown how areas ranging from a few dozen to over one thousand hectares have been incorporated into the informal land market in municipalities which, as a result, have been incorporated into the sprawling Mexico City conurbation (Legorreta 1994). There has been a clear acceleration in the cycle of illegal settlement and regularization in areas such as the Chalco Valley.[12]

On the other hand, the increased emphasis on regularization must also be viewed in the context of the relationship between the residents of the *colonias populares* and the state. In this context, it must be considered along with the financial and organizational resources brought to this relationship between 1989 and 1994 by PRONASOL. At one level, the results soon became apparent: in Chalco, for example, where the PRI had lost the presidential elections in 1988, it won the mid-term congressional elections just three years later with apparent ease.

It is more difficult, however, to ascribe long-term objectives, as regards the relationship between the state and the urban poor, to the government's regularization policies, which, unlike PRONASOL, survived the Salinas administration and will no doubt continue for many years. Our recent research leads us to agree with other authors that regularization channels community mobilization in pursuit of tenure security and settlement upgrading along lines chosen by the state, and according to rules of the game laid down by the state (Varley 1993). We should add, moreover, that the manipulation of residents' demands for public goods and services does not stop with regularization. Tenure regularization does not, as we have seen, necessarily ensure that residents will receive services, nor does it ensure an adequate level of supply or adequate infrastructure main-tenance once services have been provided.

Conclusion

Land tenure regularization in Mexico may be understood primarily as a means for routine, low-cost, state intervention in the production of urban land and housing for the low-income population, but this does not mean that it cannot, at the same time, be used in the pursuit of short-term political objectives. Although the researcher will not find any explicit policy statements to this effect, regularization programmes give clear expression to the predominant *laissez-faire* approach to housing the poor: official tolerance of illegal subdivision ensuring an abundant supply of inexpensive housing plots, and the *post hoc* legitimization of this process in tenure regularization programmes.

This policy – *the* policy for low-income housing – converts an enormous number of poor families into home-owners, but it is a form of access to home-ownership which appears to be something other than what it really is: rather than the product of an active low-cost land market and of the labour and savings of the low-income population, it appears to be the result of a benign government attitude towards the poor and their needs. It helps to reproduce a dualistic urban social order, in which the housing needs of the majority are satisfied, and their access to urban services ensured, by tortuous means which require, time and time again, 'one-off' or 'exceptional' government interventions – even though these are in practice *routine* interventions – permitting low-income housing areas to be recognized as a legitimate part of the urban public order.

That the effects of this policy should be (*inter alia*) to protect the illegal land market and ensure its continued existence – to the detriment of the government's ability to control the process of urban expansion – does not seem to have been taken into consideration by those responsible for setting official priorities in this area in recent years.

The consequences of mass regularization programmes will surely reduce the room for manoeuvre in policy-making in future years. Be that as it may, it is important, in conclusion, to emphasize that none of the principal forms of state intervention in the creation and upgrading of low-income housing areas is based on an acknowledgement of specific obligations towards their residents, who are not acknowledged as having any particular rights in this respect. The result is that government authorities continue to enjoy considerable discretion in taking new initiatives, defining new policies and, in the end, choosing whether or not to legitimate property-ownership in low-income settlements.

Notes

Translated from Spanish by Ann Varley.

1. Reforms to the agrarian laws in 1992 made it possible to privatize *ejido* lands without resorting to expropriation. To date, however, *ejido* lands continue to be sold illegally, before they have been converted into the private property of individual *ejidatarios*. We believe, therefore, that the government will continue to use expropriation to regularize low-income settlements on *ejido* lands, and continue to use agrarian rather than civil law for this purpose.

2. During the 1980s Mexico City saw the massive eastwards expansion of low-income settlements into the 'Valle de Chalco' area. The municipality of the same name housed a few thousand people in the 1960s but around 200,000 by the 1990s. Chalco was the 'birthplace' of President Carlos Salinas de Gortari's National Solidarity Programme (PRONASOL), which brought major investments in the provision of infrastructure and services into the area.

3. CORETT regularization programmes operate in three different phases, with twenty-two stages and thirty-nine different procedures (see CORETT 1992).

4. It is worth noting, however, that the first massive regularization programme in Mexico City took place during the 1970s in what is now the Netzahualcoyotl municipality of the State of Mexico.

5. Information provided by officials of the State of Mexico General Directorate of Housing and Urban Development.

6. The term 'social property' here refers to *ejidos*.

7. For example, purchasing water from informal vendors who distribute it by tanker to unserviced settlements.

8. In the Federal District and the city of Puebla, for example – even though urban property taxes cannot in theory be imposed in settlements on *ejido* lands before they have been regularized (Varley 1987; Melé 1994).

9. As the housing destroyed in the earthquake had mostly been multi-family

rental properties, a number of housing units were built in each property in the reconstruction programme; all the residents at a particular address would form a residents' association for their property.

10. In 1992, *ejidatarios* were given the power to transform *ejido* property into civil property, and thus to change its use (although the decision to privatize must still be taken collectively, by majority vote at an *ejido* general assembly). Where changes of use are sought by government agencies rather than the *ejidatarios* themselves, however, expropriation will still be necessary.

11. Among local leaders, however, the prevailing opinion is that with the DGRT 'regularization becomes more difficult'; this may be explained by the fact that regularization of private property is generally more complex than regularization of *ejido* lands.

12. The huge expansion of low-income settlement in the Chalco Valley took place mostly during the 1980s, and expropriation decrees began to be issued for the regularization of these settlements as early as the end of that decade.

References

Azuela, A (1989) *La Ciudad, la Propiedad Privada y el Derecho*, El Colegio de México, Mexico City.

— (1994) 'Corporativismo y privatización en la regularización de la tenencia de la tierra', in D. Hiernaux and F. Tomas (eds), *Cambios Económicos y Periferia de las Grandes Ciudades: El Caso de México*, Institut Français d'Amérique Latine and Universidad Autónoma Metropolitana-Xochimilco, Mexico, 79–92.

Córdoba, A. (1980) *La Ideologia de la Revolución Mexicana*, Era, Mexico.

CORETT (Comisión para la Regularización de la Tenencia de la Tierra) (1992) 'Modelo de regularización de la tenencia de la tierra', mimeo.

De Soto, H. (1989) *The Other Path: The Invisible Revolution in the Third World*, Tauris, London.

DGRT (Dirección General de Regularización Territorial, Departamento del Distrito Federal) (1994a) *La Regularización Territorial en la Ciudad de México: Soluciones de un Gobierno Solidario*, Department of the Federal District (DDF), Mexico City.

— (1994b) *Programas de Regularización del Suelo en la Ciudad de México: PROGRESSE*, DDF, Mexico City.

— (1994c) *Una Ciudad Para Todos. La Consolidación de la Propiedad en el Distrito Federal*, DDF, Mexico City.

Duhau, E. (1991) 'Las organizaciones no gubernamentales en la reconstrucción', in P. Connolly, R. Coulomb and E. Duhau (eds), *Cambiar de Casa Pero No de Barrio: Estudios sobre la Reconstrucción Habitacional en la Ciudad de México*, CENVI, Mexico, 349–428.

— (forthcoming) *Urbanización Popular, Formas de Acceso al Suelo y Política Urbana*, Universidad Autónoma Metropolitana, Mexico City.

Duhau, E. and Schteingart, M. (1996) 'Políticas sociales, gobernabilidad y pobreza', mimeo.

INTERURBA (1995) '*L'Intégration des Quartiers Irréguliers. Un Etat du Débat en Asie et en Amérique Latine*', special issue of *Pratiques Urbaines*, Vol. 12.

Iracheta, A. (1989) 'Diez años de planeación del suelo en la Zona Metropolitana de la Ciudad de México', in G. Garza (ed.), *Una Década de Planeación Urbano-Regional en México, 1978–1988*, El Colegio de México, Mexico City, 255–85.

Legorreta, J. (1994) *Efectos Ambientales de la Expansión de la Ciudad de México*, Centro de Ecología y Desarrollo, Mexico City.

Melé, P (1994) *Puebla: Urbanización y Políticas Urbanas*, Universidad Autónoma de Puebla and Universidad Autónoma Metropolitana-Azcapotzalco, Puebla/Mexico City.

Varley, A. (1987) 'The relationship between tenure legalization and housing improvements: evidence from Mexico City', *Development and Change*, Vol. 18, no. 3, 463–81.

— (1993) 'Clientilism or technocracy? The politics of urban land regularization', in N. Harvey (ed.), *Mexico: Dilemmas of Transition*, Institute of Latin American Studies, University of London, and British Academic Press, London, 249–76.

World Bank (1994) *Vivienda: Un Entorno Propicio para el Mercado Habitacional. Documento de Política del Banco Mundial*, IBRD/World Bank, Washington, DC.

CHAPTER 10

The Political Uses of Illegality: Evidence from Urban Mexico

Ann Varley

The Mexican government has provided property titles for millions of families living in illegal housing areas around many of the nation's cities. This chapter argues that land tenure legalization or 'regularization' has played an important part in maintaining political stability in urban Mexico. The political implications of regularization are overlooked by most of the international debate about the virtues of promoting legalization of ownership as a strategy for improving housing conditions in so-called 'squatter settlements'. Analysts associated with the World Bank argue for legalization on the grounds that it increases land and housing values and provides access to credit for housing improvements (Struyk and Lynn 1983; Jimenez 1983; 1984; Dowall and Leaf 1991; Friedman et al. 1988; Dowall and Clarke 1996). They do so in spite of growing evidence that tenure legalization is not required for investment in housing improvements (Angel 1983; Varley 1987; Razzaz 1993; Payne 1997). Squatters may even consolidate their houses faster than those with formal tenure (Garr 1996). Both the advocates of legalization and the more sceptical, however, have concentrated their attention on 'technical' questions,[1] and overlooked the political uses of illegality.

I argue that regularization is a strategy employed by the Mexican state to bring about the 'social integration' of the urban poor – meaning, in practice, their *political* integration into a system dominated for many decades by the Institutional Revolutionary Party, the PRI. I present two main lines of argument. The first concerns the significance of the times at which regularization has received particular government emphasis at the national level; the second, the selection of particular cities and settlements as targets for legalization programmes. I concentrate on two particular periods: the early 1970s and the end of the 1980s. These are the periods during which urban land tenure regularization has been promoted most enthusiastically by the Mexican government, as shown by Tables 10.1 and 10.2. The tables provide information concerning the regularization of *ejido* land by the national expropriation agency, the Commission for Land Tenure

Table 10.1 Expropriation of *ejido* land for tenure regularization, 1973–94

President	No. of decrees	Percentage	Area expropriated (hectares)	Percentage
Echeverría (1970–76)	139	11.9	27,995.0	24.9
López Portillo (1976–82)	87	7.4	7,311.0	6.5
De la Madrid (1982–88)	210	17.9	18,835.0	16.7
Salinas de Gortari (1988–94)	735	62.8	58,388.2	51.9
All (1970–94)	1,171	100	112,529.2	100

Source: Calculated from presidential decrees authorizing expropriations, as published in the *Diario Oficial de la Nación* to the end of the Salinas presidency in November 1994.

Table 10.2 Length of time taken by expropriations and area expropriated for CORETT, 1973–94

President	Mean time taken: 'all' (months)	Mean time taken: 'complete' (months)	Mean area expropriated: 'all' (hectares)	Mean area expropriated: 'complete' (hectares)
Echeverría (1970–76)	10.7	10.7	201.4	204.4
López Portillo (1976–82)	36.3	35.0	84.0	93.1
De la Madrid (1982–88)	54.8	30.3	89.7	109.4
Salinas de Gortari (1988–94)	54.5	28.5	79.4	60.7
All	48.1	25.2	96.1	101.0
N	1,159	601	1,171	601

Source: As Table 10.1. A few publications do not provide information on the date on which the expropriation was requested.

Note: time taken = length of time from request to approval of expropriation; 'all' = all expropriations completed between 1973 and the end of November 1994; 'complete' = expropriations completed during the administration in which they were requested.

Regularization (CORETT), set up in 1973.[2] Since *ejido* land regularization is a federal responsibility carried out, since the mid-1970s, by a single agency,[3] it is possible to collect statistics for the whole nation. During this period, most low-income settlement in Mexican cities has taken place on *ejido* property. The regularization of illegal settlements on private lands has also, however, received greater attention since the late 1980s (for reasons that will be discussed below).

Table 10.1 shows that there was a massive expansion of *ejido* regularization during the government of Carlos Salinas de Gortari, which accounted for over three-fifths of the area expropriated for regularization up to 1994. The emphasis placed on regularization by the different administrations may also be gauged from Table 10.2. The process clearly accelerated under Salinas, but the administration of Luís Echeverría, during which CORETT was set up, appears to have placed even greater emphasis on the policy in this respect. On the other hand, the Salinas administration accounted for the major share (59 per cent) of expropriations requested and authorized within a single administration, as well as by far the largest number overall. In addition, under Salinas, the average area of land expropriated fell to its lowest level, as a larger proportion of expropriations involved very small areas of land: 11 per cent of expropriations requested and completed under Salinas were under 10 hectares, compared with only 3 per cent or less in earlier administrations. It is clear, overall, that the Echeverría and Salinas administrations were those that, in their different ways, promoted regularization most. The first question to be addressed, therefore, is why regularization emerged as a national policy while Echeverría was President of Mexico.

The Emergence of Regularization as a National Policy

Although the government had been regularizing illegal settlements on both private and *ejido* land since the 1940s (Azuela and Cruz Rodríguez 1989; Varley 1985a), regularization was, on the one hand, a sporadic, unsystematic form of intervention in urban development on private land, and, on the other, one element in the routine operation of the 'agrarian' agencies responsible for the *ejido*. It did not become part of a systematic, well-publicized, national urban policy until the 1970s,[4] when the government started to use expropriation as its chosen tool for the regularization of *ejido* land. The predecessor to the national policy was the expropriation, in 1970, of land belonging to several *ejidos* in the north-west of Mexico City by a State of Mexico agency, the Institute for Urban Action and Social Integration (AURIS). AURIS sold the expropriated land to the residents, who had bought their housing plots illegally from the *ejidatarios*. After completing their payments to AURIS they could now receive land titles. This set the pattern for the national policy established by incoming President Luís Echeverría, who set up CORETT in 1973.

The emergence of regularization as a national policy was a response to the political and economic problems facing the incoming government in 1970. By the end of the 1960s, the 'Mexican miracle' of industrial and economic growth with low inflation was faltering, calling into question the existing development model, especially when growth in agricultural output started to decline (Philip 1988). Peasant dissatisfaction with empty promises of agrarian reform and government policies favouring large-scale commercial agriculture led to a series of rural land invasions during the early 1970s. The urban poor had likewise failed to receive their share of the fruits of 1960s growth. Income had been redistributed towards the middle classes and wage levels were now falling, at a time of renewed inflation (Ward 1986). In addition, the existing model of urban development was clearly in difficulties. Public housing was scarce and expensive, and the urban poor – their numbers swollen by migration – were increasingly having to house themselves illegally. Residents of illegal settlements petitioned for services to be installed, but their petitions were passed from one agency to another with the argument that, since the settlement was illegal, it fell outside the jurisdiction of the agency in question (Varley 1989).

Conditions were clearly ripe for a 'groundswell of public protest in low-income areas of the cities' (Ward 1986: 18). The political climate was highly conducive to this groundswell. The upheavals of 1968 and 1971, in which students played a leading role, questioned the durability of rule by the PRI; many student activists sought involvement in the emerging *colonos'* movements, which filled a gap in the political landscape. The PRI's 'popular' wing, the CNOP, had lost credibility as a result of clientelism, top-down imposition of leaders and failure to encourage links with other organizations. The new movements pursued strategies diametrically opposed to those of the CNOP, fostering links between a wide range of different groups which were often formalized in the creation of new umbrella organizations (*Frentes*) (Ramírez Saiz 1986). The early 1970s therefore saw the arrival on the political scene of a major new actor: the independent 'popular' movement.

The Echeverría government reacted in a highly populist fashion. This involved, on the one hand, tolerance of some 'protest outside the established channels' (Castells 1982: 271) and, on the other, 'a thorough and wide-ranging restructuring of the assorted policies needed to tackle the serious housing problems affecting a wide sector of the population' (García and Perló 1984: 109). A plethora of different housing agencies were created, and several were briefed to carry out legalization of *ejido* settlements and private land.

The place of regularization in Echeverría's policies can therefore be linked to land invasion and the new political movements. His populist response to rural invasions was a renewed wave of agrarian reform and the creation of new *ejidos*; to urban invasions, legalization.

Picking off the Opposition: Land Invasions and the Urban Popular Movement

A clear indication of the political significance of tenure legalization is the way it was targeted at particular settlements: land invasions and/or the most 'conflictive' settlements, in which independent political organizations were active.

Mexico City The capital had not witnessed widespread land invasions since the 1940s but, in the early 1970s, they emerged with new vigour in response to the economic burdens on the poor, the new political movements and Echeverría's populist politics. When the President promised to support the urban poor in their efforts to find a home, his words were taken to mean that invasions would be tolerated (Ward 1986). A series of invasion attempts in the south of Mexico City at the start of the 1970s led to major invasions in Santo Domingo de los Reyes and Padierna. The resulting settlements were the first to be expropriated for legalization under Echeverría, not only in the capital, but in the whole of Mexico.[5] They elicited an urgent response from the highest levels of government. The President toured Santo Domingo by helicopter in November 1971 and the Minister of Agrarian Reform visited Padierna, only to hear *colonos* threaten to kill his employees (Varley 1985b). These were not, perhaps, idle threats: there had been violent clashes between squatters and the police, and radical students and some of the new revolutionary groups were known to be involved.

Radical student groups associated with the independent popular movement were also involved in the first two settlements in Mexico City expropriated by CORETT, at the end of 1975. Like Santo Domingo and Padierna, both the Tlalpan and San Bernabé Ocotepec *ejidos* were located in the predominantly middle-class south-west of Mexico City.[6]

Such intervention stands in sharp contrast to government reaction to other illegal settlements. Some *ejido* settlements were more than twenty years old, and most had developed in a relatively peaceful fashion. While the regularization agencies encountered strenuous opposition in the south-west, to the extent that the police were brought in to protect their officials, settlers elsewhere were pleading for legalization. Residents of settlements established on *ejido* land in Cuautepec, in the north of the city, for example, had been petitioning for regularization since 1970. Action was promised, and the head of the regularization agency FIDEURBE even visited Cuautepec in early 1974 to discuss residents' problems; but nothing came of the visit.

The political rationale behind regularization has been confirmed by former agency officials.[7] The more co-operative settlements were of little interest to Echeverría's 'trouble-shooting' agencies, but the experience these agencies gained in dealing with 'difficult' settlements was highly valued. Consequently, FIDEURBE representatives were sent to Cuernavaca to advise on the response to the independent organizations which had appeared there, particularly in the radical *colonia* Rubén Jaramillo, where the army had been sent in, killing a number of leaders, and arresting many residents, in late 1973.[8]

Chihuahua Verbeek (1987) documents the experience of Chihuahua. In 1968, the Communist Party promoted an invasion of *ejido* land in the north of the city. The formation of *colonia* Francisco Villa gave rise to other invasions and one of the largest urban movements in Mexico, the Comité de Defensa Popular. In addition to the thirty-five settlements it controlled by 1974, the CDP also included trade unionists and militant students. It had long-term revolutionary goals, but concentrated on labour activism, workers' co-operatives, and communal labour for the installation of urban services. Residents acquired water and electricity illegally and prevented the police from entering their settlements.

The authorities tried to undermine the movement by offering Francisco Villa residents relocation to other sites, but when this failed, they tried to drive a wedge between the squatters and the student and trade union elements of the CDP by providing housing benefits for the settlers. One of the first projects by the housing agency INFONAVIT was completed in Chihuahua in 1972, but the limited scale of such projects left regularization at the forefront of efforts to weaken the CDP. It was intended to create 'a bilateral patron/client relationship between the individual households and the state' and although the settlers initially rejected regularization, eventually 'more and more households were tempted to accept the state's offer of legalization' (Verbeek 1987: 98). The CDP had to struggle to survive into the second half of the 1970s.

Monterrey In Monterrey, a number of major invasions from 1971 onwards were organized by a group of disaffected PRI leaders and activists from the 1968 student movements (Vellinga 1989). The largest, in 1973, gave rise to *colonia* Tierra y Libertad, which became the focus for a much broader political movement and a Popular Front of the same name founded in 1976. This was qualitatively and quantitatively different from many other organizations appearing at this time. It included more than thirty settlements (with over 50,000 residents, known as *posesionarios*), tenant groups, *ejidatarios* and other organizations, such as an independent taxi drivers' union, and developed close links with radical trade unions (Pozas Garza 1989). The movement's most unusual feature, however, was its policy of 'isolation from official structures', reflecting the Maoist ideology of the university activists (Vellinga 1989; Castells 1977). It rejected all state benefits in order to avoid the co-optation of settlers. The *colonias* had their own schools, a radio station, medical services, an internal 'police' service and co-operative shops. Tierra y Libertad thus came to be seen as a 'state within a state' or 'red island' (Vellinga 1989: 167).

Regularization was one of the 'benefits' rejected by Tierra y Libertad, on economic, ideological and political grounds (Castells 1977). Economically, the Front argued that land should be made available for free. Ideologically, it argued that settlers should not passively accept concessions from the state, but extract what they required from the state by class struggle. Most importantly, in political terms, regularization would establish an individualized relationship between settlers and the state, leading to the disintegration of the movement and incorporation into the existing regime.

The Front was right to be wary. After two government agencies were set up to offer housing and regularization benefits to the settlers, its support declined.[9] By 1981, the Popular Front controlled less than one-fifth of *posesionario* settlements and residents (Vellinga 1989). The state also used regularization to exploit internal differences within the movement. Two groups with conflicting attitudes towards regularization appeared (Villarreal and Castañeda 1986).[10] The State Governor played up their differences and undermined the movement by expropriating part of Tierra y Libertad in 1983.

Analysts are unanimous in concluding that the principal aim of regularization was to counter the political influence of the opposition movements: 'to systematically disintegrate forms of organization which are different from those controlled by the State' (Villarreal and Castañeda 1986: 57). As a government representative announced on the occasion of a Presidential visit to give out land titles: 'in Tierra y Libertad ... serious problems developed over a period of many years, to the extent that the settlement broke its relationship with the government and nominated its own authorities ... [but, as a result of legalization, the settlement] changed its relationship with the government of the State and achieved its integration' (Presidencia de la República 1985: 178).[11]

Regularization as Remobilizaton

I have argued that regularization serves to *demobilize* urban popular movements constituting a potential threat to the political regime (Varley 1985b). 'Independent' settlements are not, however, the norm. In the majority of settlements, which are not formed by invasion and are not politically radical, Melé (1988) correctly argues that regularization *re*mobilizes political activity along established channels of demand-making. It prolongs negotiations for security of tenure and services, keeping residents in a dependent position *vis-à-vis* local authorities and the PRI.[12]

An excellent illustration of this process is provided by Florita Moreno Armella (1988). It concerns La Libertad, an illegal settlement founded in 1982 on *ejido* land in the north of Mexico City. The municipal planning department refused to recognize the existence of La Libertad on the grounds that the land was reserved for agricultural uses. Residents were therefore unable to obtain services until they accepted help from their local Federal Deputy, representing the PRI. She enabled the settlers to set up the formal 'Council for Municipal Collaboration' needed to pursue their demands, but when the elections to the council were won by the opposition, regularization by CORETT was held back until the residents affiliated with the PRI, whereon the municipality refused to recognize the elected Council. Given that the settlers' first interest was in obtaining title to their land, they held new elections, and PRI candidates were duly elected.

The experience of La Libertad is representative of what may be described as the 'state of the art' concerning the political uses of land tenure regularization during the 1980s. At the end of that decade, however, regularization policies underwent a dramatic change. This change was associated with the political upheaval – described as a 'political thunderclap' by Alan Knight (1993: 31) – at the time Carlos Salinas became President. In 1988, the PRI suffered a near-defeat in federal elections for Congress and the presidency. A low turnout resulted in the PRI officially winning the election with 51 per cent of the votes, but the validity of these results was widely and severely impugned (Gómez Tagle 1993).

Two points should be made about the 1988 elections. First, they followed six years of severe economic crisis after the oil price collapse of 1982 ended the boom of the late 1970s. The result was a 15 per cent decline in Mexicans' standard of living, with 'an unprecedented drop in wage levels, in employment opportunities, and in income distribution, accompanied by soaring numbers of people living in poverty' (Cordera Campos and González Tiburcio 1991: 28; Lustig 1992; Tello 1991). Although Knight (1993) questions the automatic linkage of this economic crisis with a particular political outcome, the adjustment policies pursued by the government led to both a decline in the quality of life and 'a significant decline in popular expectations for continued economic and social development' (Cordera Campos and González Tiburcio 1991: 20). This loss of confidence in the economic future was paralleled by the loss of belief in the PRI's prospects of continuing as the party of the state which played a major role in explaining voter defection from the PRI in 1988. While 'changing public perceptions of *political* issues', rather than economic ones, were the key factor in the electoral outcome (Domínguez and McCann 1992: 220), the social consequences of the economic crisis nevertheless offered the party fertile grounds on which to pursue the remobilization of the popular vote in favour of the PRI.

The second point is that in 1988 the political challenge to the PRI was primarily an *electoral* challenge. The radical groups which had been active in the early 1970s, in some cases employing anti-democratic means to gain their ends, would not re-emerge as significant features of Mexico's political landscape until the mid-1990s. With such low overall levels of endorsement (only half the electorate voted in 1988), the PRI government's response to the 'new political reality' (Knight 1993: 31) would accordingly need to have a broad general appeal *as well as* being targeted at particular 'problem' groups.

Regularization and 'Solidarity': Expansion and Intensification

While Salinas was still the PRI's presidential candidate, he announced his plans to establish a new social policy guaranteeing equal opportunities for all Mexicans as regards nutrition, education, health and housing. This speech heralded the establishment, in the first days of his government, of the National Solidarity Programme, PRONASOL: 'a programme of immediate attention to the most pressing needs and demands of sectors of the population in conditions of extreme poverty' (Consejo Consultivo del Programa Nacional de Solidaridad 1994: 57). 'Solidarity' was to be targeted primarily at indigenous groups and peasants living in extreme poverty, with the urban poor as a third group of beneficiaries.

Regularization was incorporated into the Solidarity programme. The results, as regards *ejido* lands, can be seen from Tables 10.1 and 10.2. The nature of the change that occurred was not, however, by any means limited to increases in the area expropriated. The chosen strategy was to speed up the entire process and extend it to other types of property.

In 1991, a CORETT representative claimed that within one year of expropriation, the agency was providing titles for 80 per cent of plot-owners (*El Día*, 23 April 1991).[13] Even allowing for exaggeration, this represents a considerable advance on previous achievements; it was not uncommon for such progress to take at least five or six years (Varley 1985b). The acceleration reflected a strong top-down insistence on speeding up existing procedures, plus some important technical innovations. As a result, CORETT produced titles to 1.10 million plots from 1989 to 1993, almost four times the number regularized from 1974 to 1988 (Consejo Consultivo del Programa Nacional de Solidaridad 1994; SEDESOL 1993). In all, however, 2.12 million plots are reported to have been regularized under Salinas, because CORETT's efforts were supplemented by those of state governments legalizing plots in illegal settlements on private or government-owned land. In addition, the federal housing agency

INFONAVIT undertook the regularization of its housing projects in various states, and titles for former rental property purchased under the Casa Propia programme of the housing agency FONHAPO were also handed out by Solidarity (*El Día*, 11 September 1992). The great increase in the number of plots regularized was thus achieved by (a) a strong central directive to speed up the process, (b) procedural modifications, and (c) an extension of the regularization initiative to other state and federal agencies.

Regularization: Restoring the Credibility of the PRI

Regularization within 'Solidarity' must be interpreted primarily as part of the political response to the 'political thunderclap' of 1988. For the first time, a real challenge to the PRI had very nearly succeeded, and had been prevented from doing so only at the cost of a dramatic loss of credibility for the regime. Any chances of recovering legitimacy depended on an ability to persuade the disaffected population that the Salinas government really had something new to offer Mexico, and that something was Solidarity – although most of the key elements of the programme, like regularization, were anything but new (Dresser 1991; Knight 1996; Varley 1996).

That 'something new' had to be closely associated with Salinas himself. An analysis of voter defection from the PRI in 1988 showed that, in addition to scepticism about the prospects for the PRI's future noted above, voters' opinions of Salinas's personal characteristics were a decisive factor (Domínguez and McCann 1992). Solidarity therefore had to convert a 'no-can-do' candidate into a 'can-do' President.

In addition, the 'something new' had to take account of the geographical variation in the PRI's electoral fortunes in 1988. Since the 1960s, there had been an increasingly negative relationship between urbanization and electoral support for the PRI (Molinar Horcasitas 1991). Although the PRI was able to retain its ability to manipulate the results of the election in many rural areas in 1988, the same was not true of the urban areas, and it was openly acknowledged to have lost the elections in Mexico City.[14]

PRONASOL was, then, 'a vehicle for reasserting presidential power ... in order to legitimize the regime' (Dresser 1994: 160). Regularization was an extremely useful tool with which to woo the urban poor. It was inexpensive[15] and well received by the population, and delivery of titles was the ideal pretext for staging a large number of public ceremonies in which thousands of families could be presented as direct beneficiaries of the President's personal dedication to implementing his social policy. This last was particularly important, because Solidarity's success in achieving its political objectives depended heavily on its *visibility*. Consequently, Salinas spent one or two days a week on Solidarity, travelling throughout the Republic to attend such ceremonies. The emphasis on direct interaction between residents and President is strongly reminiscent of Echeverría's populist 'open-door' policies, designed to cultivate personal loyalty to the President (Ward 1981). The high visibility of PRONASOL projects, carefully nurtured by publicity campaigns (Dresser 1991; 1994; Braig 1994), was also addressed to the middle classes. Here, the objective was to restore a sense of normality, of the viability of the political regime and its capacity to solve the country's problems, quelling the doubts which had been so important in defection from the PRI in 1988.

These changes paid off: the PRI easily won the Congressional elections of 1991, the first national elections after the 1988 débâcle and therefore a key milestone on the road to rebuilding the PRI's electoral credibility. Access to PRONASOL benefits was significantly correlated with the PRI vote among lower-class voters, and it was among these voters that the PRI registered its greatest gains. Voting responded directly to 'satisfaction with the performance of the Salinas administration' (Davis and Coleman 1994: 364). The public image of PRONASOL and of Salinas himself played a key role in producing this satisfaction. In just three years, effective changes in government policy towards the poor had made a major contribution to changing the popular assessment of the President's capacity to govern. In doing so it had ensured continuity in the political regime.

With respect to regularization, the success of the PRONASOL strategy depended on changing the way in which tenure legalization operated. The final section therefore demonstrates how a new model of regularization was established under Salinas.

A New Model of Regularization in Mexico City

Solidarity was 'born' in Mexico City, in the Chalco area which came to symbolize both urban poverty and the success of the Solidarity programme, and which has been extensively discussed elsewhere (Dresser 1991; Varley 1996). Chalco was not, however, the only part of Mexico City to feel the impact of the new social policies. One of the main targets was Ixtapalapa, the Federal District's largest *delegación*,[16] with almost 1.5 million inhabitants. Ixtapalapa, one of the poorest and most poorly serviced areas, was part of the band of poorer districts in which the PRI performed worst in 1988 (Ward 1990). Over the next few years the *delegación* consequently benefited from a series of servicing and regularization projects. There was much to be done: one half of the Federal District's illegal plots were in Ixtapalapa, constituting, according to the President, the major concentration of land tenure problems in the whole of Mexico (DGRT 1994b; *La Jornada*, 3 August 1991).

Ixtapalapa offers a good example of the modifications to the process of regularization adopted in the push to improve the PRI's electoral fortunes. During Salinas's election campaign, a public meeting held in Ixtapalapa to evaluate government achievements in regularization and housing had yielded a clear conclusion – people didn't trust the government: 'It was a question of endless to-ing and fro-ing: when people thought they'd finally got hold of a paper guaranteeing their right to their plot, it turned out that it was only a promise ... it gave an extremely bad impression of government actions' (DGRT 1994b: 8).

One particular problem had been the practice of '*inmatriculaciones administrativas*' of plots in the Public Property Register. This meant simply reserving a number in the Register for plots without a previously recognized owner; after five years, if there were no rival claims, the occupants could become the legal owners, but meanwhile their status remained undefined and the documents they held did not guarantee their property rights. This had provoked widespread cynicism about legalization on the part of Ixtapalapa residents.[17]

From the administrative point of view, the main problem had been the extreme legal complexity of regularization on private land. The problems were particularly acute in areas which had been the subject of unrecorded inheritance, intra-family cessions or subdivisions, and sales. In these circumstances, the danger of conflicts between rival claimants resulting in injunctions undermining the whole process was considerable (DGRT 1994b).

The response was to extend the use of expropriation to these cases. This was a radical innovation. Expropriation had not been used for this purpose since the 1940s (Azuela 1989), although the expropriation of properties damaged in the 1985 earthquake had shown how effective it could be. Experience gained in the housing agency FONHAPO by Manuel Aguilera Gómez, then head of the Federal District's internal affairs department, led the General Directorate of Land Regularization (DGRT, a dependency of his department) to adopt this strategy, on condition that prior approval was gained from residents and subdividers. During the Salinas administration, more private land than *ejido* land was expropriated in the Federal District; expropriation by the city authorities led to the regularization of 3,325 hectares (DGRT 1994a), compared with 2,909 hectares expropriated for CORETT. Fifty-five per cent of the DGRT area and 35 per cent of the *ejido* land was located in Ixtapalapa.

Other changes involved legal and administrative simplification, including a legal measure exempting residents from taxes on the transfer of ownership (*Diario Oficial*, 5 April 1989). The DGRT's work was decentralized as four local offices improved accessibility for residents (DGRT 1994b). Finally, the problem of conflicts over the dimensions of individual plots, a major cause of delay, was reduced by getting residents to sign a plan showing the relationship between all the plots in their block before any individual documents were produced.

What is particularly interesting about these innovations is that they were successfully transferred from the DGRT to CORETT's operations within the Federal District. DGRT methods and personnel were employed by CORETT's Federal District offices under the direction of a close associate of Aguilera Gómez.[18] She told her staff that Aguilera Gómez had given her one instruction to obey above all else: to improve the government's image. Meticulous attention was to be paid to the manner in which officials dealt with the public, emphasizing work 'on the ground' and personal contact with residents, and there was to be *no* corruption (CORETT was a byword for corruption and inefficiency).[19]

The new 'get it done and get it done fast' mentality did not, however, prevent a political logic from continuing to shape CORETT's activities in Ixtapalapa. All sorts of tactics were used on an everyday basis to appease or undermine opposition groups within the regularized areas. When inaccurate surveying led to a substantial area being omitted from expropriations for both CORETT and the DGRT, it 'coincided' with an area in which the left-wing opposition enjoyed particular support and in which its local leaders lived. Officials would bend the rules for individual families (for example, allowing 'invasion' of an unclaimed plot) on condition that they participated in the ceremonies in which titles were handed out. At these ceremonies, areas dominated by opposition groups were under-represented in the number of titles handed out. Many of their residents would have their titles withheld until nearer or even after the elections to encourage them to vote for the PRI. At a ceremony held in Ixtapalapa just before the August 1991 elections, a representative of the main opposition group commented ironically that although the documents had in some cases been ready as early as March, 'they preferred to wait until now, a week before the elections [to hand out the titles] – I can't *think* why …' (*La Jornada*, 12 August 1991).

Conclusion

There is an interesting discrepancy in the amount of attention paid to the 'economic' and 'political' aspects of tenure legalization in the debate about its advantages and disadvantages. Those who argue for the economic benefits of providing clear title seem unwilling to acknowledge the existence of any dissenting view, although an excellent recent review by Geoffrey Payne (1997) documents the reasons why a little more scepticism about legalization's capacity to improve life for the poor might be wise.[20] The proponents of regularization apply sophisticated econometric modelling techniques to survey results to estimate the increase in land or housing values that may be attributed to the possession of formal title to land, isolating this analytically from the effect of infrastructural improvements.[21] Yet the attention dedicated to teasing out these impacts stands curiously at odds with the lack of interest shown in the political impact of legal-ization. In this chapter, I have gone into considerable detail in reviewing the history of recent land tenure regularization programmes in Mexico in order to show the political logic at work. The political uses of illegality, as evidenced in tenure legalization, are easy to assert but not always easy to demonstrate, although the occasional government official can be found who is happy to show off by publicly declaring that regularization is and always has been used for political ends in Mexico.[22] The question that arises is whether or not, when it takes such minutely sophisticated analysis to demonstrate the economic benefits of legalization, overlooking its political consequences, or failing to take them into account when evaluating the *overall* desirability of the policy, can be justified. There are, I believe, other reasons to endorse the provision of tenure security in this way, particularly in societies whose more privileged members automatically assume that full legal title to land and housing is their right. Whether or not these justify the (political and economic) costs involved will depend on the range of considerations at play in particular local circumstances and no general recommendation is likely to be possible. In any case, a broader perspective on the issues raised by legalization is surely essential.

Notes

This chapter draws on material published in two articles that have appeared in publications intended primarily for a 'Mexicanist' audience (Varley 1993; 1996).

1. See for example Dowall and Clarke (1996) and Payne (1997).

2. Over 24,000 *ejidos* together occupy approximately one-half of the national territory (Zaragoza and Macías 1980). Although the *ejido* was intended for agri-cultural use by the beneficiaries of the agrarian reform, *ejidatarios* have sold land illegally for urban development. *Ejido* lands thus account for approximately one-quarter of the built-up area of Mexico City (Varley 1985a) and (together with communal property) one-third of that of Guadalajara, the country's second largest city (Becerra 1997).

3. Until, that is, the reforms to Article 27 of the Constitution in 1992. Following these reforms, other options have opened for regularization of *ejido* land. Ex-propriation by CORETT still continues to be the norm, however, and for this reason, as well as the complex consequences of the new alternatives, they will not be discussed further in this chapter. For further information on the urban aspects of the reforms, see Austin (1994); Melé (1994); and Jones and Ward (1998).

4. This has led some analysts to argue, mistakenly, that there was no govern-ment response to illegal settlement before the 1970s (see, for example, Iracheta 1988: 52). This underlines the lack of importance attributed to regularization by government officials before 1970.

5. Santo Domingo was expropriated in November 1971 for regularization by INDECO, the National Institute for Community Development and Popular Hous-ing. Padierna was expropriated by the Federal District urban development and regularization agency FIDEURBE in late 1973.

6. Echeverría had a house near San Bernabé.

7. Interviews with former directors of INDECO and FIDEURBE by Peter Ward and Ann Varley respectively.

8. For an analysis of the situation in Cuernavaca, see Montaño (1976).

9. FOMERREY was set up in 1973 to relocate settlers to site-and-service projects or regularize existing settlements. Plan Tierra Propia was established in 1979 by a state governor committed to eliminating the 'red island'. It concentrated on the older independent settlements, whose residents would be unimpressed by the offer of relocation (Villarreal and Castañeda 1986).

10. Regularization has elicited contrasting responses from activists (Ramírez Saiz 1986). Some argue that it incorporates settlements into the land market, driving out the original settlers, and should therefore be rejected. Others point to the vital role security of tenure plays in mobilizing settlers, arguing that this is a legitimate individual demand.

11. In private, government officials may be more outspoken. A national CORETT official interviewed in 1989 compared opposition activists with the dogs that laze around in low-income neighbourhoods until an outsider (a state agency) enters the area and succeeds in making them look foolish.

12. Political activism falls away sharply once residents' immediate demands are fulfilled (Cornelius 1975; Ramírez Saiz 1986; Castillo 1986).

13. A rate of 60 per cent within one year was claimed by a CORETT official in the Federal District interviewed in August 1991.

14. Gómez Tagle (1993: 77) notes that Salinas gained many of his votes in rural areas reporting 100 per cent voter turnout and 90–100 per cent support for the PRI. There is debate about the rural/urban distribution of the Solidarity programme's benefits, but it seems likely that urban communities benefited far more than might be expected, given the programme's stated priorities (Varley 1996).

15. Regularization of *ejido* land is largely self-financing: compensation for expropriation is fixed at low levels and although *ejidatarios* receive a small share of the profits, administrative expenses are deducted from the proceeds of sale (Varley 1985b, Azuela 1989).

16. The *delegación* is the Federal District equivalent of the municipality.

17. Interview with former CORETT official, 8 August 1991.

18. This was understood by those involved to be a 'concession' by Salinas to Mayor Manuel Camacho Solís, in the context of Camacho's ambitions to become the next presidential candidate and Aguilera Gómez' corresponding designs on the Federal District mayorship. Source as note 17.

19. During the Salinas years, CORETT personnel in the Federal District were paid unusually high salaries to minimize the temptations of corruption. Source as note 17.

20. Other than the argument that legalization displaces the original residents, a claim that usually goes unsupported by any evidence to this effect.

21. The sophistication of the analytical techniques employed may be at odds with the conceptual sophistication of the methods by which data are collected in the first place. As Payne (1997: 65–6) notes with respect to Jimenez (1984), for example: 'Any research which asks residents how much they are willing to pay for security of tenure inevitably reduces a mass of intangible, subjective and often conflicting considerations to the point where it would be dangerous to draw any conclusions with confidence.' There is also an issue about asking leading questions, as in the method employed by Dowall and Leaf (1991: 708). Asking real estate brokers to estimate the likely sale price of residential plots with different 'grades

of tenure claim' signals to these informants an expectation that there is likely to be a difference between the values in each case, raising questions about the validity of findings that match what the informants may think they were expected to deliver.

22. See, for example, *UnomásUno*, 13 March 1991.

References

Angel, S. (1983) 'Land Tenure for the Urban Poor', in S. Angel, R. W. Archer, S. Tanphiphat and E. A. Wegelin (eds), *Land for Housing the Poor*, Select Books, Singapore, 110–42.

Austin (1994) 'The Austin Memorandum on the Reform of Article 27 and urbanisation of the *ejido* in Mexico', *Bulletin of Latin American Research*, Vol. 13, no. 3, 327–35.

Azuela, A. (1989) *La Ciudad, la Propiedad Privada y el Derecho*, El Colegio de México, Mexico City.

Azuela, A. and M. S. Cruz Rodríguez (1989) 'La institucionalización de las colonias populares y la política urbana del DDF, 1940–1946', *Sociológica*, Vol. 9, 111–13.

Becerra, O. G. (1997) *La Propiedad Social del Suelo en el Área Metropolitana de Guadalajara: Su Origen y Evolución*, Cuadernos de Difusión Científica no. 48, Universidad de Guadalajara, Guadalajara.

Braig, M. (1994) 'Continuity and change in Mexican political culture: the case of PRONASOL', Paper presented to conference on 'La cultura política en México', University of Utrecht.

Castells, M. (1977) 'Marginalité urbaine et mouvements sociaux au Mexique: le mouvement des "posesionarios" dans la ville de Monterrey', *International Journal of Urban and Regional Research*, Vol. 1, 145–50.

— (1982) 'Squatters and politics in Latin America: a comparative analysis of urban social movements in Chile, Peru and Mexico', in H. Safa (ed.), *Towards a Political Economy of Urbanization in Third World Countries*, Oxford University Press, Delhi, 249–82.

Castillo, J. (1986) 'El movimiento urbano popular en Puebla', in J. Castillo (ed.), *Los Movimientos Sociales en Puebla II*, Universidad Autónoma de Puebla, Puebla, 201–360.

Consejo Consultivo del Programa Nacional de Solidaridad (1994) *El Programa Nacional de Solidaridad: Una Visión de la Modernización de México*, Fondo de Cultura Económica, Mexico City.

Cordera Campos, R. and E. González Tiburcio (1991) 'Crisis and transition in the Mexican economy', in M. González de la Rocha and A. Escobar Latapí (eds), *Social Responses to Mexico's Economic Crisis of the 1980s*, Center for US–Mexican Studies, University of California, San Diego, 19–56.

Cornelius, W. A. (1975) *Politics and the Migrant Poor in Mexico City*, Stanford University Press, Palo Alto.

Davis, C. L. and K. M. Coleman (1994) 'Neoliberal economic policies and the potential for electoral change in Mexico', *Mexican Studies/Estudios Mexicanos*, Vol. 10, 341–70.

DGRT (Dirección General de Regularización Territorial, Departamento del Distrito Federal) (1994a) *La Regularización Territorial en la Ciudad de México: Soluciones de un Gobierno Solidario*, Department of the Federal District (DDF), Mexico City.

DGRT (1994b) *Programas de Regularización del Suelo en la Ciudad de México: PROGRESSE*, DDF, Mexico City.

Domínguez, J. I. and J. A. McCann (1992) 'Whither the PRI? Explaining voter defection in the 1988 Mexican presidential elections', *Electoral Studies*, Vol. 11, 207–22.

Dowall, D. E. and G. Clarke (1996) *A Framework for Reforming Urban Land Policies in Developing Countries*, UMP Paper no. 7, World Bank, Washington, DC.

Dowall, D. E. and M. Leaf (1991) 'The price of land for housing in Jakarta', *Urban Studies*, Vol. 28, no. 5, 707–22.

Dresser, D. (1991) *Neopopulist Solutions to Neoliberal Problems: Mexico's National Solidarity Program*, Center for US–Mexican Studies, University of California, San Diego.

— (1994) 'Bringing the poor back in: National Solidarity as a strategy of regime legitimation', in W. A. Cornelius, A. L. Craig and J. Fox (eds), *Transforming State-Society Relations in Mexico: The National Solidarity Strategy*, Center for US–Mexican Studies, University of California, San Diego,143–65.

Friedman, J., E. Jimenez and S. K. Mayo (1988) 'The demand for tenure security in developing countries', *Journal of Development Economics*, Vol. 29, no. 2, 185–98.

García, B. and M. Perló (1984) 'Estado, sindicalismo oficial y políticas habitacionales: análisis de una década del INFONAVIT', in J. A. Alonso (ed.), *El Obrero Mexicano 2: Condiciones de Trabajo*, Siglo Veintiuno, Mexico City, 94–133.

Garr, D. J. (1996) 'Expectative land rights, house consolidation and cemetery squatting: some perspectives from central Java', *World Development*, Vol. 24, no. 12, 1925–33.

Gómez Tagle, S. (1993) 'Electoral reform and the party system, 1977–90', in N. Harvey (ed.), *Mexico: Dilemmas of Transition*, Institute of Latin American Studies, University of London, and British Academic Press, London, 64–90.

Iracheta, A. (1988) 'Los problemas del suelo y la política urbana en la zona metropolitana de la ciudad de México', in R. Benítez Zenteno and J. Benigno Morelos (eds), *Grandes Problemas de la Ciudad de México*, Plaza and Valdés, Mexico City, 47–95.

Jimenez, E. (1983) 'The magnitude and determinants of home improvements in self-help housing: Manila's Tondo Project', *Land Economics*, Vol. 59, no. 1, 70–83.

— (1984) 'Tenure security and urban squatting', *Review of Economics and Statistics*, Vol. 66, no. 4, 556–67.

Jones, G. A. and P. M. Ward (1998) 'Privatizing the commons: reforming the *ejido* and urban development in Mexico', *International Journal of Urban and Regional Research*, Vol. 22, no. 1, 76–93.

Knight, A. (1993) 'State power and political stability in Mexico', in N. Harvey (ed.), *Mexico: Dilemmas of Transition*, Institute of Latin American Studies, University of London, and British Academic Press, London, 29–63.

— (1996) 'Salinas and social liberalism in historical context', in R. Aitken, N. Craske, G. A. Jones and D. Stansfield (eds), *Dismantling the Mexican State?*, Macmillan, Basingstoke, 1–23.

Lustig, N. (1992) *Mexico: The Remaking of an Economy*, Brookings Institution, Washington, DC.

Melé, P. (1988) 'Cartographier l'illégalité: filières de production de l'espace urbain de la ville de Puebla (Mexique)', *L'Espace Géographique*, Vol. 4, 257–63.

— (1994) 'Mexique: réforme agraire, fin et suite', *Etudes Foncières*, Vol. 63, 27–34.

Molinar Horcasitas, J. (1991) *El Tiempo de la Legitimidad: Elecciones, Autoritarismo y Democracía en México*, Cal y Arena, Mexico City.

Montaño, J. (1976) *Los Pobres de la Ciudad en los Asentamientos Espontáneos*, Siglo Veintiuno, Mexico City.

Moreno Armella, F. (1988) 'Política y territorio: la presencia del poder político institucional en el proceso de expansión del Area Metropolitana de la Ciudad de México', in A. Iracheta Cenecorta and A. Villar Calvo (eds), *Política y Movimientos Sociales en la Ciudad de México*, Plaza and Valdés, Mexico City, 77–95.

Morris, S. D. (1993) 'Political reformism in Mexico: past and present', *Latin American Research Review*, Vol. 28, no. 2, 191–205.

Payne, G. K. (1997) *Urban Land Tenure and Property Rights in Developing Countries: A Review*, Intermediate Technology Publications and Overseas Development Administration, London.

Philip, G. (ed.) (1988) *The Mexican Economy*, Routledge, London.

Pozas Garza, M. d. l. A. (1989) 'Land settlement by the poor in Monterrey', in A. Gilbert (ed.), *Housing and Land in Urban Mexico*, Center for US–Mexican Studies, University of California, San Diego, 65–77.

Presidencia de la República (1985) *Las Razones y las Obras: Gobierno de Miguel de la Madrid, Crónica del Sexenio 1982–1988 Segundo Año*, Presidencia de la República, Mexico City.

Ramírez Saiz, J. M. (1986) *El Movimiento Urbano Popular en México*, Siglo Veintiuno Editores, Mexico City.

Razzaz, O. M. (1993) 'Examining property rights and investment in informal settlements: the case of Jordan', *Land Economics*, Vol. 69, no. 4, 341–55.

SEDESOL (Secretaría de Desarrollo Social) (1993) *Solidarity in National Development*, SEDESOL, Mexico City.

Struyk, R. J. and R. Lynn (1983) 'Determinants of housing investment in slum areas: Tondo and other locations in Metro Manila', *Land Economics*, Vol. 59, no. 4, 444–54.

Tello, C. (1991) 'Combating poverty in Mexico', in M. González de la Rocha and A. Escobar Latapí (eds), *Social Responses to Mexico's Economic Crisis of the 1980s*, Center for US–Mexican Studies, University of California, San Diego, 57–65.

Varley, A. (1985a) 'La zona urbana ejidal y la urbanización de la ciudad de México', *A: Revista de Ciencias Sociales y Humanidades*, Vol. 6, 71–95.

— (1985b) '*Ya somos dueños: ejido* land development and regularisation in Mexico City', Unpublished PhD thesis, University College London.

— (1987) 'The relationship between tenure legalization and housing improvements: evidence from Mexico City', *Development and Change*, Vol. 18, no. 3, 463–81.

— (1989) 'Settlement, illegality and legalization: the need for re-assessment', in P. M. Ward (ed.), *Corruption, Development and Inequality: Soft Touch or Hard Graft?*, Routledge, London, 156–74.

— (1993) 'Clientilism or technocracy? The policies of urban land regularization', in N. Harvey (ed.), *Mexico: Dilemmas of Transition*, Institute of Latin American Studies, University of London, and British Academic Press, London, 249–76.

— (1996) 'Delivering the goods: Solidarity, land regularisation and urban services', in R. Aitken, N. Craske, G. A. Jones and D. Stansfield (eds), *Dismantling the Mexican State?*, Macmillan, Basingstoke, 204–24.

Vellinga, M. (1989) 'Power and independence: the struggle for identity and integrity in urban social movements', in F. Schuurman and T. Van Naerssen (eds), *Urban Social Movements in the Third World*, Routledge, London, 151–76.

Verbeek, H. (1987) 'The authorization of unauthorized housing in Cd. Chihuahua, Mexico', in O. Verkoren and J. van Weesep (eds), *Nederlandse Geografische Studies, 37: Spatial Mobility and Urban Change*, Geografisch Instituut, Rijksuniversiteit te Utrecht, 89–102.

Villarreal, D. R. and V. Castañeda (1986) *Urbanización y Autoconstrucción de Vivienda en Monterrey*, Centro de Ecodesarrollo, Mexico City.

Ward, P. M. (1981) 'Political pressure for urban services: the response of two Mexico City administrations', *Development and Change*, Vol. 12, no. 3, 379–407.

— (1986) *Welfare Politics in Mexico: Papering Over the Cracks*, Allen and Unwin, London.

— (1990) *Mexico City: The Production and Reproduction of an Urban Environment*, Belhaven Press, London.

Zaragoza, J. L. and R. Macías (1980) *El Desarrollo Agrario de México y su Marco Jurídico*, Centro Nacional de Investigaciones Agrarias, Mexico City.

CHAPTER 11

A Tale of Two Cities: Policy, Law and Illegal Settlements in Kenya

Winnie V. Mitullah and Kivutha Kibwana

The 'illegal city' is an important aspect of urban development. In most developing countries, poor economic performance caused by both internal and external factors has led to the proliferation of illegal settlements. Ignoring the legal requirements of most national and urban governments, most housing is built outside the law. Informal settlements provide cheap accommodation and economic opportunities for a large part of the population. The 'illegal city', in short, is a response both to housing needs and to the search for economic engagement.

The architects of the illegal city seem to be more innovative than the managers and planners of the legal city. They have come up with innovative 'solutions' that are able to accommodate and provide services for the majority of urban residents. In Nairobi, the capital city of Kenya, illegal settlements provide accommodation for over half the urban population. A similar proportion is engaged in economic activities within these settlements. In this respect, one is led to query the illegal status of such areas. The illegal city should be accommodated within the legal city if reality on the ground is to be reflected in the law, because the credibility of the law will be seriously undermined if the majority of citizens or residents are classed as illegal.

In spite of the significant role played by the 'illegal city', it has been viewed as a disgrace, the shame of the 'official city'. For decades, most governments in developing countries took punitive measures against informal settlements, with the aim of either stopping their growth or totally eliminating them (UNCHS 1991; Juppenlatz 1970). Such efforts proved futile and it has taken much scholarly persuasion to convince governments that enabling approaches should be applied in addressing informal settlements (Abrams 1964; Turner 1967; Mangin 1967; Rosser 1971).

As a result of pressure from international agencies, most governments responded to the growth of illegal settlement by concentrating on providing public housing. Houses were built according to the required building standards and attendant planning regulations. The building standards and planning regulations were, however, too stringent and colonially oriented and did not reflect the situation on the ground. Housing developed according to official building regulations proved too costly for the poor and this furthered the growth of illegal settlements; hence these policies led to a transfer of houses intended for the poor to the middle and sometimes the upper classes.

During the 1970s, further examination of the problem of illegal settlements resulted in quasi-government target-beneficiary programmes. Through them governments aimed to support residents of informal settlements in housing themselves. This was done through site and service, upgrading and low-income tenant-purchase housing schemes. These programmes also failed to reach their target beneficiaries.

As the 1980s came to an end, and the international pressure applied through Structural Adjustment Programmes (SAPs) mounted, most governments withdrew from direct participation in housing development. Instead they shifted the focus of their programmes to the provision of infrastructure and services, an option which may be appropriate for the growth of the general economy but is detrimental to low-income groups residing in illegal settlements, who deserve to receive housing subsidies.

A Conceptual Framework

In Kenya, as in other African countries, urban growth has been riddled with contradictions between the legal and the illegal city. This is reflected in the nature of settlement and the activities undertaken by residents of the two cities. Prior to the 1980s the distinction between the legal and the illegal city was quite clear and one could easily identify the two. At this point city governments were barely coping with the management of rapid urbanization. Since the mid-1980s, when urban management in most African cities reached a dead end, it has, however, become impossible to differentiate a planned from an 'unplanned' area, particularly as far as planned low-income settlements are concerned.

Although heterogeneous in terms of the quality and quantity of services enjoyed by residents, the legal city is 'exclusively planned' and inhabited by the comparatively wealthy. It has housing built according to planning and building by-laws with most services provided. The illegal city, on the other hand, is the home and workplace of the majority of city-dwellers. The housing units are not planned in the usual sense of planning and are not built according to the required building standards. Urban services are not provided and the residents largely rely on services available in neighbouring planned areas and those provided by NGOs and community-based organizations. To this extent, illegality and legality can be conceptualized purely on professional lines: the cities which the poor build and in which they live and work are different from and unrelated to what the city authorities want built.

The divide between the legal and the illegal city owes its origin to the colonial period. Colonial policies segregated residential areas for the colonial administrators and their African employees. The two areas had different types of houses and services. Whereas the administrators lived in houses with several rooms, their employees, who were mostly men, shared single rooms with only bed spaces. The expectation was that the employees were transient urban dwellers who belonged to the rural areas and were not supposed to bring their relatives or spouses into urban areas.

The strict regulation of movement and vagrancy laws did not stop non-formally employed Africans from moving into the urban areas. Most of them built their parallel city on the periphery of the official city in areas referred to as 'native zones'. They conducted all sorts of economic activities ranging from commercial sex work to hawking vegetables to petty manufacturing. Residents of such areas were considered illegal immigrants and had to cater for their own housing and services (Parker 1948).

At independence, the Kenyan government further entrenched the restrictive policies pursued by the colonial government, thereby perpetuating the legal–illegal city divide. As with the colonial government, the official policy was to demolish nascent settlements within the so-called 'illegal native zones' (Republic of Kenya 1965; 1966; Haldane 1971; Hake 1977). This resulted in the government demolishing more housing units than it provided.

From 1970 onwards, the demolition policy began to be questioned and the 1974/78 Development Plan abandoned the policy, at least on paper. The policy was based on a mistaken assumption that the government could manage to control rural–urban migration by augmenting rural development and providing adequate urban housing. These aspirations have not to date been fulfilled and the search for innovative approaches has continued as illegal settlements continue to proliferate.

Since the termination of the demolition policy, the Kenyan government has attempted to accommodate the residents of the illegal city, adopting several different approaches to the provision of low-income housing. These include site and service, upgrading and low-income tenant-purchase schemes. The goal was supposedly to eradicate illegal settlements, but so far this has failed and alternative approaches are still being sought.

The persistence of informal settlement may suggest that the legal and illegal cities have a symbiotic relationship. At any rate, it has so far proved impossible to eradicate informal settlement. We should not assume, however, that no planning whatsoever exists when poor people build an illegal settlement, since a rudimentary informal or customary form of planning is evident, although it is inadequate by the standards of the legal city. Some of this informal planning ethos is derived from rural housing standards and socio-economic and environmental dictates in relation to the availability of building materials.

Since the owners of property in the legal city often invest in the housing market of illegal settlements, an entrepreneurial and economic logic that cannot be ignored is clearly at work. If such realities are acknowledged, they may suggest that one viable route for dealing with the illegal city is to build incrementally on its informal/customary planning, in a context in which any agents of change emphasize methods of intervention based on community participation.

A Brief History of Urbanization in Kenya

Since 1948, when Kenya had its first population census, there has been rapid population increase in both urban and rural areas, as reflected in Table 11.1.

Table 11.1 Kenya: rural and urban population 1948–89

Year	Total	Rural	Urban	Urban as % of total	Number of urban centres
1948	5,406	5,121	285	5.2	17
1962	8,636	7,965	671	7.8	34
1969	10,943	9,861	1,082	9.9	47
1979	15,327	13,020	2,307	15.0	90
1989	21,433	17,556	3,877	18.1	139

Source: Government census data. Population figures in thousands.

In 1948 there were only seventeen urban centres with a population of 285,000, representing 5.2 per cent of the national total. Most of this population was concentrated in Nairobi and Mombasa, accounting for 83 per cent of the urban population. This left only 17 per cent of the urban population spread across the other fifteen urban centres.

By the time of Kenya's second census in 1962, the number of urban centres had increased to thirty-four, with a population of 671,000, 7.8 per cent of the national population. By 1979 there were ninety urban centres, with a population of 2.3 million. An analysis of the inter-censal period from 1969 to 1979 showed that urban centres with 2,000–4,999, 10,000–19,000, 20,000–99,000 and above 100,000 people had growth rates of 7.5

per cent, 7.1 per cent, 5.7 per cent and 5.6 per cent respectively. About two-thirds of the urban population were still, nevertheless, located within the major municipalities of Nairobi, Mombasa and Kisumu.

The most recent census, in 1989, revealed a total of 139 urban centres. Of these, forty-six had 10,000 people or more, compared with twenty-five such centres in 1979; thirty-two centres had 5,000–9,999 people; sixty-one, 2,000–4,999 people and seventy-six, fewer than 2,000 people. The census also indicates that the smaller towns have continued to experience higher growth rates than the main urban areas. Nevertheless, the major urban centres still have the lion's share of the urban population.

With the exception of a few towns within the coastal areas, most urban centres owe their origin to colonialism. Urbanization within the coastal areas dates back to before the ninth century. More than forty distinct administrative autonomous market centres thrived along the coast and on the off-shore islands before the European conquest. Malindi, the oldest urban centre in the coastal area, dates back to AD 470.

Periodic markets in pre-colonial Kenya can also be included in the early urban system urbanization (Krapf 1860; Obudho and Waller 1976). The history of urbanization in Kenya has emphasized pre-colonial urbanization along the Kenyan coastal area and colonial urbanization, and the existence of periodic markets prior to colonization is often down-played, although some of them were quite developed and could qualify as urban centres. They largely disappeared, however, with the development of colonial urban centres, perhaps because they were left out as business shifted to the newly developed centres (Hull 1976). A similar process has been witnessed more recently, even after independence. Small market centres have been known not to grow, or even to disappear completely, when new roads are developed away from them. On the other hand, new market centres are known to develop along new roads.

British colonization during the nineteenth century and the subsequent construction of the railways contributed to the development of a number of trading centres (Soja 1968; Obudho 1975). The centres introduced by the colonial administration were classified into three categories: towns or 'bomas' (these are the current urban centres with populations of 2,000 people or more), trading centres and the periodic markets which had existed before colonization.

The colonial urban centres developed as administration and transport centres connecting the centre and the periphery. Most developed along the railway lines, with hardly any relation to or influence on local economic conditions. They were not meant for Africans, except for employees of the railways or colonial administration.

The Vagrancy Act (Chapter 58 of the Laws of Kenya) was used to exclude Africans who were not formally employed, but it was not possible to keep them away from the city altogether. Instead they were pushed to areas on the urban periphery. Such areas were viewed as the proper place for Africans whose presence in the towns was no longer required. The initial development of urban areas in Kenya was thus highly controlled. Africans were restricted to African reserves located on the urban fringe where the necessary infrastructure and services were not provided. This was the origin of the illegal city.

The early colonial urban centres were not able to generate capital for themselves or for the nation. Instead, they siphoned resources out of the country, leaving the urban areas without the economic resources required for development. After independence, many industries remained in foreign ownership and retained very little capital within the urban areas or the country at large. The integration of multinational companies and the inherently unequal terms of trade also continued (Trainer 1989). All these factors contributed to the inability to deal with the issue of illegal settlements. Instead blame was placed at the door of urbanization *per se*.

Urbanization has been widely regarded as the cause of most problems relating to service provision and management within urban areas. In its original context, urbanization meant progress: the migration and concentration of population in particular centres was a response to industrial development and thus to the availability of income-earning opportunities. Urban development in countries such as Kenya has, however, been very different from that in the industrialized world. It has been a response, not to industrial development, but to the expectation of better economic opportunities to be found in the urban areas. Over the years the expectations of migrants have not been fulfilled, as demonstrated by the large numbers resorting to the informal or 'illegal' sector of the urban economy.

Nairobi: Legal and Illegal City

Origins, growth and planning Nairobi owes its origin to the construction of the Mombasa–Kisumu railway line, which opened the hinterland for European settlement in the Kenyan highlands. From a modest beginning as a railway depot with only 18km^2 of land in 1896, Nairobi later became an administrative and economic centre for colonial administrators (Amis 1983).

In 1920 the boundary was expanded to include an area of 25km^2. Further expansion at independence (1963) brought the total land area to 688km^2. The initial area of 18km^2 consisted only of the central administrative and business district and its environs. The latter had clearly marked, separate, areas for Africans and Europeans. This was a small controlled area and problems of developing infrastructure and providing and managing services did not arise. As the boundaries of the city expanded, however, the population grew, placing extra burdens on the provision of infrastructure and services.

Residential areas and the type of services offered were segregated on a racial basis. The colonial white residents occupied the better, hilly, parts of the city, to the north and west. These areas had adequate infrastructure and services. On the other hand, the Africans were located on the flat eastern part of the city, with minimal services provided. These were the formally employed Africans who were allowed to have temporary accommodation and were not expected to stay with their families. In the eyes of the colonial administrators, Africans belonged to the rural areas and were in towns only temporarily. This perception, which to some extent remained even after independence, significantly distorted management strategies for urban areas.

Other Africans who happened to be in the city and were not employed by the railway or the colonial administration were viewed as surplus to city needs and were 'officially' not catered for; they thus became the nucleus of the population of the illegal city. This population continued to pose problems for the city authorities as it settled in peripheral areas of the city. By 1900 the problem of management beyond the railway administration started to become evident. In response to this, a Township Committee of six members was formed to be responsible for city management. This was the birth of local government in Nairobi.

In 1919, Nairobi was upgraded to Municipal Council status, but the council did not have a full mandate for managing services. It was not until 1934 that the council took over the African Hospital (Lee-Smith 1989). In the following year it also took over the child welfare services and clinics. These were indications that the city authority needed to have the full control and planning of the city. This was partly realized after the 1948 census, which showed that Africans comprised 54 per cent of the population. This population could not be ignored and in the same year a comprehensive plan for the city was conceived. The resulting master plan recognized the presence of non-formally employed Africans and initiated changes in the provision of services.

In 1950, at the height of the nationalist movement, Nairobi became a city; the first African mayor was elected in 1962. The city had long been developing into an outstanding commercial centre, transport node, national metropolis and political centre. This attracted many migrants, making it almost impossible for the city managers to cope with the provision and management of services.

The commissioning in 1973 of the Nairobi Urban Study Group, funded by the UNDP, was a response to the deteriorating situation with unco-ordinated planning based on sectoral and political issues. The group came up with another master plan, referred to as the 'Nairobi Metropolitan Growth Strategy' (Nairobi Urban Study Group 1973). The intention was to devise methods of putting an end to the problems associated with urbanization and come up with guidelines for city growth. Location of industries and housing was a key concern of the Strategy, with an emphasis on integrating employment and housing in an effort to alleviate transport problems. In addition to the traditional industrial area, another four areas within the city were designated as new, decentralized, industrial areas. These areas have not materialized to date, as illegal subdivisions continue to encroach on the areas supposedly reserved for industrial development. It has been observed that 'since 1980 most areas designated for metropolitan growth have been sub-divided into plots by cooperatives and companies, sometimes according to approved plans and sometimes not' (UNCHS 1987: 10). Workers still have to travel long distances to work.

Master plans are meant to guide development and should not be taken as exact blueprints. In Nairobi, neither the 1948 nor the 1973 master plans has been respected by the city authorities. Instead, the authorities have emphasized the production of plans and regulations at the expense of managing development. Where illegal settlements have been upgraded or redeveloped, this has been done within a context of unco-ordinated planning and policy implementation. In some cases, the authorities themselves have been a contributing factor to the inability to achieve planned development targets.

The City Planning Department was established in 1981, on the recommendation of the Nairobi Urban Study Group, to ensure proper planning. The department has performed very poorly, especially in the area of land allocation and housing development. Similarly poor performance is characteristic of most other departments of the Nairobi City Council. Most are run on a patron–client or 'godfather' basis without any serious consideration being given to the public interest.

In response to the poor performance of the Planning Department, in 1983 the then City Commission came up with a task force to evaluate the planning policy of the city government. The objectives of the task force were, *inter alia,* to redevelop derelict land, encourage high-rise housing development, maximize use of existing infrastructural services, reduce distance from home to work and develop a balanced urban environment (Ngari 1995). This whole exercise was an attempt to increase residential densities, in a rational, planned fashion, in response to the demands placed on the city by a growing population.

The failure of urban policy and master plans is reflected in housing development. The city government has failed to provide sufficient housing or to assist urban residents, especially the low-income groups, to house themselves. The proliferation of illegal settlements on the periphery and the development by formal sector private developers of middle- and high-income housing without the necessary infrastructure and services are clear signs of the problems facing the city.

The housing problem within the city has been exploited not only by the informal private developers responsible for the growth of illegal settlements but also by property developers in the formal sector. Although these formal sector developers have sufficient resources to do otherwise, they have been developing housing without making adequate allowance for infrastructure and services. This makes such formal sector developments similar in some ways to the illegal settlements. The only difference lies in the fact that those living in areas developed by formal sector developers can afford private services or use their influence to obtain some services from the city authorities.

The housing problem has been escalating in spite of several programmes (upgrading, sites and service, tenant-purchase and mortgage schemes) funded by international financial institutions such as the World Bank, CDC and USAID. The city government has been unable to cope with private developers, especially those developing illegal settlements. These developers are commercializing housing and have nothing to do with the intended policies of the City Council such as those advanced by both the Urban Study Group and the 1990 task force on planning.

Legal or illegal citizens? The distribution of Nairobi's population

Since its inception in 1896, the population of the city has been increasing. By 1901 the population was only 8,000 but by the 1948 census it had grown to 118,976. In 1962 the population had reached 343,500, rising to 827,800 in 1979. The most recent census (1989) revealed a population of 1,324,570 with a total male and female population of 752,597 and 571,973 respectively. In all, there were 382,863 households in Nairobi, occupying a total area of 693km² and with an average population density of 1,911 per square kilometre (Republic of Kenya 1989b). The latter varies across residential areas, with low-income illegal settlements having the highest densities and high-income settlements, the lowest.

Illegal settlements have been growing faster than the official city. It has been observed that illegal settlements in Kenya have annual population growth rates of between 4 and 6 per cent. Kibera Laini Saba, one of the largest illegal settlements in Nairobi, has been recorded as having the highest annual growth rate: 12 per cent. The increase in population can be explained by a number of factors including rural–urban migration, natural increase (partly due to improvement of health services, although the current structural adjustment programmes have been reversing the trend), extension of city boundaries and government policies relaxing controls on movement into towns.

Nairobi's population figures have been controversial and the city authorities have often put forward higher figures. In 1988, when government estimates showed a population of 1.35 million, city estimates gave the population as 2 million. If the 1989 national population census showing Nairobi's population as 1,324,570 is used as a reference, the figure from the city authorities is way above the national census figure. The city

Table 11.2 Nairobi: estimated population and area of informal settlements

Administrative division	Population	Area covered by informal settlement (hectares)
Makadara	102,480	85
Langata (Kibera)	251,040	229
Kasarani	158,115	227
Dagoretti	186,250	373
Embakasi	31,890	73
Pumwani	11,890	14
Parklands	7,326	24
Total	748,991	1,025

Source: MATRIX 1993.

authorities have explained this discrepancy by arguing that Nairobi's transient population should be included in the calculations: that part of the population which does not necessarily reside within the city but uses services provided by the city authorities.

The growth of illegal settlements has contributed significantly to the rapid growth of the city. Records of illegal settlements do not exist prior to 1952. The available information shows, however, that Africans lived in unregulated areas 'in many ways more like rural villages than urban suburbs' (Bujra 1973: 10). Such settlements were eventually demolished and both landlords and tenants had to move to demarcated 'native locations'. Pumwani (place of rest), established in 1922, was one such location. Within such areas both Africans and Arabs were expected to rent plots from the Municipal Council and build lodging houses out of traditional materials.

Although Pumwani was a legal place of residence for both Africans and Arabs, not many Africans lived there. The same could not be said of Pangani, an illegal settlement, but in 1938 Pangani was demolished and its African residents had to move elsewhere. Most of them moved to the adjacent settlement of Mathare, now one of the longest-lived of illegal settlements. For decades Mathare has suffered demolitions but the residents keep coming back, and they have been joined by newcomers. The new residents are those who have suffered demolitions elsewhere in Nairobi and new migrants into the city. To date, illegal parts of Mathare still survive, despite several government programmes to integrate it with the legal city.

Another old quasi-legal settlement, whose legal status differs from Pumwani, is the Nubian village in Kibera. It dates back to 1912, when ex-Nubian soldiers were settled in Kenya and given residence permits. As in Pumwani, houses were supposed to be built with temporary materials, as there was an intention of eventually redeveloping the area.

In 1952 Nairobi was estimated to have only about 500 residential units within illegal settlements. By 1972 the number had increased to 22,000 (Chana and Morrison 1973), reaching 110,000 and housing about 40 per cent of the city population by 1979 (Amis 1984). An inventory of illegal settlements undertaken in Nairobi in 1993 showed that they had a total population of 748,991 residing in an area of 1,025 hectares (MATRIX 1993; see Table 11.2). They account for 55 per cent of the Nairobi population but, as the MATRIX study notes, that population occupies only 5.5 per cent of the area used for residential purposes in Nairobi.

The Functions of Nairobi's Illegal City

The illegal city has been a response to a changing rate of socio-economic development accompanied by rapid population growth. It provides employment, incomes and housing to over 50 per cent of the population of Nairobi and has become the base for informal sector activities for both rural migrants and city-born residents (Ondiege and Dondo 1991).

The role of the informal sector in creating employment has been noted and documented since 1972 (ILO 1972). The 1989–93 Development Plan estimated that informal self-employment was growing at 40–60 per cent annually (Republic of Kenya 1989a). Although the illegal sector provides the higher share of job opportunities, formal employment is still given priority.

Urban development has witnessed an expansion of the urban labour force that has taken place faster than the creation of employment opportunities. Where job opportunities have been created, they are often restricted to skilled workers. The untrained and less educated are thus left to build the illegal city and create jobs for themselves within the illegal settlements. The implication is that they are expected to fend for themselves outside the formal sector.

In Nairobi, informal self-employment grew by 28 per cent per annum between 1980 and 1984; whereas formal employment grew by only 18 per cent during the same period. Illegal settlements in Nairobi are littered with small-scale businesses where the unskilled are able acquire skills on the job and generate income for their families. By 1993 it was estimated that there were 40,000 small businesses in Nairobi, most of them located within illegal settlements (MATRIX 1993).

The small-scale businesses range from basic hawking of perishable goods to petty manufacturing and trades, including welding, metal work, mechanics, carpentry and construction work. These activities provide employment at low capital cost and generate an output which contributes to the economy of Nairobi (MATRIX 1993). The income earned from these business activities is comparatively low (Mitullah 1990).

A high percentage of families depend on earnings from the small-scale business activities located within the illegal settlements. A study conducted in Nakuru, one of the major urban centres of Kenya, showed that 65 per cent of the respondents interviewed were dependent on the sector for employment and income (Malombe 1993). Only 35 per cent had other sources of income.

In the area of housing, the informal sector has played a key role. Between 1979 and 1989, it is estimated that housing construction in the sector accounted for between 60 and 80 per cent of all new housing constructed (Hoek-Smit 1989).

Characteristics of Nairobi's Illegal Settlements

Illegal settlements house a large percentage of the city residents and have unique characteristics and features. These include poor location, low incomes, high population densities, housing constructed largely of temporary materials, poor sanitary conditions, minimal or non-existent urban services and quasi-legal tenure. These characteristics and features 'differ slightly from settlement to settlement, depending on the age of the settlement, the type of land tenure, geographical location, the vibrancy of the informal sector and access to wage employment' (MATRIX 1993: 13). The settlements on private land are less crowded and have better houses and a cleaner environment.

Illegal settlements are largely located in poor areas which attract hardly any demand. They have high population and housing densities and most people earn low incomes. In most areas the growth rate is higher than for the city as a whole. The settlements have an average of 250 dwelling units per hectare and 750 persons per hectare. On the other hand, the upper- and middle-income areas have between ten and thirty dwelling units per hectare and 50 to 180 persons per hectare (MATRIX 1993).

The forms of housing in illegal settlements differ from those in the legal city. Most housing is built of materials referred to in official circles as 'temporary'. The concept 'temporary' is a colonial legacy: it views local traditional materials as non-durable, because they do not conform to the Western standards of the building code – standards which do not reflect reality on the ground and have a negative influence on housing development. Building materials referred to as temporary have been known to last for many years.

The requirements of the building code, before its revision in July 1995, were beyond the means of the majority of urban dwellers. Planning and building regulations have contributed to squatting on both public and private land.

Poor sanitation is another characteristic of illegal settlements. Most rely on water vendors and communal water supply points. The residents purchase water at higher prices than those paid to the Nairobi City Council in any legal part of the city. A basic needs survey carried out in 1992 by the Kenya Consumers Organization showed that 75 per cent of the population in four illegal settlements (Mathare, Kawangware, Soweto and Kibera) purchased water from vendors while 21 per cent had access to water through communal pipes.

Water is a necessity for life but can also be a health hazard when it is not well managed. In most illegal settlements there are hardly any drainage and solid waste disposal services. In the few cases where rudimentary and deficient open drains have been provided by communities with the assistance of NGOs, they are often blocked by garbage, causing particular problems during the rainy season.

In almost all illegal settlements sanitation is inadequate. The Metropolitan Household Survey showed that 94 per cent of the population in such areas does not have access to adequate sanitation (UNICEF 1989). Poorly constructed pit latrines shared with up to twenty-five households and over fifty people make the sanitation situation worse. At the same time, they are used as bath/shower facilities. This makes them fill up very rapidly, requiring evacuation, but as this is expensive it is rarely carried out.

In the rare cases where water-borne sanitation exists, it is often non-operational because of a lack of water or low pressure. By its nature water-borne sanitation requires high capital investment in physical infrastructure, and this is not affordable to residents of illegal settlements.

Solid waste is hardly collected, a problem which has affected most parts of the city in recent years. Whereas both the high- and middle-income legal settlements have opted for private solid waste collection, those resident within illegal settlements cannot afford private services.

Apart from drainage and solid waste collection services, the illegal settlements lack other basic services provided to the formal areas, such as schools, health services and recreation facilities.

Most illegal parts of the city are assumed not to have any title to land. Research has shown, however, that most owners of the residential units have some form of tenure, although this may not be recognized. Some have temporary occupation licences or letters from chiefs on public land or some agreement with landowners on private land. These quasi-legal tenures have been thought to contribute to the settlements' lack of improvement. They show that there is very little if any 'typical squatting'. In any case, the majority of illegal settlement residents are tenants who may not have any idea about the title of the land on which they are living.

Policy Development and Illegal Urban Centres in Kenya

At independence, most African states viewed rural–urban migration as the major cause of urban population growth. In response to this, most governments, Kenya included, pursued policies of 'decongestion' focusing on development of rural areas and alternative growth poles. The aim of 'decongestion' policy was to reduce population in the major urban areas and keep potential migrants away from them. The growth centres were also supposed to provide markets for agricultural produce, other exchange goods, small-scale food processing, manufacturing, social interaction and information exchange. They were, in short, to play the role of regional centres. A United Nations survey of 126 countries in 1987 indicated that three-quarters of the countries covered were attempting either to slow or to reverse migration to major urban areas.

In spite of the policy focus on the rural areas and alternative growth centres, urban growth and related problems continued to outstrip the capacity of African governments to plan ahead and provide services for the urban population. The policy focus did not address inherent problems of urbanization such as illegal settlements. It failed to retain population within the rural/regional growth centres, because these areas also lacked the required infrastructure and services.

'Decongestion' policies take a long time to achieve their aims, although studies in other parts of the world (Latin America and India) have shown that they do work. Annual growth rates of intermediate cities are becoming equal to, or greater, than those of the larger cities, as in the developed economies (Harris 1984; 1988). It has been argued that this trend may be explained by the presence of many larger cities in both Latin America and India. This is thought to provide more options for potential migrants and results in a spread effect, reducing growth in the major urban centres.

By contrast, Africa has a limited number of larger cities. Most countries have at most only one city with over half a million people. Since the mid-1980s, when economic pressures became intense, with high unemployment, some migrants have been giving the smaller urban centres a try. In Kenya, as mentioned above, the smaller urban centres have recorded higher population growth rates since 1988. If this trend continues, Kenya might eventually share the experience of Latin America and India.

The Kenyan government has not been able to address urban issues effectively and there are hardly any policy papers giving a coherent overall policy direction. Urban policy guidelines appear in bits and pieces in different government documents such as the Development Plans and related Sessional Papers. Housing is one of the sectors which has been addressed using this approach. The 1965 housing policy paper remains, to date, the single policy paper explicitly addressing housing issues, despite the fact that housing is a major problem, with more than half the city population living in conditions considered unacceptable.

After independence, however, most urban policies hinged on housing, broadly aiming to improve conditions in illegal settlements. The policies were restrictive, as they were still dominated by the colonial legacy of high building standards and planning regulations accompanied by punitive measures, including demolition of illegal settlements. The city authorities seem not to have appreciated that those developing illegal settlements and those who rent their homes within them relieve the city authorities of their responsibility and should not be harassed.

After the ILO study of 1972, the government, with the support of the UN and other international organizations, began to pursue enabling housing policies. Pragmatic approaches such as the upgrading of illegal settlements, encouraging individual and group initiatives, were considered. In practical terms the government provided building sites (and sometimes materials) with basic services under the site and service schemes. Low-income groups were expected to move into such areas, while those staying put within illegal settlements had their areas upgraded. While these two policy approaches were positive moves, they still suffered from the delusion that it was possible to provide 'decent homes to every Kenyan whether privately built or state sponsored'. This resulted in an insistence on high planning and building standards contributing to the inability of low-income groups to afford the schemes.

The independent Kenyan government, then, still entertained the notion that it would be able to provide all citizens with decent housing (Republic of Kenya 1974). This was to be achieved through the National Housing Cooperation and the Housing Finance Company of Kenya, institutions established immediately after independence to assist Africans to house themselves. Government ambitions, however, were out of tune with economic realities, and yet policies to promote urban employment growth and better standards of living were neglected. Instead, the government relied on loans and grants which in most cases did not benefit the most needy.

In its pursuit of decent housing for all, the government has insisted on ensuring basic standards of health, privacy and security in all programmes in which it participates or which it supports (Republic of Kenya 1974). The housing, infrastructure and services provided have to respect planning regulations and building standards. Most urban residents cannot meet these exacting requirements and have no choice but to settle in areas that are not officially endorsed. Although such individuals and groups cater for themselves, and government policy states that they should not be harassed, they continue to be viewed as 'illegal' residents.

Before some aspects of the planning and building codes were revised in 1995, they still bore the traces of their colonial legacy. In addition, the 1995 reforms have not been ratified and adopted by the relevant local authorities. Most councils are therefore still using the old planning regulations and building standards, leaving many urban residents unable to develop or rent a legally acceptable housing unit.

On the other hand, after independence the government continued to provide over-subsidized rental housing while demolishing informally built settlements. The majority of urban dwellers could not afford such dwellings and the government could no longer afford to provide subsidized housing. Its role as a provider of housing began to dwindle with the publication of an official policy paper on 'Economic Management for Renewed Growth' in 1986. This paper articulated a policy according to which the government would refrain from being the main provider of public goods. In the area of housing, the paper, like the ILO report, acknowledged the importance of the informal sector. The government should stop subsidizing the poor and promote equity by charging market prices to the few who benefit from government services in order to expand provision to many others who are still in need (Republic of Kenya 1986).

The 1986 paper was followed by preparation of a National Housing Strategy document in celebration of the International Year of Shelter for the Homeless. Subsequently a Housing Policy Document was developed out of the National Strategy Paper and a Sessional Paper prepared, but to date this has not been put to parliament.

Law and the Illegal City: the Case of Nairobi

In answering the question of 'what is the problem of land in the city?', Patrick McAuslan (1994: 560–1) observes that 'the crisis [is] of inadequate amounts of land being made available for urban development and in particular for urban development by and for the urban poor'. He further comments:

> Too many countries, particularly, it must be said, in Africa, still approach issues of urban land management in ... terms [of rigid notions of legality and illegality] and it is distinctly unhelpful. [U]se of these terms and action taken in pursuance of them is much more of a socio-political rather than a legal matter – it benefits the urban elite who wield the law – but the point needs to be made that policies and their implementation which are predicated on the basis that the majority of urban dwellers are in some way living 'illegally' have not succeeded in dealing with the problems of urban land in the past and are not likely to succeed in the future ... concepts of legality and illegality obfuscate rather than illuminate. (McAuslan 1994: 582, 584)

Victor Nkiwane (1994: 610) arrives at the conclusion that: 'The legal framework itself remains highly inadequate. Squatters, if we accept that they are driven not by mere want of squatting but by need, need as much protection from the law as the owners of land occupied ... People who have access and means to obtain land or housing legally will not resort to illegal squatting.'

A close examination of the relationship between the law and all aspects of urban land management – land availability, the setting and maintenance of building standards, services provision, the creation of space for economic activities and socio-cultural life – demonstrates that the law is heavily biased against the poor inhabitants of illegal settlements. Urban land-related law recognizes and protects first and foremost those who control the central business district or the urban core; the support it offers dwindles as we journey to the urban periphery and beyond. In Kenya, the seventeen or so laws that concern or affect slums or illegal settlements are outrightly hostile and unaccommodating; their unabashed goal is to bulldoze such settlements and facilitate the wholesale legalization and 'gentrification' of urban centres.

These laws are, first of all, Chapter IX (Trust Land) of the Constitution of Kenya, followed by the Town Planning Act (Chapter 134), Land Planning Act (Chapter 303), Public Health Act (Chapter 242), Local Government Act (Chapter 265), Government Lands Act (Chapter 280), Trust Lands Act (Chapter 288), Registered Land Act (Chapter 300), Land Control Act (Chapter 302), Land Acquisition Act (Chapter 295), Valuation for Rating Act (Chapter 283), Rent Restriction Act (Chapter 266), Housing Act (Chapter 296), Vagrancy Act (Chapter 117), Trust of Lands Act (Chapter 58), and the Building Codes 1968 – Grade I and II (under/ pursuant to the Local Government Act).

Illegal settlements and the individual housing units within them are not recognized by the law because the land they occupy is often owned or controlled by the state, local authorities or private landowners. Where landlords rent out housing units within illegal settlements, these structures are tolerated, partly because they are often the property of the elite and partly because they provide affordable accommodation to people who must live close to where they supply their labour. At the behest of the landlords or the central or city government, however, these illegal structures may routinely be demolished to make way for the building of structures that will attract higher rents or free the land for sale. More illegal structures can be built with the proceeds, or legal structures can replace illegal ones. Law is thus used to sanction the demolition of squatter settlements and the eviction of slum dwellers.

Where the land on which illegal settlements and structures are built is state land, when official allocations occur, they favour the already advantaged, politically well-connected elite, the only group able to mobilize officials and use the law and, therefore, land (*Daily Nation*, 10 April 1995; 29 April 1995; 16 May 1995; and 4 July 1995). Indeed, given the recent (1990s) feverish but illegal land-grabbing mania in Nairobi and other urban centres, there will be very little land available to meet the future needs of the urban poor, unless acceptable mechanisms can be devised to free this land for use by the poor or for other legal purposes.

Where a person who owns land in Nairobi builds a structure which does not meet the required building standards, the resulting structure is counted as belonging to the illegal city. Given the origins of the building standards, they cannot have been meant to accommodate the urban poor or even most of the middle class. Moreover, we have seen that the majority of buildings in Nairobi and other urban centres currently fail to respect the building standards. If the majority of people cannot meet a given standard, the standard ought to be reconsidered.

Kenya's urban poor face a vagrancy law which can disqualify them from living in the urban environment since it defines a vagrant as 'a person having no fixed abode and not giving a satisfactory account of himself' (Section 2 [b]); the 'vagrant' can then be arrested by a police officer, without a warrant (Section 3). This law, if rigorously enforced, would lead to many of the urban poor being relocated and consigned to rural areas. Ironically, this law may perhaps encourage the urban poor to construct slums so as to avoid falling foul of its provisions: if they hastily construct a cardboard house – as, for example, in Nairobi's Carton City slum – they have, legally, a fixed abode.

If the urban poor are to overcome the vagrancy hurdle, they have to contend with the laws that can bestow on them title to land on which to build their structures. If the land is state land, then the government, through the Government Lands Act, can give preference to the urban poor in the allocation of this land. It would be good policy to reserve state land in or adjacent to urban centres for the development of housing by the urban poor, especially through co-operatives. Trust land could also be set aside or the government could compulsorily acquire land for such purposes.

If the Kenyan government eventually traces illegally obtained land in the urban centres, the land it recovers should in the first instance be put at the disposal of the urban poor, although schemes to purchase and develop such land would first have to be established. Poor landowners could be exempted from any rates due on such land under the Valuation for Rating Act or Rating Act.

A 1986 'Kenya Low-income Housing By-laws Review' study undertaken by the Ministry of Works, Housing and Physical Planning recommended revision of some specific building standards and by-laws, for low-cost housing development in particular. The study concluded, *inter alia*:

> 1.00 The issue of adoption of appropriate standards applicable to Urban Housing and particularly to low-cost housing have been unresolved to date because the existing building code currently in use is in some places cumbersome to apply as it sets too high standards or is out of date. The result has been that it has been difficult to provide healthy and affordable low-cost housing to the majority of the low-income earners ...
>
> 3.00 The result of the analysis has revealed that there are revisions that can be implemented immediately without the need to change, revise or amend the existing legislation's (*sic*), while others will require changes to the existing Building

Code and the Public Health Act in order to make that legislation compatible with the needs of low-income housing in Kenya and the government's low-cost housing policies.

4.00 It is thus expected that the new form of building legislation that in effect relates to low-cost housing development will be such that whilst the basic requirements may remain fixed, the technical means of satisfying them can easily and speedily be revised to accommodate various changing needs and resources of our country.

The study gave general examples of the main areas requiring change in the current building laws. These were the need to ensure clarity in legal requirements, the unification of multiple legislation, simplification of the administrative system, the harmonization of different authorities' responsibilities in this area, the need to streamline standards, and the development of a comprehensive building law.

The study also proposed a review of the Local Government (Adoptive By-laws) (Building) (Amendment) Order of 1968, as regards performance specification by-laws 216 to 232, to relax building standards for high-density or low-cost (low-income) residential areas. The proposed relaxation would certainly make it easier for the urban poor who own land to meet the standards required, and, if complemented by the use of locally available building materials and construction techniques, it could lead to a substantial increase in the proportion of buildings erected by the urban poor that could be considered legal.

Another area requiring attention is the availability of funds for housing purposes. Mortgage interest rates usually run at about 30 per cent annually. Perhaps under the Housing Act, under which loans and grants of public moneys are provided for the construction of dwellings, cheaper money could be made available to the urban poor.

Under the Rent Restriction Act, tenants of slum dwellings are protected since the rent for these premises is below the 2,500 shillings standard rent. Most tenants will not, however, be aware of this protection and illegal evictions are commonplace in slums.

Kibwana (1989) examined in detail the legal regulation of the informal sector, paying particular attention to informal sector activities within the illegal city. Once again, in spite of policy commitments to support the informal sector, the law has lagged behind policy intentions with serious consequences for economic activities by informal sector operators. Most are routinely harassed by the authorities and denied the space to undertake their business activities. Administrative practice and the law thus contradict positive policy intentions. Genuine official commitment to supporting the informal sector is needed, especially in illegal settlements.

Conclusion

Continuous rapid population growth in Kenya will continue to put pressure on housing provision. This will necessarily be reflected in the proliferation of illegal settlements. The architects of illegal settlements have come up with housing approaches which integrate the poor with the legal city, albeit inadequately, and which are capable of standing the test of time. Both national and city governments, however, have failed to come up with appropriate laws, policies and strategies to accommodate the poor. What needs to be done is to rationalize the reality of illegal settlements by making them legal forms of accommodation. The relevant policies, laws and regulations should constantly be kept under review, and revised as necessary.

The existence of illegal settlements should be acknowledged and all necessary support given. They should be understood as a source of economic support and income for residents, investors and the national and city governments. The latter two should be prepared to build incrementally on the informal/customary planning methods applied within such settlements. This should enable residents and investors to participate effectively in the everyday management of urban life, instead of having to participate in programmes that do not reflect their needs or desires. It will presumably keep legislators on their toes, given the challenge of coming up with laws that mirror the reality of illegal settlements.

Existing laws and regulations tend to protect landowners, formal investors and the politically well-connected elites, who also happen to be the wealthy. The poor, who normally only have the most basic of movable assets, such as clothing, bedding and household goods, have largely been ignored. It has to be understood that the poor squat out of need and not mere want. Therefore, they need national and city government protection at all levels.

Most of the seventeen or so laws relating to illegal settlements are biased against the poor residents of the illegal city. The laws are hostile and unaccommodating and yet these illegal settlements house over 50 per cent of the urban population. We can conclude that if the majority of people cannot meet a given standard, then the standard ought to be reconsidered. This should be a priority for both national and city governments.

References

Abrams, C. (1964) *Man's Struggle for Shelter in an Urbanizing World*, MIT Press, Cambridge MA.

Amis, P. (1983) 'A Shanty Town of Tenants: The Commercialisation of Unauthorised Housing in Nairobi, 1960–1980', Unpublished PhD thesis, University of Kent at Canterbury.

— (1984) 'Squatters or tenants? The commercialization of unauthorized housing in Nairobi', *World Development*, Vol. 12, no. 1, 87–96.

Bujra, J. (1973) 'Pumwani: the politics of property', Institute of Development Studies, University of Nairobi, mimeo.

Chana, T. and H. Morrison (1973) 'Housing systems in the low-income sector of Nairobi, Kenya', *Ekistics*, Vol. 36, no. 214, 214–22.

Hake, A. (1977) *African Metropolis: Nairobi's Self Help City*, Chatto and Windus for Sussex University Press, London.

Haldane, D. (1971) *Those Without*, National Christian Council, Nairobi.

Harris, N. (1984) 'Some trends in the evolution of big cities: studies of the USA and India', *Habitat International*, Vol. 8, no. 1, 7–28.

— (1988) 'Economic development and urbanization', *Habitat International*, Vol. 12, no. 3, 5–15.

Hoek-Smit, M. C. (1989) 'Evaluation of Umoja II: An Experimental Housing Project in Nairobi', Report prepared for USAID, Nairobi.

Hull, R.W. (1976) *African Cities and Towns Before the European Conquest*, Norton, New York.

ILO (International Labour Office) (1972) *Employment, Incomes and Equality: A Strategy for Increasing Productive Employment in Kenya*, ILO, Geneva.

Juppenlatz, M. (1970) *Cities in Transformation: The Urban Squatter Problem of the Developing World*, University of Queensland Press, St Lucia.

Kibwana, K. (1989) 'Critical aspects regarding the legal regulation of the informal sector', *Lesotho Law Journal*, Vol. 5, no. 2, 357–87.

Krapf, J. L. (1860) *Travels, Researches and Missionary Labours During an Eighteen Years Residence in Eastern Africa*, Trübner, London.

Lee-Smith, D. (1989) 'Urban management in Nairobi: a case study of the *matatu* mode of public transport' in R. E Stren and R. R. White (eds), *African Cities in Crisis: Managing Rapid Urban Growth*, Boulder, Westview Press, 276–304.

McAuslan, P. (1994) 'Land in the city: the role of law in reforming urban land markets' in Y. Vyas, K. Kibwana, O. Owiti and S. Wanjala (eds), *Law and Development in the Third World*, Faculty of Law, University of Nairobi, 560–90.

Malombe, J. (1993) 'Informal sector and housing provision for the urban poor in Kenya', Paper presented to seminar on 'Small and Intermediate Size Enterprises in African Industrialization', Nairobi.

Mangin, W. (1967) 'Latin American squatter settlements: a problem and a solution', *Latin American Research Review*, Vol. 2, no. 1, 65–98.

MATRIX (Matrix Development Consultants) (1993) *Nairobi's Informal Settlements: An Inventory*, MATRIX, Nairobi.

Mitullah, W. V. (1990) 'State Policy and Urban Housing: The Case of Low Income Housing in Nairobi', Unpublished PhD thesis, University of York.

Nairobi Urban Study Group (1973) *Nairobi Metropolitan Growth Strategy*, Nairobi City Council, Nairobi.

Ngari, J. (1995) 'Urban management experiences in Kenya: the case of Nairobi City Council', Paper presented to workshop on 'Urban and Regional Planning Policy and Development Strategies', Nairobi.

Nkiwane, V. (1994) 'The problem of urban squatting in African countries', in Y. Vyas, K. Kibwana, O. Owiti and S. Wanjala (eds), *Law and Development in the Third World*, Faculty of Law, University of Nairobi, 591–614.

Obudho, R. A. (1975) 'Urbanization and development planning in Kenya: historical appreciation', *African Urban Notes*, Series B, Vol. 1, no. 3, 1–56.

Obudho, R. A. and P. P. Waller (1976) *Periodic Markets, Urbanization and Regional Planning: A Case Study from Western Kenya*, Greenwood Press, Westport.

Ondiege, P. and A. Dondo (1991) 'Informal sector assistance policies in Kenya', Department of Urban and Regional Planning, University of Nairobi.

Parker, M. (1948) *Political and Social Aspects of the Development of Municipal Government in Kenya with Special Reference to Nairobi*, Colonial Office, London.

Republic of Kenya (1965) *Sessional Paper on Housing Policy*, Government Printer, Nairobi.

— (1966) *Development Plan for the Period 1965/66–1969/70*, Government Printer, Nairobi.

— (1974) *Development Plan for the Period 1974–1978*, Government Printer, Nairobi.

— (1986) *Economic Management for Renewed Growth*, Government Printer, Nairobi.

— (1989a) *Development Plan for the Period 1989–1993*, Government Printer, Nairobi.

— (1989b) *Kenya Population Census*, Government Printer, Nairobi.

Rosser, G. (1971) 'Housing for the lowest income groups: the Calcutta experience', *Ekistics*, Vol. 31, no. 183, 126–31.

Soja, E. W. (1968) *The Geography of Modernization in Kenya: A Spatial Analysis of Social, Economic and Political Change*, Syracuse University Press, New York.

Trainer, T. (1989) *Developed to Death: Rethinking Third World Development*, Green Print, London.

Turner, J. F. C. (1967) 'Barriers and channels for housing development in modernizing countries', *Journal of the American Institute of Planners*, Vol. 33, no. 3, 167–81.

UNCHS (United Nations Centre for Human Settlements, Habitat) (1987) *Case Study of Sites and Services Schemes in Kenya: Lessons from Dandora and Thika*, Habitat, Nairobi.

— (1991) *Global Strategy for Shelter to the Year 2000: Implementation of the First Phase*, Habitat, Nairobi.

UNICEF (United Nations Children's Fund) (1989) 'Urban Basic Services Project Strategy: Programme Recommendation for 1989/93', UNICEF Kenya Office, Nairobi.

CHAPTER 12

Law and Urban Change in the New South Africa

Stephen Berrisford

South African towns and cities starkly reflect the legal and political orders under which they were built. In order to achieve political and ideological goals of racial segregation and of tightly restricted access to urban areas, an extraordinarily elaborate set of laws was promulgated at every level of government. The often absurd and uniformly repugnant minutiae of this legislation do not warrant discussion here. Rather, this chapter will look broadly at the role which law has played in South African urban development in the past and also identify some of the key legal issues currently facing urban authorities in South Africa.

Few of South Africa's urban problems are unique: rapid population increase, inadequate housing supply and rapidly growing informal settlements, contaminated and dangerous urban environments, gross inequalities in access to essential services and other opportunities, together with ineffective local government. South African cities, however, are unusual because of the direct, if complex, historical relationship between law and urban space. The law was consistently and rigorously used to ensure that particular patterns of urban land use, occupation and residence could be achieved. A chapter of this nature is unable to explore the complexities of this relationship fully. It will, however, attempt to provide an introduction to the subject.

The first section of this chapter will describe the South African urban context in order to enable a clearer understanding of the nature of South African urban law. The second section will introduce the legislation that produced this situation. Law has played a central role in the shaping of South African cities and in the determination of access to urban opportunities and resources. The recent political transition in South Africa has led to a profound shift in emphasis of state urban policy. This shift has led to the promulgation of new urban legislation. Critically important urban legal questions, however, still remain to be tackled. These will be identified and discussed in the third and final section of the chapter.

The Urban Context

Race zones South African towns and cities are dominated by the 'race zones'[1] created by the legislation implementing the notorious policy of apartheid.[2] Although none of the explicitly racial provisions used to establish and defend these race zones remains on the statute books, their products or physical manifestations do remain. Moreover, a host of other, ostensibly race-neutral provisions that effectively perpetuate racial segregation also remain. These include town-planning regulations, municipal by-laws and the different legal regimes for land, planning, housing and similar matters applicable to the different race zones within each urban area. The continued existence of these various inherited legal regimes greatly hinders processes of administrative and institutional integration, particularly at the level of local government.

The legacy of the former race zones to the post-apartheid South Africa is a grossly unequal distribution of land rights both at a national level and at that of each individual town or city. The phenomenon of rich and poor people living apart from each other is certainly not unique to South Africa. In this country, however, the separation is not only spatially more marked and extreme than in many others but is also a phenomenon deliberately created by law. The importance of the law in determining the current form and pattern of development in South African cities adds an inevitable layer of complexity to the task of drawing up new urban policies (Budlender and Latsky 1990; Republic of South Africa 1994; 1995a; 1995b; 1996).

'The apartheid city' The phenomenon of the 'apartheid city' has been well documented elsewhere (Davies 1981; McCarthy and Smith 1984; Smith 1992; Robinson 1996; Swilling et al. 1991; Christopher 1994; Dewar et al. 1990). In this chapter it will be possible only to provide a brief overview.

With negligible exceptions, South African towns and cities follow a common pattern of development. Formal commercial and business sectors co-exist alongside formal, formerly exclusively white, residential areas. Land values are generally high and land use is strictly regulated by town planning regulations. By contrast, the formerly black areas, generally located some distance away from or on the outskirts of the formerly white areas, are characterized by inadequate and frequently non-existent public services and by extremely limited access to shops and places of employment. Land values are low and tenure arrangements uncertain; there is rapid growth in the construction of illegal structures and illegal land occupations are increasingly common. There is minimal, if any, land use regulation. The residents of these areas are forced to travel to white areas for all but their most basic needs. Because of the widespread poverty it is they who are least able to afford the extra travel costs imposed by their peripheral location within the urban system.

Contemporary patterns of living, working and shopping in South African cities stand as a constant and persistent reminder of the apartheid state's determination to prohibit permanent residence of blacks in urban areas. Overcoming the legacy of a government that refused to acknowledge the permanence of blacks in urban areas until 1986 and which accordingly refused to permit investment in those areas in which blacks were living remains one of the most significant challenges facing the Government of National Unity. Accordingly, investment in infrastructure, housing and support services forms a central element of the government's Reconstruction and Development Programme (RDP) (Republic of South Africa 1995a). A significant obstacle to this element of the RDP, however, is the inadequacy, inappropriateness and even absence of a legal framework governing access to land, land use, land development and the provision of basic urban services.

Urbanization   South Africa is a rapidly urbanizing country. Already it is estimated that between 48 and 65 per cent of all South Africans live in urban areas. By 2020 this figure is likely to have risen to 75 per cent (Republic of South Africa 1995a).

The question of urbanization, particularly of blacks, was an obsession of the pre-1994 South African state. Specifically the state was preoccupied with the restriction of black migration to and residence in towns and cities. Although there certainly were pre-apartheid examples of black urbanization (Mabin 1992) and although under apartheid the patterns of urban–rural migration were not unidirectional (Dewar et al. 1991), the imposition of official apartheid in 1948 nevertheless clearly resulted, first, in increased economic pressure on rural blacks to move to the cities and, second, in legislative restrictions on their capacity to do so.

South African towns and cities cannot be seen in isolation from the history of state intervention in the process of urbanization, particularly the restriction of black urbanization.[3] Current patterns of access to land and to the range of economic, social, health and recreational benefits of urban life are all directly shaped by this history.

Since permanent black residence in the urban areas was so vigorously discouraged, minimal housing was provided for blacks and public facilities and services were all geared towards meeting the needs of white city residents. This manifests itself today in a backlog in housing and infrastructure provision in formerly black urban South Africa[4] which is proving to be one of the Government of National Unity's greatest headaches. The absence of a formal or adequate programme for the delivery of urban land or housing to blacks resulted in widespread land invasions and rapidly growing informal settlements.

Following the state's formal rejection of legislative means for restricting black urbanization in 1986, the processes of urbanization took on a number of new characteristics. Most of these remain under-researched and their origins uncertain (Mabin 1992). The post-1986 urbanization process has, however, been characterized by the rapid growth of informal and illegal settlements. Ironically, the bulk of this increased and ongoing growth of illegal settlements is concentrated on land that is close to existing black townships,[5] that is, on the urban periphery and spatially removed from the established and predominantly white suburbs. The essential structure of the apartheid city is, thus, effectively replicating itself despite the time elapsed since the scrapping of the legislation. The urban poor continue to be located on the fringes of urban areas in shanty ghettos without access to essential services, facilities and opportunities. This suggests that other factors might determine locational choices exercised by the urban poor.

Local government transition The Government of National Unity began its period of transitional rule in May 1994 under the leadership of President Nelson Mandela. Local government transition has, however, taken somewhat longer, with local elections taking place only in October 1995 in most of the country.[6]

The apartheid era created a plethora of bodies exercising the various functions of local government. The formerly white areas were mainly governed by town or city councils operating within tightly circumscribed legislative mandates from central government. Only since 1982 has there been provision for black local authorities. These authorities have been widely regarded, not least by their constituents, as illegitimate and have been crippled by years of opposition to their authority, including boycotts of their service charges and rates. Coloured and Indian areas had either municipalities or Management Boards, which suffered from similar legitimacy and capacity problems. Within any one functional urban area there were likely to be a range of such bodies, each of which owed its existence to a different statutory basis and each of which ostensibly exercised a range of similar powers and functions but with vastly different resources available to it.

By 1994 local government, especially in black, coloured and Indian areas, was in a chaotic state. The Government of National Unity responded with the Local Government Transition Act (no. 209 of 1993), a statutory framework to guide the process of local government transition. The Act provides for the establishment of transitional local authorities created through amalgamation of the previously racially determined bodies into new authorities with new areas of jurisdiction. The complex processes of amalgamating different administrations, as well as providing for metropolitan government in the metropolitan areas, have created widespread short-term uncertainty and inefficiency, with detrimental effects on reconstruction and development projects.

South African Urban Legislation

The apartheid policies of the National Party's rule from 1948 until 1994[7] were predicated on a belief in racial superiority and domination which is now notorious. The direct and fundamental impact of these policies on the nature, rate and form of urbanization and urban development in South Africa is well known and well documented.[8] This section will outline the specific legal instruments used by the apartheid state to create the patterns of land use and occupation that are now so extraordinarily difficult to change. It will also mention recent, post-apartheid, legislation aimed at redressing these patterns.

The apartheid state was determined to preserve at least a veneer of legality for its actions. Where law proved insufficient to achieve state goals, the physical removal of people and destruction of their shelter became a frequently used permutation of state policy (Posel 1991). Despite this tendency the state considered the 'rule of law' to be of great ideological importance and accordingly persisted in implementing apartheid through an intricate and complex web of rules and regulations, administered by a burgeoning bureaucracy.[9] Until the 1980s the implementation of apartheid policies was characterized not so much by the 'random terror of the death squad, but by the routine and systematic processes of courts and bureaucrats' (Chanock 1989: 265). This resulted in a proliferation of complex, often internally contradictory, laws and regulations attempting to control different aspects of the urban system. Apartheid legislation was characterized by the wide discretionary powers placed in the hands of state officials, thereby reducing the chances of judicial challenge to state action.

It is not possible to examine the South African urban context without locating it squarely within a national context of land segregation. The 1913 Land Act (no. 27 of 1913) saw the first formal division of the national territory along racial lines. With this Act the right of blacks to live or work in both the urban areas and the commercial farmland became extremely precarious. Towns and cities were considered the exclusive domain of whites, with specific areas within them reserved for 'coloureds' and Indians. For economic reasons – primarily the need for an accessible and cheap labour force – limited black urban residence was permitted but subject to harsh controls (Savage 1986; Corder 1984; Dean 1984). Inevitably the state's preoccupation with racial separation created widespread legislative duplication as it strove to provide distinct frameworks for the various race zones.

Key elements of post-1910 urban legislation

The 1913 Land Act This statute provided the foundation for almost eighty years of segregation and deprivation. Essentially it divided the country into two broad categories of land: areas where blacks could own land and areas where they could not enjoy any form of right in land (Bundy 1990). This Act was the source of the now oft-quoted statistic of 13 per cent of the population owning 87 per cent of the land. The land where blacks were entitled to hold land rights represented an initial 8 per cent of the national territory and was later increased to 13 per cent by subsequent legislation (Development Trust and Land Act, no. 18 of 1936). The 1913 Act effectively demolished all but the most precarious rights held by blacks in land outside of the 'reserves' set aside for black occupation. These reserves were inadequate to provide for the numbers of people they contained and were located in remote rural areas far from urban employment centres. The inevitable consequences of this Act were thus over-crowding and extreme poverty in the reserves and an increased urbanization rate.

No account of urban law and South African would be complete without a reference to the Land Act. It was the linchpin on which so many of the subsequent and well-documented horrors of apartheid turned.[10] In later years it provided the basis for the establishment of the 'bantustans', the 'national states' contrived by the South African state to provide a physical and constitutional home for black South Africans. This strategy simultaneously stripped blacks of their citizenship and their rights to live permanently in the urban areas. Only in 1978 did the state indicate a willingness to contemplate permanent urban residence by blacks and, in limited circumstances,[11] to permit blacks to hold ninety-nine-year leaseholds on urban land.[12]

The pass laws and influx control   Once the racial boundaries of national space were established by the 1913 Land Act it became necessary for the state to devise ways of ensuring compliance. A central element of this strategy was the notion of 'influx control', of controlling the influx of blacks into urban areas. The 'battery of pass laws and influx control regulations'[13] drawn up by the state were not only used to regulate the flow of blacks into the urban areas; they were also integral to its overall approach to policing and repression of blacks (Savage 1986: 85, 181). It is conservatively estimated that between 1916 and 1984 almost 18 million people were affected either by arrests or prosecutions made under this legislation (Savage 1986).

Influx control took various forms, especially after the establishment of 'independent' bantustans, beginning in the mid-1970s. The access to and presence in urban areas of blacks was prohibited if they did not possess a permit or 'pass'. Economic pressure from business interests together with the ongoing defiance by illegal urban residents of places such as Crossroads in Cape Town finally brought about the end of formal influx control in 1986.[14] Despite the formal end to influx control, the legacy of inadequate land, infrastructure and housing provided for blacks in urban areas – because of the official denial of the legitimacy or lawfulness of their physical presence in the towns and cities – continues to represent an urgent political and social problem.

The Group Areas Act[15] Originating in nineteenth-century health and sanitation legislation, the Group Areas Act was the chief mechanism for dividing individual urban areas into race zones. It applied to all parts of South Africa in which Africans were prohibited from owning or occupying land (Robertson 1990). The Act divided urban areas into zones for the exclusive occupation of specific groups and established the classification criteria for belonging to such a group.

Despite the formidable discretionary powers vested in the authorities by this legislation and the vigour with which they enforced it, defiance became widespread, peaking in the 1980s. While the state refused to allow for the growth in the urban black population, so the conditions of over-crowding in the townships became utterly intolerable. Black workers in certain areas began to leave the townships and move into various white areas such as Hillbrow in Johannesburg. The state's inability to stem such flows meant that the Act was in a number of areas effectively dead well before its official repeal in 1991.[16]

Prevention of Illegal Squatting Act[17] Despite the barrage of legislation prohibiting and restricting black occupation and ownership of land, further laws were necessary to deal with their transgressors. The Prevention of Illegal Squatting Act was widely used by the apartheid state, and indeed remains on the statute books today, to remove people from land that they were occupying illegally. Together with the Trespass Act (no. 6 of 1959) and Slums Act (no. 76 of 1979 and its predecessors), two other ostensibly race-neutral statutes, it greatly enhanced the state's powers to remove people forcibly from illegally occupied land. In a country where 87 per cent of the land was reserved for 13 per cent of the population, such legislation clearly had a significant impact.

Planning legislation Alongside and often supplementing the race zones into which the country was divided were numerous town and regional planning statutes. With the exception of the Physical Planning Act, these enactments were drawn up by the four provincial governments of white South Africa.[18] The various bantustans also promulgated their own planning legislation. The national Physical Planning Act of 1967[19] authorized metropolitan guide plans for physical development which reinforced and strengthened the urban race zones established under the more overtly racist legislation. This legislation also played a key role in promoting the state's doomed policy of industrial decentralization, an attempt to reinforce the restrictions on black urbanization. The Act also did not apply at all in non-urban black areas.

At a provincial level the various ordinances each provided for 'town-planning' or 'zoning' schemes which enabled the provincial administration and certain local authorities to zone the land within their areas of juris-diction, i.e. the primarily white race zones, in terms of desired land uses. These ordinances remain in force today. Once a piece of land was zoned for a particular use, a number of specific use and development rights then adhered to it. These rights cannot be removed without the payment of compensation by the local authority. Within the residential zones the schemes stipulate high standards and strict controls. These schemes have effectively entrenched a pattern of highly lucrative use and development rights (predominantly for commercial or industrial use), almost all of which are held by white landowners. In addition they entrench exclusive standards for residential areas which make entry to such areas by lower-income people extremely difficult and unlikely. Given the complexity of such schemes, moreover, local authorities are required to allocate substantial financial and human resources to their management and enforcement. Since the primary product of these schemes are rights with a compen-satable value, the local authorities cannot afford to ignore their existence. Accordingly, the resources which would be optimally allocated for the relief of previously unmanaged black areas are instead used to preserve the assets and environmental quality of white areas.

In theory, land use planning in black race zones was to be executed in terms of regulations issued under the Black Administration Act (no. 38 of 1927) and the Black Communities Development Act (no. 4 of 1984 and its predecessors). In practice, however, the professional capacity, the political will or a conducive political climate for the implementation of land use planning in black race zones simply did not exist.

Post-apartheid legislation The post-apartheid Government of National Unity faces an extraordinarily complex task in unravelling the legislative web spun around the cities by decades of segregatory and discriminatory legislation. Simply removing formal racial barriers to land ownership and occupation is a relatively straightforward process when compared with that of using the law to influence positively the complex patterns and dynamics of urban development in rapidly growing towns and cities. The law has created an inequitable, inefficient and hostile urban environment. To date, two significant legislative developments have been the promul-gation of the Restitution of Land Rights Act (no. 22 of 1994) and the Development Facilitation Act (no. 57 of 1995). These are discussed below.

Restitution of Land Rights Act The Restitution of Land Rights Act, which fulfils a mandate established in the Interim Constitution,[20] provides for the restitution of land rights to those people, or their descendants, who lost such rights as the result of racially motivated state action between 1913 and 1994. The scale of the dispossession that took place and the large numbers of households affected make it extremely difficult for the state to restore to each and every claimant full compensation for their, or their antecedents', losses. In attempting to redress one of the most serious and politically sensitive consequences of apartheid, the Act nevertheless plays an important symbolic role.

Handling restitution claims in urban areas is generally more complex than in rural areas. Unlike the situation in rural areas, claims in urban areas are likely to arise from the dispossession of individuals or households who would not necessarily have occupied their premises for a long period of time. Testing the validity of a claim thus becomes difficult, particularly where there is more than one claimant for a single property and the existing records are either incomplete or unavailable, as is frequently the case. South African cities have grown and changed rapidly, particularly over the last fifty years. In addition, state officials hastily strove to remove physical traces of removals, especially in the more visible urban areas. These two factors have resulted in areas subject to urban restitution claims bearing little physical resemblance to their pre-removals state. The actual restitution of the land itself thus becomes very difficult. Where actual restitution is not possible a claimant is entitled to monetary compensation or a comparable land right in another piece of land provided by the state.

This Act cannot fully redress the injustices of apartheid land dispossessions. It will nevertheless have a significant impact on a significant number of households. In urban areas the processes of restitution have great potential to contribute to the restructuring and integration of towns and cities.

Development Facilitation Act   A priority of the Government of National Unity is the development of and investment in the bantustans and townships of black South Africa. Recognizing the current legislative morass to be a major obstacle to the achievement of this goal, the government proposed transitional 'development facilitation' legislation which was promulgated in late 1995. The Development Facilitation Act is premised on an acknowledgement that the process of disentangling existing urban legislation and then of formulating new legislative frameworks for urban development requires significantly more time and resources than are currently or immediately available. Accordingly it was decided to draft the Act as a transitional and parallel statute. This Act is to remain in force until such time as a comprehensive system of planning and land development legislation has been drawn up by the various authorities vested with such responsibilities. The Act does not repeal the existing body of legislation relating to urban land development. Rather it runs parallel, providing on the one hand an alternative legislative route for certain development projects and, on the other, circumscribing the decisions taken by all public authorities through the establishment of substantive planning principles and the authorization of locally specific land development objectives.

This Act has a number of aims. Since such a short period of time has elapsed since its promulgation it is not possible to discuss any real consequences of this legislation. Its potential significance does, however, warrant a brief description of its contents.

The Act aims first to provide for swifter consideration of development applications, especially in the bantustans and townships. The first essential element of the Act for expediting consideration of development proposals is the establishment of appointed tribunals with the specific responsibility for considering all development applications opting not to use the existing legal procedures contained in the pre-1994 town planning or land development legislation and which use instead the 'fast track' mechanisms contained in the Act. These tribunals have wide powers: to subpoena witnesses and to over-ride any existing legislative impediment to the proposed development. In order to expedite the process of delivering housing, especially to the poor, the Act also provides a more streamlined process for the surveying, conveyancing and registration of land.

As a safeguard against such wide powers, the Act also provides a set of legislative principles with which all land development decisions have to be consistent, regardless of whether they are taken under the Act or under any other legislation. The principles cover an extremely wide range of planning and development issues such as the promotion of integrated development, the optimization of existing resources, promotion of mixed-use developments, discouragement of sprawl, correction of historical distortions in settlement patterns, the promotion of sustainable development and maximization of public participation in decision-making. In order to ensure that decision-making does not occur in a policy vacuum, Chapter 4 of the Act requires local authorities[21] to draw up 'land development objectives'. These objectives relate to a number of critically important urban issues such as access to services, integration of towns and cities, transportation and land use planning and co-ordination of land and economic development strategies, together with quantitative targets, particularly for housing construction. These objectives allow many existing plans and policies to be over-ridden. All authorities considering land development applications must ensure that any decision is consistent with the relevant objectives.

The long-term significance of the Act lies in its provision for the establishment of a Development and Planning Commission. This Commission has wide powers to advise the government on the formulation of new legislation and policy for urban development and planning, land surveying and land tenure, engineering infrastructure and services as well as matters relating to land development financing and taxation. Many of the ideas already established in the Act will provide some indication to the Commission of possible new approaches to South African urban law. The Commission does, however, have a relatively clean slate. The urban future of South Africa, in no small measure, rests with this Commission and its capacity to provide appropriate and effective guidance.

Critical Legal Questions

The legislative task facing the Development and Planning Commission is vast. In this section two issues are highlighted as central to the formulation of new and appropriate approaches to urban law. Although by no means exhaustive, they do represent critical challenges that have to be tackled before meaningful progress can be made in devising an effective and appropriate role and purpose for urban law in South Africa.

Constitutional protection of private property   At the root of South Africa's urban question lies the politically prickly issue of property rights. As indicated above, the urban legal history of South Africa has created a very specific land market. As long as it remains in its current form, real urban integration and restructuring will be almost impossible. Although gradual change in urban land markets is discernible, and in some areas even rapid and marked, the essential patterns of urban land use, occupation and ownership remain.

Important economic arguments have to be resolved before intervention in the operation of a market as important as that in urban land will be possible. There can nevertheless be no effective change in patterns of urban development until such intervention is made. Intervention of such a nature will inevitably have an impact on the land rights of current urban landowners.

The relatively recent Appellate Division case of the Diepsloot Residents and Landowners Association v Administrator, Transvaal[22] vividly revealed the conflicts that can arise between the public interest of housing the poor and homeless on relatively well-located land and the legally protected rights of landowners. In that case the provincial administration's attempt to establish a low-income settlement alongside an established suburb was challenged by the suburban residents on the grounds that such a settlement would detract from various of their common-law rights to use and enjoy their properties. The Appellate Division found in favour of the provincial administration. This, however, was prior to the constitutional protection of property rights entrenched in the Interim Constitution.[23] Similar scenarios are inevitable in the future. In such an event the extent and nature of the new protection afforded to landowners will be of central

importance to the effectiveness and viability of housing strategies as well
as programmes for urban integration.

Another example highlighting the relationship between property rights
and urban development is the case of the use and development rights[24]
already protected under the inherited provincial planning ordinances and
primarily attached to land in the formerly white areas. These rights play
a critical role in the commercial urban land market. They also entrench an
extremely inequitable urban form, one which was envisaged by the authors
of municipal town planning schemes over forty years ago and in which
all lucrative use and development rights are concentrated in the hands of
white landowners, and in proximity to white residential areas. Under the
inherited ordinances,[25] compensation is already payable for the taking of
any of these rights by a planning authority. Important questions need to
be answered as to the impact of a new property clause on these rights.

It is most unlikely that the constitutional authors intended to hamper
the integration and redevelopment of towns and cities. Their protection of
property rights nevertheless creates an additional obstacle for the authorities
attempting to alter current patterns of land development. For reasons of
space and because the Interim Constitution will be replaced by a final
constitution currently being drafted, it will not be useful to explore here
the precise wording of the South African property clause. It is, however,
critical that in the process of drafting a new constitution the nature and
extent of formal property protection is compatible with and indeed
complementary to the challenges facing urban policy-makers and legislators.
Regardless of the content of such a future clause, the task of giving
content to the protection of property rights in such a way as to enable
progressive planning legislation – a task which will in all likelihood fall to
the judiciary – will be of central importance to South Africa's urban future.

Land use regulation   As stated earlier, there is minimal effective land
use regulation in formerly black areas of the country. Although by no
means the sole cause, this has certainly contributed to the poor environmental quality of such areas. First, the resources and staff necessary for
the implementation of a land use planning system in these areas were
never made available. Second, major land development other than that by
the state was either discouraged or prohibited in such areas. Consequently
there was very little development to regulate. The state of the boundary
surveying and land registries in such areas was also inevitably so poor that
investment would in any event have been extremely unlikely. With the
recent political changes, many of these obstacles to development fall away.
Now sensitive and appropriate development and investment in the townships are actively encouraged and promoted, forming a cornerstone of
the national Reconstruction and Development Programme (Republic of
South Africa 1995a).

The important legal questions here relate to the conceptual bases on which to build an urban land use planning and regulation system. Development and investment are desired and necessary, particularly in the urban periphery. A planning system is thus required that not only promotes development in these areas but also ensures that this development does not further detract from an already degraded, insecure and hostile environment. This raises critical questions. First there is the need to determine what it is that ought to qualify for legislative protection in the process of urban development. Second, and following from this, an appropriate approach to the involvement of the public in the formulation of policy and decisions has to be established. Finally, there must be a determination of how, and to what extent, commercially valuable use and development rights will be identified, described, protected and allocated. In addition, the planning needs of most formerly black race zones are very different from those in the formerly white areas. A new planning system thus has to satisfy both these sets of needs without simply replicating the apartheid model of differentiated standards of urban environmental control. And, as pointed out above, the unconscionable situation in which the current legal realities of development regulation in white areas result in their receiving the bulk of available planning resources has to change.

Further legal questions   The successful handling of urban land claims under the Restitution of Land Rights Act presents a critical challenge to urban authorities. Particularly important will be the claims relating to the well-publicized forced removals such as those in District Six in Cape Town, Cato Manor in Durban and Pageview in Johannesburg.

A large number of municipal by-laws exist in formerly white residential areas, many of which effectively act as entry barriers to those areas by the poor. They also frequently reinforce the inefficient patterns of land-extensive sprawl in those areas. These by-laws are not obvious products of apartheid. They do, however, represent a substantial obstacle to the effective integration and restructuring of urban South Africa.

The proliferation and rapid growth of informal and illegal settlements requires urgent attention. The Development Facilitation Act does include provisions for the regularization of such tenure forms but they remain as yet untested.

Conclusion

South Africa is emerging from an unusual urban history, one in which law has played an extensive role. In the urban sphere, despite popular opposition, the law succeeded in establishing a physical pattern of urban growth and development that reflected the racist ideology of the apartheid state. Defiance was always present, albeit with varying intensity over time, but did not substantially challenge the fundamental map of urban rights and privileges. The current processes of political transition represent an opportunity to redefine the appropriate role of law in urban processes. At both conceptual and practical levels, the role and purpose of law in a rapidly growing, inequitable and inefficient urban context have to be identified. In South Africa, there is little doubt as to the damaging impact of urban law on generations of black South Africans. The state used the law deliberately and vigorously to achieve its racist and exploitative ideological goals.

In the current transition the law has frequently seemed to operate more as a deterrent to change than as an ally. The Government of National Unity nevertheless retains a strong commitment to developing and transforming the country's legal system in order to redress the injustices of the past and to establish a secure and prosperous future for all South Africans. In the urban context this can be seen in the importance accorded to the Development Facilitation Act, the Restitution of Land Rights Act and, obviously, the Interim Constitution. The law has not been forsaken as a means of meeting the expectations of a long-suffering public nor of realizing the political objectives of a new government. The widespread acknowledgement that the current inherited legal frameworks for urban development have to be replaced means that there is little resistance to the need for change. The important questions now revolve around how and with what these frameworks are to be replaced. Although urban law was a key weapon in apartheid's legislative arsenal, it proved to be insufficient to counter the overwhelming social, economic and political forces emanating from the inherently contradictory nature of the grand apartheid plan itself, from internal opposition and from international pressure. It has nevertheless stamped on the urban landscape patterns of development, land use and land occupation that must be changed. It is in this process of change that the determination of an appropriate and effective conceptual and practical basis for urban planning and land management law will be critically important.

Notes

1. The term 'race zone' comes from Budlender and Latsky (1990) on *rural* South Africa.

2. The term 'apartheid' was coined by the National Party (NP) prior to their election victory in 1948. It is an Afrikaans word meaning, literally, 'separate-ness'. Subsequent NP governments contrived other names for this policy, such as 'separate development'. Despite semantic changes the core of the policy remained the same and the term apartheid will be used throughout this chapter. The term was used to describe a policy of racial segregation which prohibited marriage between races, denied blacks the franchise, and allocated different racial groups separate areas in which to live, separate educational and health facilities, and access to different recreational areas and venues.

3. The legislative instruments used to enforce state urbanization strategies will be examined later in this chapter.

4. Black urban South Africa in this context means 'townships' – residential areas set aside for the exclusive residence of blacks.

5. This does not imply that there are not interesting and, unsurprisingly, well-publicized examples of informal settlements established in or near white areas. These do, however, remain the exception. For further discussion of this phenomenon, see Mabin (1992).

6. As a result of electoral boundary disputes, local elections in some areas were postponed to early 1996.

7. Towards the end of the regime's rule, the implementation of apartheid in its traditional form was less consistent and less severe. This period marked the move towards negotiation between the National Party (NP) and the outlawed African National Congress (ANC), leading to the unbanning of the ANC and other organizations and to the release of Nelson Mandela in early 1990 and culminating in the first democratic elections and the assumption of power in 1994 by the ANC-dominated Government of National Unity.

8. See, for example, Western (1981); Mabin (1991; 1992); Robinson (1996); and Budlender (1990).

9. For further information, see Chanock (1989) and Corder (1988).

10. For more information on land dispossession, forced removals and relocations, see Platzky and Walker (1985).

11. Only where the person concerned had qualified in terms of section 10 of the Blacks (Urban Areas) Consolidation Act (no. 25 of 1945).

12. Under the Blacks (Urban Areas) Amendment Act (no. 97 of 1978).

13. Key legislation in this regard was the Blacks (Urban Areas) Consolidation Act (no. 25 of 1945) and its main predecessor the Natives (Urban Areas) Act (no. 21 of 1923).

14. Abolition of Influx Control Act (no. 68 of 1986).

15. Act no. 36 of 1966, the successor to Act no. 41 of 1950.

16. Abolition of Racially Based Land Measures Act (no. 108 of 1991).

17. Act no. 52 of 1951.

18. Land Use Planning Ordinance (Ordinance 15 of 1985) (Cape); Town-Planning and Townships Ordinance (Ordinance 15 of 1986) (Transvaal); Townships Ordinance (Ordinance 9 of 1969) (Orange Free State); and Town Planning Ordinance (Ordinance 27 of 1949) (Natal).

19. This Act was repealed and replaced in 1991 by the Physical Planning Act (no. 125 of 1991).

20. See the Republic of South Africa Constitution Act (no. 200 of 1994), section 121.

21. Or, where the local authority is either unable or unwilling, the provincial authority.

22. 1994 (3) SA 336 (A).

23. The Interim Constitution introduced to South Africa its first constitutionally protected human rights, including a right to private property – see section 28 of the Republic of South Africa Constitution Act (no. 200 of 1993), to be replaced by section 25 of the Final Constitution agreed to by the Constitutional Assembly on 8 May 1996.

24. See the Appellate Division case of Sandton Town Council v Erf 89 Sandown Extension 2 (Pty) Ltd 1988 (3) SA 122 (A) for an example of the South African courts' approach to the protection of these use and development rights.

25. See note 18.

References

Budlender, G. (1990) 'Urban land issues in the 1980s: the view from Weiler's Farm', in C. Murray and C. O'Regan (eds), *No Place to Rest: Forced Removals and the Law in South Africa*, Oxford University Press, Cape Town, 66–85.

Budlender, G. and J. Latsky (1990) 'Unravelling rights to land and to agricultural activity in rural race zones', *South African Journal on Human Rights*, Vol. 6, 155–77.

Bundy, C. (1990) 'Land, law and power: forced removals in historic context', in C. Murray and C. O'Regan (eds), *No Place to Rest: Forced Removals and the Law in South Africa*, Oxford University Press, Cape Town, 3–12.

Chanock, M. (1989) 'Writing South African legal history: a prospectus', *Journal of African History*, Vol. 30, no. 2, 265–88.

Christopher, A. J. (1994) *The Atlas of Apartheid*, Routledge, London.

Corder, H. (1984) 'The rights and conditions of entry into and residence in urban areas by Africans', *Acta Juridica 1984*, 45–63.

— (ed.) (1988) *Essays on Law and Social Practice in South Africa*, Juta, Cape Town.

Davies, R. J. (1981) 'The spatial formation of the South African city', *GeoJournal* Supplementary Issue 2, 59–72.

Dean W. H. B. (1984) 'The legal regime governing urban Africans in South Africa: an administrative-law perspective', *Acta Juridica 1984*, 105–39.

Dewar, D., T. Rosmarin and V. Watson (1991) *Movement Patterns of the African Population in Cape Town: Some Implications*, Working Paper no. 44, Urban Problems Research Unit, University of Cape Town, Cape Town.

Dewar, D., V. Watson, A. Bassios and N. Dewar (1990) *The Structure and Form of Metropolitan Cape Town: Its Origins, Influences and Performances*, Working Paper no. 42, Urban Problems Research Unit, University of Cape Town, Cape Town.

McCarthy, J. and D. M. Smith (1984) *South African City: Theory in Analysis and Planning*, Juta, Cape Town.

Mabin, A. (1991) 'Origins of segregatory urban planning in South Africa, c 1900–1940', *Planning History*, Vol. 13, no. 3, 8–16.

— (1992) 'Dispossession, exploitation and struggle: an historical overview of South African urbanisation', in D. M. Smith (ed.), *The Apartheid City and Beyond: Urbanization and Social Change in South Africa*, Routledge, London, 13–24.

Platzky, L. and C. Walker (1985) *The Surplus People: Forced Removals in South Africa*, Ravan Press, Johannesburg.

Posel, D. (1991) 'Curbing African urbanization in the 1950s and 1960s', in M. Swilling, R. Humphries and K. Shubane (eds), *Apartheid City in Transition*, Oxford University Press, Cape Town, 19–32.

Republic of South Africa (1994) *White Paper – Reconstruction and Development: Government's Strategy for Fundamental Transformation*, Government Printer, Pretoria.

— (1995a) *Remaking South Africa's Cities and Towns – The Urban Development Strategy (Discussion Document)*, Government Printer, Pretoria.

— (1995b) *White Paper – A New Housing Policy and Strategy for South Africa*, Government Printer, Pretoria.

— (1996) *White Paper – Our Land*, Government Printer, Pretoria.

Robertson, M. (1990) 'Dividing the land: an introduction to apartheid land law', in C. Murray and C. O'Regan (eds), *No Place to Rest: Forced Removals and the Law in South Africa*, Oxford University Press, Cape Town, 122–36.

Robinson, J. (1996) *The Power of Apartheid: State, Power and Space in South African Cities*, Butterworth-Heinemann, Oxford.

Savage, M. (1986) 'The imposition of pass laws on the African population in South Africa 1916–1984', *African Affairs*, Vol. 85, no. 339, 181–205.

Smith, D. M. (ed.) (1992) *The Apartheid City and Beyond: Urbanization and Social Change in South Africa*, Routledge, London.

Swilling, M., R. Humphries and K. Shubane (eds) (1991) *Apartheid City in Transition*, Oxford University Press, Cape Town.

Western, J. (1981) *Outcast Cape Town*, Allen and Unwin, London.

PART III

Conclusions and Future Trends

CHAPTER 13

Law and Urban Change in Developing Countries: Trends and Issues

Alain Durand-Lasserve

I was struck, on reading the contributions to this book, both by the extraordinary diversity of the circumstances that we group together under the heading of the 'illegal city', and by the convergence that is taking place in the process of illegal urban development and the ways in which different social actors respond to this process. Until the middle of the 1980s, a unitarist approach to urban management prevailed, which assumed a unified legal system and formal land and property market practices and norms to which all 'informal' deviations would eventually have to be reconciled. By contrast, recent studies have argued that a different approach to managing the city, in all its diversity, has been emerging. Its path will not be a smooth one. The new approach presupposes state recognition of the legitimacy of 'informal' systems of property rights and social practices occurring beyond the realm of the 'rule of law', but these are associated with social groups who have until now been excluded from the formal decision-making process.

These new studies challenge our understanding of the role of the state and of the part that law plays in urban management and in the regulation of both formal and informal property markets. The observations in the following pages are based mainly on the case studies presented in this book, but I also refer, as necessary, to other recent research on the 'illegal city'.

The Illegal City: Trends and Variations

General trends In the past decade, urban policy-making in developing countries has been strongly influenced by neo-liberal economic models and a renewed emphasis on the market. The structural adjustment programmes adopted in many countries have often been accompanied by 'modernization' of the legal and institutional framework. Large urban development projects are no longer in favour and land and property markets are becoming increasingly polarized. The formal market is growing and becoming more internally differentiated. At the same time, illegal forms of housing production are also becoming more diverse and increasingly commercialized (Baross and van der Linden 1990; INTERURBA/ AITEC 1995). It is this that I wish to explore in greater depth.

'Illegal' settlements have not grown in the same way or to the same extent in different countries or even within the same country, but we estimate that they account for between 20 and 80 per cent of the growth in the urban area and between 15 and 70 per cent of the urban population in developing countries (35 per cent in Peruvian cities, 50 per cent in Nairobi or the three main Turkish cities, for example). In some countries (such as Thailand, Korea, Malaysia and Chile), rapid economic growth and the introduction of housing finance systems have permitted private sector development of housing for middle- and lower middle-income groups. Rising property prices have nevertheless caused other problems in these countries, pushing illegal settlement ever further from the city centre and making it even more difficult for the poorest households to solve their housing problems. Other countries, such as Indonesia and Mexico, have managed to integrate most illegal settlements into the city by introducing tenure legalization and upgrading programmes. Some, like India, Egypt and Jordan, are struggling to achieve similar results. These (limited) success stories, however, are still the exceptions to the rule; in the majority of large cities in developing countries, the share of the population living in illegal settlements remains largely unchanged, or may even be increasing (see Durand-Lasserve and Clerc 1996).

As the case studies in this book have emphasized, the term 'illegal settlement' is used to describe a great variety of different situations, but these can be grouped into two broad categories.

The first of these is illegal subdivision, which refers to settlements established on land in either private or public ownership that has been subdivided to produce individual plots for sale or rent. These subdivisions are illegal for a variety of reasons. The vendor may not have legal title to the property in the first place, or they may fail to obtain the necessary permits or to respect planning regulations concerning for example the provision of urban services. Usually, more than one of these conditions will apply, increasing the difficulties facing city governments trying to install services and legalize tenure in such areas.

The second category is land invasion, when land is occupied for housing purposes without the permission of the owner. This produces 'squatter settlements' – a term often applied, incorrectly, to all forms of illegal settlement. The owner whose land is invaded may be a private individual or, more often, a public body. Government attitudes to land invasion vary both between and within cities, and over time. The degree of official tolerance displayed determines the level of insecurity in a land invasion.

The residents of illegal settlements always face similar problems. They lack security of tenure; the right to transfer, sell or mortgage their property may be refused or challenged; and they are likely to be denied full access to infrastructure and services.

Although a great deal has been written about the illegal city, we still do not understand it very well. We know quite a lot about its urban landscape, its demographic importance and the characteristics of its population, but still find it difficult to understand how it develops or how it grows. It is as if reality has changed faster than the intellectual models we use to analyse and explain it.

Regional variations There are some important regional variations on the pattern described above, which I shall now discuss briefly with reference to the chapters in this book and to other research (Payne 1997; UMP 1994; UMP and Ministère des Affaires Étrangères 1993; Von Einsiedel 1995). Given the scant attention it receives in the English-language literature, I shall pay particular attention to sub-Saharan Africa.

There is considerable similarity between illegal settlements in Asian and Latin American cities as regards the poverty of their inhabitants, the services to which they have access and the extent to which their illegality and morphology set them apart from the 'formal city'. Market mechanisms prevail in the provision of low-income housing in Latin America and even more so in Asia. The dominance of market mechanisms is favoured by the comparative homogeneity of land tenure systems and the existence of a unified legal system, as state law prevails over alternative (for example, customary) legal systems. There is also an emphasis on the role of individual property developers: throughout these regions, the market tends to reduce cultural variation and differences in social practices concerning land use and property systems. This favours the emergence of standard management procedures and of similar institutions, social actors and legal norms.

The story is very different in African cities. A much higher proportion of the urban population lives in illegal settlements lacking infrastructure and the most basic urban services; but the contrast with Asia and Latin America is not only a question of quantitative differences. There are also differences in kind, given the heterogeneity of African land tenure systems and their relationship to state law. This is what makes the African case so distinctive. Although it is true that in most of the Arab states (Morocco, Jordan, Egypt and the Gulf states, for example) and to some extent in parts of Asia (Indonesia in particular), we can also observe vestiges of legal systems pre-dating modern state law, these residual alternatives have quite clearly been supplanted by the dominant legal system.

In sub-Saharan Africa, however, 'customary law' continues to have a major role to play in urban land management, in spite of all the changes it has undergone during the colonial period and since independence. It gives usufruct rights to agricultural land collectively to a particular group (an extended family network or the people who cleared the land). Such rights cannot, in theory, be sold. Although they were to some extent recognized by the colonizing powers, they have generally been ignored by post-independence governments – in vain. The recent history of African cities shows that no housing policy can afford to neglect the issue of customary tenure (Le Roy 1995; Mabogunje 1992; Le Bris et al. 1991). Faced with the enormous demand for land, and the lack of practical alternatives, people holding customary land rights have responded to the lack of state recognition of their rights by improvising procedures for subdivision and the transfer of usufruct. In doing so, they have made use of an imaginative combination of customary, market and bureaucratic practices (Tribillon 1993; 1995).

Throughout sub-Saharan Africa, and in the francophone countries in particular, the customary system displays an astonishing capacity to resist market forces and government efforts to encroach on traditional land rights, including radical property law reforms. It successfully co-exists with the market, in a context in which the structure of demand, the institutional framework and the lack of appropriate finance systems all make it extremely difficult for formal property developers or government authorities to meet the low-income population's demand for land and housing.

Current trends and the limits of conventional policy responses We can make four general observations concerning convergent trends in illegal urban development as described in this book and the wider literature.

The first of these is the growing predominance of market mechanisms: the dominant trend of the past two decades (Baross and van der Linden 1990; Jones and Ward 1994; Payne 1988; 1997; Pienaar 1996). It can be observed in all the countries discussed in this book, and has displaced the processes giving the low-income population free or nearly free access to land which survived until the mid-1970s. Squatting is on the decline virtually everywhere, albeit to a different extent in different contexts. It is declining rapidly in countries in which the informal market absorbs the excess demand that is not met by the government or by the formal private sector, but it is still important in countries where the government opposes informal commercial practices, thus preventing them from releasing the pent-up demand for land.

The second conclusion is that conditions in illegal settlements have improved only where the government has been willing to intervene and where a certain level of economic development has been achieved. Recent studies[1] allow us to identify the following trends in this respect:

a) a general worsening of conditions in countries facing economic crisis, high rates of rural-urban migration, withdrawal of the state from urban land management, a crisis in the authority of the state, or government repression of informal land and housing development processes. The conjunction of two or more of these characteristics leads to a dramatic deterioration in living conditions in illegal settlements;

b) stabilization in countries which have reached a certain level of economic development and/or implemented policies regularizing or upgrading illegal settlements or encouraging the development of an informal low-income land market;

c) improvements in a limited number of countries enjoying political stability and high rates of economic growth permitting the establishment of housing finance systems for those on moderate incomes, and in which ways have been found to accommodate, on the one hand, state law and formal sector practices, and, on the other, informal legal systems and land development practices.

A third conclusion concerns the inability of the formal private sector to meet the demand for land and housing of the majority of urban residents. In the Philippines, for example, Asteya Santiago notes that, in 1993, 90 per cent of housing production by the formal sector was directed to only 15 per cent of the urban population. With few exceptions, recent research confirms this trend.

The fourth conclusion concerns the limitations of conventional policy responses. Their legitimacy and efficiency have recently been questioned (UNCHS 1993b; Farvacque and McAuslan 1992; ESCAP 1990; World Bank 1983). They require government intervention in the provision of land, housing, infrastructure and services, in housing finance systems and in urban planning, as the basis for a rational, unified form of urban management. Such policy responses express a particular technical logic (based on a belief in social actors making rational choices), an economic logic (based on the need to reduce costs) and a political logic (based on the notion that all social actors should obey the same rules of the game, as guaranteed by the authority of the state). They vary remarkably little from city to city or region to region (Durand-Lasserve and Clerc 1996; UNCHS 1992).

Prior to 1970, the emphasis was on the creation of public land management and housing agencies. These were to undertake housing and urban development projects with the support of the World Bank and the United Nations Development Programme. During the 1970s, a new approach emerged, emphasizing tenure legalization in informal settlements, 'site and service' schemes and settlement upgrading (USAID 1991; Payne 1988). More recently, the emphasis has been on urban management, improving institutional performance, decentralization, privatization, public–private partnerships and social policy 'safety nets' to ensure political stability.

This policy emphasis will probably continue for the foreseeable future. The chapters on Turkey and the Philippines in particular illustrate the evolution of these different policy approaches.

Recognizing policy limitations The remarkable similarity in problem definition and policy design and implementation from one country to another is the product, not of a shared policy *model*, but rather of a consensus between governments and international financial institutions on a common policy *objective*: promoting the development of the formal market. It is primarily this that has motivated legal reforms over the course of the past decade, minimizing direct state intervention, bringing informal housing production into the market, reducing subsidies on service provision so that user charges reflect actual costs, and promoting the emergence of private companies and public–private partnerships (Dowall 1995; Dowall and Clarke 1996; PADCO 1990; World Bank 1991; 1993). Where tenure regularization is emphasized, it is primarily because illegal tenure is believed to hinder the operation of market forces, and secondly as a means of maintaining social peace.

Official intervention has traditionally involved 'pilot projects' of limited duration in a limited number of settlements, seeking to demonstrate that a particular policy is appropriate and effective before it is adopted elsewhere. Such projects suffer from a number of limitations, and can rarely be reproduced on a broader scale (Doebele 1994; Skinner et al. 1987; Fondation pour le Progrès de l'Homme 1991). The Philippines provides a good illustration of the shortcomings of regularization and servicing policies. Only in India, and, until recently, in Peru, have such policies been seen as a national development priority, rather than mere 'sectoral' policies. Their implementation has lacked coherence and consistency; local governments have proved incapable of effective intervention; and the insistence on seeing land problems as a *rural* issue has distorted policy responses.

Such policies pay insufficient attention to the diversity of local circumstances. This reveals a lack of flexibility in the legal and institutional framework. Technical and legal norms are unrealistic; allocation procedures are overly complex and lack transparency; and the recognition of tenure rights runs into innumerable administrative barriers (UNCHS 1993a; UMP 1994; UMP et al. 1995; UMP and Ministère des Affaires Étrangères 1993). Questions about the role of law and its ability to lend coherence to national housing policies while recognizing diversity have come to occupy centre-stage in debate on policy responses to illegal settlement (Durand-Lasserve 1990).

The demise of the unitary approach to urban management For a long time, it was believed that new housing areas should be developed according to a particular technical and planning logic. This started with a plan or project, followed by the servicing of the land in question, construction, the allocation of the finished houses to future residents and finally the arrival of the new occupants. This was the model to be found, until recently, in operational manuals for housing and urban development projects, and it is still generally followed by formal private and public sector developers today.

This ideal model has, however, less and less to do with the reality of urban development in the world's poorer countries. The 'planning–servicing–construction–occupation' sequence is, in practice, turned upside down, as the production of urban land obeys a quite different logic (Baross and van der Linden 1990; Bolívar 1995; Connolly 1994).

In most cities, the control of urban growth by conventional planning norms and regulations is becoming less and less effective. A radical change of perspective is needed, one that allows for the servicing and improvement of areas that are already occupied. Studies reviewing policies for the regularization and servicing of illegal settlements suggest such a change is already under way (Durand-Lasserve and Clerc 1996; UNDP 1996; Van den Hoff and Steinberg 1992).

In general, more pragmatic approaches are being adopted towards illegal settlements. Less intensive programmes emphasizing infrastructure provision or improvement reach a larger number of people. Less rigid cost-recovery policies are being adopted, together with a more realistic approach to the question of standards, including legal standards (such that legal tenure is no longer a precondition for servicing). Local organizations capable of taking on part of the growing responsibility for the management of illegal settlements are emerging (Gilbert et al. 1996; Vanderschueren et al. 1996), and new responsibilities are being delegated to community associations, often supported by NGOs providing technical and strategic assistance (Abbott 1996; Fondation pour le Progrès de l'Homme 1991; UNCHS 1992).

These changes challenge the notion of the state as repository and guarantor of a unitary model of urban management, with a single, unified, legal system and a single model for the production of urban space. This notion of the state derived its legitimacy from a technocratic way of thinking based on 'universal' legal principles and colonial and subsequently modern international urban planning norms and practices. This model of the state makes it very difficult for the ways in which the low-income population gain access to urban land and housing to be recognized as legitimate; but it has been discredited by recent trends, as the state's ability to control urban development is everywhere being challenged by the 'spontaneous' process of illegal settlement. Nowadays, fewer and fewer national and city governments try to deny the existence of informal land markets. They are close to accepting the informal market as a legitimate means of satisfying the basic human need for shelter, even if they continue to oppose the development of particular 'sensitive' locations (Arandel and El Batran 1996; Azuela 1995; UNCHS 1994; Van den Hoff and Steinberg 1992).

Managing the Illegal City: Choices and Constraints

The illegal city is first and foremost the product of a form of society in which the logic of production and exchange is associated with unequal access to resources and wealth. It is also the result of levels of housing production and service provision that are clearly inadequate, the result either of a deliberate political strategy or simply of economic constraints preventing social actors and public authorities from keeping up with the needs of a rapidly growing urban population.

Policy responses to illegal settlement There are four main policy approaches to dealing with illegal settlements: legalization; re-blocking and densification; upgrading; and prevention (Durand-Lasserve and Clerc 1996; USAID 1991).

The first approach entails official tolerance of illegal settlement followed by periodic 'amnesty' regularizations. This very common policy has been applied in Turkey, Egypt and some parts of Brazil, for example. It is the easiest and, in the short term, the least expensive response. It has political advantages for the government in power and provides a certain degree of control over the illegal city (since legalization can be presented as a sanction imposed on people who have broken the law). It is often needed to smooth over past irregularities. Nevertheless, even where it is technically feasible and economically viable, this type of legalization does not solve the chief problem facing the residents of illegal settlements: obtaining access to infrastructure and services. This approach also fails to do anything about overly rigid and inappropriate legal and institutional frameworks. Instead of dealing with the root cause of the problem, the authorities try to skirt around it. This can lead to further difficulties, given the complexity of identifying and registering property rights in such areas. As the Turkish case study demonstrates, moreover, it can have a negative effect on the city as a whole if its distributional consequences are ignored: in the longer term, the social and urban planning costs of these 'amnesties' can be very high.

The second form of intervention seeks to promote settlement upgrading by establishing a more rational pattern of land use. This is often needed to ensure the viability of upgrading projects, particularly in central and inner city areas. Part of the population is relocated within the same area, thus releasing land for urban services and amenities and, where possible, for commercial activities. The land freed for other uses can be sold at market prices to purchasers from outside the settlement. The proceeds can then be used to cross-subsidize the installation of services (as well as the costs incurred in redesigning the settlement).

The third form of intervention provides access to infrastructure and services. The limited achievements of many regularization and servicing projects come from their being too ambitious in the first place. Over-ambitious projects are generally a product of three mistaken beliefs: first, that it is necessary, at a stroke, to make up for the accumulated deficit in provision of services and infrastructure; second, that upgrading projects must operate to the highest standards, both technically (to meet planning regulations) and in financial and administrative terms (to ensure full cost recovery); and, third, that legalization requires the production of individual land titles. The case studies suggest, however, that simpler and less expensive approaches should be favoured, emphasizing minimum standards of service provision – a drinking-water supply, sanitation and street paving (UMP et al. 1995; UMP and Ministère de la Construction et de l'Urbanisme 1994).

The fourth form of intervention stresses prevention rather than cure. This requires a little explanation. Traditionally, urban management has meant the management of a given area of land: a perimeter is defined and land development within that perimeter is then controlled. An alternative, perhaps more appropriate, approach would be to 'work outwards' from the key elements structuring urban space. For the city as a whole, this means the key infrastructure networks, such as major water mains. At the level of the neighbourhood, it means the local infrastructure network serving individual homes, streets, schools and markets. Such an approach would allow the informal modes of housing development employed by the urban poor to be incorporated into the realm of legality from which they are otherwise excluded (Tribillon 1993; 1995).

This policy approach combines three forms of intervention: the production of a primary infrastructure network, the incorporation of informal subdividers into the production process, and the progressive servicing of areas that are already occupied, with plenty of scope for community mobilization and self-help (Nientied and van der Linden 1990; Skinner et al. 1987; UNCHS 1994; Van den Hoff and Steinberg 1992).

In sub-Saharan African cities in particular, this approach has the advantage of allowing the authorities to side-step the problems presented by customary land ownership, as it involves customary authorities at every stage of the process.

Such infrastructure-led and 'structuring' approaches to planning, which I describe as 'preventive' measures, emphasize *progressive* development and servicing of illegal settlements, stimulating constant downwards revision of norms and standards. The population contributes directly to the provision and management of infrastructure and services. Such approaches also favour a less centralized form of urban management, promoting community organization at the settlement and block level (Gilbert et al. 1996; Marulanda and Steinberg 1991).

Managing the illegal city: a decentralized approach In most of the cases analysed in this book, land management still depends on central or federal government, even where responsibilities for urban management have been transferred to local governments as a result of decentralization policies. Land tenure, taxation systems and the registration of property rights and transactions are generally regulated by national governments and administered by the regional delegations of central government agencies. Central governments, however, generally lack the financial and administrative resources to ensure effective implementation of their policies throughout the country. At the same time, intermediate level management agencies with genuine decision-making power are generally weak or absent (Pienaar 1996).

With regard to the role of central government, we can say that state agencies have a clearly defined and very wide field of influence in urban land management, but that they do not have the resources to ensure observance of their rules, the will to modify them, or the will to delegate these responsibilities to other bodies.

At the local level, residents and community authorities often devise innovative approaches to land management issues – conflict resolution, the management of relocation projects, informal credit systems or the provision of labour for upgrading projects – but the lack of a suitable legal or institutional context for their efforts denies them a more lasting role in the process of settlement consolidation.

Between these two levels there is a void which is rarely filled by local government. This is unfortunate, since municipal governments have a strategic role to play in the establishment of effective long-term upgrading and regularization policies. The creation of public bodies to act as inter-mediaries between central government and community organizations – the National Housing Authority in the Philippines or the Bangalore Development Authority, for example – has achieved only limited results. By contrast, the evidence suggest that it is regularization policies carried out in close collaboration with local authorities, or by those authorities themselves, that succeed best. These authorities are in the best position to develop new approaches to land management: they possess impressive negotiating skills and sensitivity to the needs of the low-income population (Durand-Lasserve and Clerc 1996; Tribillon 1993). They are better placed than central government to identify problems and vested interests involved in projects for the legalization and upgrading of illegal settlements. They are also better placed to identify the most appropriate and socially accept-able regulatory instruments and physical improvements, and to assess beneficiaries' ability to pay.

A new relationship with law The policies discussed above imply that the government's role is primarily to improve access to land by groups whose needs are not met by the market or conventional public housing programmes. Its role in the land market does not have to be a direct one (making housing plots available for acquisition by the poor). Instead, the state should regulate the supply of land for housing, ensuring that land can be acquired by different means and that the norms it establishes are respected. This requires a new type of relationship with the law, and it is to this that I shall now turn my attention, focusing on the question of appropriate standards and security of tenure.

Appropriate norms and standards Urban planning norms concerning design, construction and servicing standards are singularly ill-adapted to the needs of most of the population. Together with conventional legal and procedural norms, they increase social segregation by 'creating' illegality.

This question has been the subject of much comment in recent years (Dowall 1991; Farvacque and McAuslan 1992; Gilbert 1990). Conventional standards and norms are based on an ideal model for planning the organization of space and regulating the relations between social actors. They have virtually always been part and parcel of an overall urban management system and regulate formal sector activities taking place within this system. They are the product of a technocratic or bureaucratic way of thinking that is out of touch with reality. In practice, their main function is often to provide government agencies with a means of exercising their power and to allow certain professional groups (surveyors, public notaries and architects) to profit from the operation of the land market. Cultural models and vested interests on the part of bureaucrats, professional bodies or corporations therefore hinder the reform of existing norms and standards. To propose reform means questioning the model which legitimizes existing norms and challenging the powerful interests that benefit from them.

Take the case of procedural norms determining the recognition of land rights. Even if people know about the regulations and wish to observe them, the administrative machinery does not allow them to do so, since it does not have the necessary resources. This is particularly problematic in sub-Saharan Africa (Le Roy 1995; Mabogunje 1992; Mosha 1993; UMP and Ministère de la Construction et de l'Urbanisme 1994) but is also apparent in other regions. The time it takes for subdivision requests to be approved, building permits granted or requests for regularization agreed, together with the cost and complexity of the procedures involved, have led to a general condemnation of this type of procedure (Durand-Lasserve and Clerc 1996; Tribillon 1995). Since legal and procedural norms are difficult for most people to understand or observe, they are simply ignored.

The modest results of experiments with administrative simplification suggest that attention should be paid, not so much to the norms and procedures themselves, as to their underlying objectives. It is these that need redefining. It is not possible, for example, to simplify procedures for the registration of title to land without undermining their ability to fulfil the purpose for which they are intended. Senegal is currently learning this in the course of its large-scale legalization programme. But it is possible – as has been realized in India, Indonesia and Peru – to redefine the objectives of legalization, since guaranteeing security of tenure does not necessarily require the formal provision of individual land titles.

Security of tenure and alternatives to private property Although the main problem with illegal settlement is the lack of urban services, it is not possible to provide these unless the residents have a certain security of tenure. From a conventional legal perspective, security of tenure can be achieved only by the use of slow, complex and costly procedures (INTERURBA/AITEC 1995; UMP et al. 1995). The belief that it requires full individual title is still widely held, even though different interest groups do not share the same priorities (property developers and government authorities oppose any alternative, whereas the residents of illegal settlements would generally prefer a simpler solution meeting their basic requirement of freedom from the fear of eviction). An emphasis on the virtues of private property is characteristic of situations in which market pressures marginalize illegal settlements or people lack confidence in the authorities' ability to guarantee their security of tenure.

It is not always possible, however, to provide full legal title to land, since the agencies in charge of land management do not have the necessary resources. Nor is it always desirable, because it can make the task facing regularization agencies even more complex, producing the opposite effect to the one intended by *reducing* residents' security of tenure. In many cases, in particular in sub-Saharan Africa, it is so difficult to meet all the requirements for the provision of full legal title to land that the regularization process can never be completed.

The problem of finding a form of legalization that will be acceptable to all concerned and compatible with existing norms and procedures is the most common difficulty. Debates in this area centre on two issues: how residents' security of tenure can be guaranteed and who should be responsible for identifying, registering and protecting property rights. In general, more flexible methods of recognizing occupancy rights are being favoured at present.

The most popular option involves local or central governments simply recognizing the status quo. This removes the threat of eviction hanging over the residents of illegal settlements. It does not, however, provide any specific rights or guarantees for the people concerned, and this can discourage them from investing in housing improvements or starting small businesses.

The second option entails the recognition of occupancy rights without formal tenure legalization. This requires a more active involvement by the authorities, although relatively simple procedural measures will often suffice. The owners of land that has been occupied illegally must recognize the legitimacy of such procedures and agree not to undertake legal measures to recover their property without first coming to some sort of agreement with the occupants.

A third option involves recognizing the legitimacy of the process by which the low-income population has acquired land for housing, without insisting on full legalization of tenure. This requires negotiation with residents and landowners. Property becomes a political right: a right to build, a 'right to the city'. This right is made effective with the authorities' approval of a particular housing area's location and layout. The accent is on negotiation rather than regulation. It requires the simplification of procedures for the registration of land rights; the most successful experiment of this kind has been carried out in Peru (Forsyth 1991).

The fourth option is full formal legalization. This incorporates informal practices into the sphere of formal property transactions and market processes. It requires procedures for the identification of property rights to be speeded up, primarily by simplifying them. Experience shows that this is difficult but by no means impossible, particularly where there is a strong government commitment to the process, as in Mexico at the end of the 1980s (INTERURBA/AITEC 1995; UMP and Ministère des Affaires Étrangères 1993; Tomas 1995; see Chapter 9 by Azuela and Duhau and Chapter 10 by Varley).

Registering and protecting tenure rights There is nothing to stop governments from developing simple but effective procedures for recognizing the physical existence of particular goods and the fact of possession (as distinct from ownership) of the goods in question. There is also nothing to stop agents other than central government from undertaking these procedures.

We should note that different interest groups have different needs in this respect. The first consists of investors, property developers and financial interests. For them, government involvement is essential. The second group consists of residents – for whom central government involvement is not always essential. Records of who lives where and of municipal acts recognizing the existence of their settlement will meet most of their needs. Such records can be kept by local government offices, community organizations or even the residents of individual blocks. This community-based approach to registration can respond to most of the problems that may occur, without pretending to provide full legal certainty (UMP et al. 1995).

Parallel registration systems are therefore needed to meet different requirements with different degrees of formality at different scales and in the interests of different actors. The aim should be to ensure compatibility between these parallel systems, leaving open the option of movement towards the creation of a single, formal, registration system should the necessary resources become available.

Towards a New Understanding of Law

I wish to return to the question of the role of law to make certain observations – not as a lawyer but as a social scientist who, in recent years, has been involved in a number of legalization and upgrading projects in illegal settlements.

Law formalizes and entrenches illegality Laws on property, urban planning or construction give legal expression to the social relations conditioning access to land, housing and urban services. In doing so, law may, in a sense, be seen as formalizing and perpetuating illegality. It enables illegal settlements to be categorized – or stigmatized – as areas falling outside the law, whose residents are liable to legal sanction. In this sense, law presents obstacles to the search for appropriate ways of integrating these areas in the city by providing services or security of tenure for their inhabitants.

State law has negative implications for the illegal city. The origins, occupation and organization of illegal settlements are all a consequence of legal requirements that the low-income population cannot hope to meet. Planning laws, for example, help to regulate urban space but also widen the gulf between the legal city and the real city. Their ability to regulate the organization of space depends on government agencies' ability to apply the law effectively. Failure to plan effectively may be blamed on technical, political or cultural errors or misunderstandings, but the underlying problem is often a tendency to overestimate the power of the public authorities, resulting in the setting of unrealistic objectives and standards.

Even where the law is successfully applied, urban planning legislation, and zoning regulations in particular, shape urban space at the broad scale (Singh 1992). *Within* planning zones, however, law plays a positive role only in areas that have received official approval because they conform to property and planning regulations. In 'non-conforming' areas, however, where the residents occupy the land and build their houses illegally, state law plays an essentially negative role. Everywhere they turn, residents find that they are not allowed to do something, or that it is impossible for them to do something, or that they may be liable to prosecution if they do it.

It would be mistaken to regard illegal settlements as 'outlaw' areas in which law has no role to play. Residents often comply with some laws so as not to reinforce their settlement's lack of legitimacy, and in order to make it easier for the authorities to recognize and eventually regularize it. They seek formal recognition for their property transactions, avoid building out on to the pavement and respect areas set aside for services and amenities. Residents also defend the legitimacy of the way in which they have housed themselves by appealing to a higher legal order – including constitutional law – to assert their right to housing. Alternatively, they may invoke customary practices that pre-date modern legal systems, arguing that their legitimate rights to a particular area have been wrongly disregarded by colonial authorities or post-independence governments (UNCHS 1993a; Mabogunje 1992; Mosha 1993).

Is legal reform the answer to the problems posed by the illegal city? Research invariably underlines the limitations of legal reforms in this context. Changing the laws concerning land acquisition, valorization and sale does not solve the problems of unequal access to urban services and amenities. Such reforms will be effective only as part of a broader package of urban policy measures concerning services, credit and taxation. It is not land or planning law alone that shapes urban development, but the entire body of legislation affecting urban social relations (Fernandes 1995; Mabogunje 1992).

All the available evidence indicates that legal reform is a necessary but not a sufficient condition for improving urban living conditions, especially if, as Asteya Santiago notes in her chapter on the Philippines, the reforms are confined to property, planning and building regulations. The greatest potential for legal reform to make a significant contribution lies not in this area but in decentralization, more effective taxation, amendments to the law of contract and the creation of housing finance systems (as in Thailand, Turkey, Chile and the Philippines).

Further comment is required on the question of legal pluralism and diversity.

Legal pluralism often hinders both the application and reform of existing laws The reasons for legal pluralism vary. Before we can assess the impact of legal reform on the illegal city we must first consider the historical evolution of the legal system and the relationship between state law and alternative legal systems within the same country and city.

STATE LAW AND LEGAL COMPLEXITY All the chapters in this book underline the complex and sometimes contradictory nature of land and property law and urban planning regulations. This results from the accumulation of laws and regulations on similar or overlapping issues, particularly where some colonial laws remain on the statute books of independent nations. Each change of government or policy direction adds to the amount of legislation. This issue is raised in the case studies on India, Turkey, the Philippines and South Africa. Some urban management agencies seemingly compensate for their inability to make any real difference to city life by devising more and more regulations, in a frenzy of activity whose only results are excessive growth of the bureaucracy and public cynicism. The chapter on Nairobi provides a good example of this phenomenon.

What makes simplification of the legal framework so problematic is that it has been built up into such a complex edifice that to modify or repeal any of its elements can undermine the logic and coherence of the structure as a whole. This is why legal reform is so difficult, particularly when strong economic, political and bureaucratic interests are at stake, as is generally the case with legislation on land and property rights, and, to a lesser extent, urban planning. As experience in Côte d'Ivoire has shown, it can be even more difficult to 'tidy up' the legislation than to undertake a radical reform (not that the latter is any more likely to be effective).

DIVERGENT PRACTICES WITHIN A SINGLE LEGAL SYSTEM   In attempts to reform and modernize the legal framework, another difficulty arises with respect to different legal practices. This is a particularly sensitive issue in sub-Saharan Africa, where Jean-François Tribillon (1993) distinguishes three different 'levels' on which the law operates. First, there is state law: the law of the constitution, of civil codes and government decrees. Second, there is administrative law, which is based on and operates within the context of state law, but is subject in its application to a complex set of administrative regulations and entrenched bureaucratic practices ('the way we have always done things') which frequently have very little to do with the law *per se*. Finally, there is the interpretation and practical implementation, by government officials and the population, of the different laws and administrative regulations. These three 'levels' are interdependent but they do not change in the same way or at the same time.

ALTERNATIVE LEGAL SYSTEMS   This already complex situation may be made even more complex when other legal systems compete with state law (and the different interpretations and practices to which it gives rise) – legal systems which obey a different logic and derive their legitimacy from other sources. Some of them are survivals of legal traditions pre-dating the development of the modern nation-state. These may be termed 'residual' legal systems, like customary law (Le Roy 1995). Alternatively, they may stem from the reinterpretation or distortion of modern (state) law by marginalized groups who 'do not find a place' within it or who are actively excluded from it.

State law and alternative legal systems Reconciling state law and alternative legal systems requires an impressive combination of 'legal engineering' and social mediation, particularly where there are competing legal systems with different sources of legitimacy.

If we consider, for example, how to reconcile modern and customary legal systems in sub-Saharan Africa, it is clear that the only realistic alternative is to think, in modest terms, of finding ways to ensure the peaceful resolution of conflicts of interest between different urban stakeholders. This must be done in a pragmatic, open-minded way, encouraging the parties to redefine their long-term objectives and modes of behaviour. Diversity, here, is only an advantage in so far as it allows ways to be found of regulating practices lying outside state law and the formal market. Failure in this respect will perpetuate inequality and instability.

The task for the state, then, is to find ways of applying the law that will be to some extent compatible with alternative legal systems. Compatibility exists, for instance, when a government directive does not hinder the workings of another, residual or popular, legal system. The different systems must *articulate* with each other. Compatibility also exists when the law is sufficiently *flexible* to allow movement between different systems in everyday urban management. Legal devices acting as *bridges* between the different systems are needed. Usufruct rights or local forms of tenure may then, with government consent, be transformed into full, duly-registered, property rights (UNCHS 1993a). One example of this approach comes from Turkey where, in the 1980s, 'village ownership documents' were used in property transactions.

Research has shown that both community intermediaries and government officials can testify to local property rights and enable informal practices to be legitimized within the formal legal framework. The chapter on Jordan provides a good example. It is in sub-Saharan Africa, however, that the pragmatic articulation of different legal systems is best developed. Even so, this is rarely the product of deliberate policies to this effect. Instead, the explanation seems to lie in the strength of customary legal traditions and the practices adopted, for better or worse, by government officials.

In this respect, South Africa is faced with an enormously complex situation involving the reform of laws whose legitimacy is undermined by their inheritance from the apartheid regime, and the articulation of the existing legislation with a new legal system deriving its legitimacy from the new constitution, community traditions and customary law. Alan Mabin (1996) rightly describes this situation as 'a tyranny of difference'.

In general, however, the global tendency is for alternative legal systems to be supplanted by state law. The role of intermediation, in this context, is to ensure a certain orderliness and logic in processes of transition and integration which may take several decades to complete (UMP et al. 1995).

Changes in the law   State law defines a framework for action according to the power relations existing in society at a given moment. As such, it reflects a set of circumstances inherited from the past.

The changes that take place in the legal system, by contrast, reflect new social and economic needs and constraints. Change may take place slowly, over a long period, or changing political circumstances may lead to new policy directions or even a radical redefinition of land and planning policies. Change then takes place much more rapidly and may be spectacular (the furore caused by some reforms, particularly those concerning property rights, is often deliberately courted by those in power).

Recent case studies have identified the main factors leading to change in the laws on land, housing and urban management. First, direct pressure from the population, particularly in favour of elections. Second, changes in the political regime, involving democratization (as in South Africa), a socialist land and housing system (as in two-thirds of the sub-Saharan African countries in the past two decades – for example, the agrarian and land ownership reforms of 1984 in Burkina Faso) or ultra-liberal economic policies (as in Peru in the early 1990s or Chile during the 1980s). Liberalization often takes place in the context of structural adjustment policies and is accompanied by property law reforms, more efficient land and property tax systems, support for the private sector and state withdrawal from direct intervention in urban land management. Third: the establishment of a dictatorship, which may lead either to repressive policies (as in India from the end of the 1960s or Brazil and Chile during the 1970s) or to populist ones, as in the Philippines from 1972 to 1986 or Peru from 1968 to the early 1970s. Fourth: the implementation of decentralization policies. It is worth observing, in this context, that the decolonization of sub-Saharan Africa rarely led to radical changes in the property laws, as post-independence governments simply took over from the colonial authorities, retaining their privileges in this area (UMP et al. 1995; Tribillon 1993).

As a general rule, it is not the needs and demands of the poor that lead to changes in the property laws, but those of the dominant classes. Given that reforms to property law affect production, exchange, capital accumulation, income distribution and civil service graft, they are difficult to implement (particularly if pursued by a weak government). Law generally changes slowly, although sometimes less slowly than the urban reality to which it is applied. Changes can, however, be rapid when radical reforms establish new 'rules of the game' to modify the balance of power in society. Yet highly interventionist property reforms, or those with socialist overtones, virtually always fail. They are 'out of sync' with reality, and they fail to modify that reality (Mabogunje 1992).

Managing diversity

Legal hierarchies   I do not think we can realistically speak of the emergence of a 'new legal order' arising from the progressive incorporation into state law of alternative, residual or popular, legal systems. Even if we acknowledge that in the long term the tendency is towards a subordination of alternative legal systems to modern state law, we cannot ignore the current diversity of property rights and practices. Urban land and housing policies must therefore seek to manage and regulate this diversity.

Let me explain. All legal systems are global, unitary and exclusive: they cover the whole of a given field and apply to all social actors intervening in that field; they uphold the same principles and presuppositions; they leave no area untouched; they are hegemonic and mutually exclusive. The relationship between state law and older legal systems is necessarily one of domination and subordination: the state tolerates the alternative systems when it cannot displace them but does not abandon its ambition to take over from them entirely. The pressure on residual legal systems is strongest when the economic stakes are high and the government has the means to pursue its expansionary ambitions, even by force. In other cases, governments may accept or even encourage a certain degree of legal dualism.

When it has the upper hand, the government should still be open to compromise, even if it sees any accommodation with alternative legal systems as merely temporary or transitory. Legal pluralism can allow the government to shed some of its responsibility for urban management and property matters by letting other social actors manage some issues, such as minor local property disputes. In sub-Saharan Africa, for example, governments may transfer responsibility for property matters to customary authorities in three different circumstances (UMP et al. 1993). First, the survival of a relatively intact and widely respected customary legal system (as in Ghana, Uganda and some francophone countries). Second, partial withdrawal by the state because of a lack of resources (as in Cameroon, Zaïre and the Congo). Third, the lack of major economic or political vested interests.

The national authorities may go so far as to re-establish the rights of former customary landholders, as they have done in Ghana, Botswana and Benin. In such cases, however, customary autonomy in property matters is limited. The authorities may police local land matters and resolve some local disputes. They will remain under the tutelage of central government, however, unable to dispose of their lands or change land use patterns without its approval. Might we consider this a reconstructed, modern and 'democractic' form of 'native reserve'?

Local responses to illegality Managing diversity also entails local management of property questions (INTERURBA/AITEC 1995; Skinner et al. 1987; Schübeler 1996; UNCHS 1994). In the sub-Saharan context in particular, centralized management of property matters (including the identification of people with title to land, property registration, cadastral systems and so on) has shown its limitations. The complexity and lack of transparency of the procedures mean that property registers are unable to keep up with demand. This tends to dissuade people from using official property management systems and encourages corruption. It causes particular problems for land tenure legalization programmes (Fernandes 1995; UNCHS 1993a; Royston 1996). Local management of property matters is, therefore, being presented as both more effective (since it allows less complex procedures to be used, making it easier to keep registers up to date) and less arbitrary (it is less anonymous, and local officials do not find it so easy to evade accountability as their central government counterparts).

In most cities, new legislation and fiscal reforms since the early 1980s have increased local governments' land and property management powers. This is true, for example, of reforms undertaken in Turkey during the 1980s, particularly the New Reconstruction Law of 1985. Such reforms operate at two levels. They stimulate the development of the formal sector (in particular, via the establishment of housing finance systems) and they regularize illegal settlements, speeding up their integration into the market but blocking further expansion. Similar patterns have been reported in India, Brazil and Egypt. Management of illegal settlements may be entrusted to different types of agency: municipal governments, neighbourhood associations or block committees. What is important is that those responsible should be able to ensure the articulation of different legal systems: customary landholders, religious leaders, elected officials, community representatives or other intermediaries (in particular, those subdividing land for sale) (UMP et al. 1993; UMP et al. 1995).

The problems central governments tend to transfer to local authorities are the problems they cannot solve. While current thinking favours decentralization and community participation in urban management, it is important to avoid merely shifting responsibility for intractable problems on to the shoulders of local authorities. Some governments experiencing acute economic and financial crises see decentralization as a means of dumping their responsibilities for the management, regularization and servicing of illegal settlements on to local government, with the pretext of 'empowering' the community. The legal basis for local authorities' new roles remains ambiguous, however, and they are not given the resources to discharge their new responsibilities adequately. This leads to confusion and great insecurity over property rights (UMP et al. 1995).

It seems, moreover, that the forms of local land management favoured are those which preserve central government prerogatives: local authorities are drawn into the decision-making process, but their role remains a consultative one. Their job is to provide information about local landholding patterns, but central government retains the right to validate property rights.

Finally, as the Indian and Turkish case studies indicate, local management of illegal settlements encourages clientelism. As Ayse Yonder (this volume, citing Oncu 1988) notes, 'selective enforcement and relaxation of regulation ... became "the most expedient way of dispensing patronage" in return for votes in both the formal and informal districts of the city'.

Although there is a general tendency for urban land management responsibilities to be transferred to local authorities, it is worth pointing out that there are some notable exceptions – in particular, in Peru, where the 1993 Constitution reduced the powers of local government by making their decisions subject to prior approval by the traditionally centralist Congress.

Current trends in the relationship between law and the illegal city
The ways in which law is changing are related to the forms of urban management and land management towards which we are currently heading.

The 'statist' model of government intervention in this area is under threat from 'above' and 'below'. From above, governments are threatened and marginalized by globalization, which converts cities, now required to manage their own affairs, into the linchpins of the new global economic order. From below, they see their ability to intervene in urban areas, and especially in urban land management, undermined because they lack appropriate legal instruments and resources. Areas suitable for urban development are generally already occupied, and on such a scale that it is simply not possible to 'free' them for planned development.

In this new context, it seems, more and more often, that urban land is no longer a major issue. Urban land seems to be losing its importance as a key sector in the process of capital accumulation. The growing transfer of responsibility for land management to local authorities testifies to its diminished importance, as does the almost universal government tolerance of illegal settlements. There are virtually no evictions any more, and where evictions do still take place, they are limited to areas of 'strategic' importance (high-value central locations, commercial or industrial zones) and environmentally sensitive or protected areas. With the blessing of central government (which is withdrawing from intervention in urban affairs) and local government (which does intervene, but lacks the resources to do so effectively), the management of the illegal city is coming to depend more and more on its inhabitants and informal sector actors.

The urban authorities favour a dualistic model of land management. On the one hand, they promote the development of a modern real estate sector by means of deregulation and the establishment of housing finance systems. On the other hand, they try to contain the demands made on them by the inhabitants of the illegal city, pursuing selective regularization and upgrading programmes to integrate illegal settlements into the legal city. All the case studies in this book, and in particular those on the

Philippines, Turkey and India, indicate, however, that the integrationist approach to illegal settlement will be pursued only as long as it does not hinder the development of the formal land and housing market.

As far as law is concerned, it seems as though the changes that are taking place concern the implementation of new legal practices at least as much as legislative reform or the emergence of a new legal order with the appropriate new instruments and procedures to go with it. They require, on the one hand, a more flexible use of existing legal instruments, and, on the other, innovative implementation procedures for urban projects supported by new social actors – or rather, to be precise, by new social relations within the city. They presuppose the establishment of negotiation and mediation procedures in the management of illegal settlements and, above all, a form of decision-making which takes account of the wishes expressed by the residents of the illegal city.

Notes

Translated from French by Ann Varley.

1. See, for example, Durand-Lasserve and Clerc 1996; INTERURBA/AITEC 1995; UMP and Ministère des Affaires Étrangères 1993; UMP et al. 1995; Von Einsiedel 1995.

References

Abbott, J. (1996) *Sharing the City: Community Participation in Urban Management*, Earthscan, London.

Arandel, C. and M. El Batran (1996) 'The informal housing development process in Egypt', Report submitted to PIR-Villes, CNRS, Paris.

Azuela, A. (1995) 'La propriété, le logement et le droit', *Les Annales de la Recherche Urbaine*, Vol. 66, 2–11.

Baross, P. and J. van der Linden (eds) (1990) *The Transformation of Land Supply Systems in Third World Cities*, Avebury, Aldershot.

Bolívar, T. (1995) 'Construction et reconnaissance des barrios urbains du Venezuela', *Les Annales de la Recherche Urbaine*, Vol. 66, 81–7.

Connolly, P. (1994) 'Urban planning and segmented land markets: illustrations from Cancún', in G. A. Jones and P. M. Ward (eds), *Methodology for Land and Housing Market Analysis*, UCL Press, London, 251–65.

Doebele, W. A. (1994) 'Urban land and macroeconomic development: moving from "access for the poor" to urban productivity', in G. A. Jones and P. M. Ward (eds), *Methodology for Land and Housing Market Analysis*, UCL Press, London, 44–54.

Dowall, D. E. (1991) 'Less is more: the benefits of minimal land development regulation', in USAID, *Regularizing the Informal Land Development Process,* USAID Office of Housing and Urban Programs, Washington, DC, 9–20.

— (1995) *The Land Market Assessment: A New Tool for Urban Management*, UMP Paper no. 4, World Bank, Washington, DC.

Dowall, D. E. and G. Clarke (1996) *A Framework for Reforming Urban Land Policies in Developing Countries*, UMP Paper no. 7, World Bank, Washington, DC.

Durand-Lasserve, A. (1990) 'Articulation between formal and informal land markets in cities in developing countries: issues and trends', in P. Baross and J. van der Linden (eds), *The Transformation of Land Supply Systems in Third World Cities*, Avebury, Aldershot, 37–56.

Durand-Lasserve, A. and V. Clerc (1996) *Regularization and Integration of Irregular Settlements: Lessons from Experience*, UMP Working Paper no. 6, World Bank, Washington, DC.

ESCAP (United Nations Economic and Social Commission for Asia and the Pacific) (1990) *Case Studies on Metropolitan Fringe Development with a Focus on Informal Land Subdivisions*, United Nations, Bangkok.

Farvacque, C. and P. McAuslan (1992) *Reforming Urban Land Policies and Institutions in Developing Countries*, UMP Paper no. 5, World Bank, Washington, DC.

Fernandes, E. (1995) *Law and Urban Change in Brazil*, Avebury, Aldershot.

Fondation pour le Progrès de l'Homme (1991) *La Réhabilitation des Quartiers Dégradés. Leçons de l'Expérience Internationale. La Déclaration de Caracas*, Fondation pour le Progrès de l'Homme, Caracas.

Forsyth, A. A. (1991) 'The Institute for Liberty and Democracy's Property Rights Program', in USAID *Regularizing the Informal Land Development Process*, USAID Office of Housing and Urban Programs, Washington, DC, 21–7.

Gilbert, A. (1990) 'The costs and benefits of illegality and irregularity in the supply of land', in P. Baross and J. van der Linden (eds), *The Transformation of Land Supply Systems in Third World Cities*, Avebury, Aldershot, 17–36.

Gilbert, R., D. Stevenson, H. Girardet and R. Stren (1996) *Making Cities Work: The Role of Local Authorities in the Urban Environment*, Earthscan, London.

INTERURBA/AITEC (eds) (1995) *Cities in Developing Countries. Integration of Irregular Settlements. Current Questions in Asia and Latin America*, INTERURBA, Paris.

Jones, G. A. and P. M. Ward (eds) (1994) *Methodology for Land and Housing Market Analysis*, UCL Press, London.

Le Bris, E., E. Le Roy and P. Mathieu (1991) *L'Appropriation de la Terre en Afrique Noire. Manuel d'Analyse, de Décison et de Gestion Foncière*, Karthala, Paris.

Le Roy E. (1995) 'Irrégularités et illégalités foncières dans quelques situations urbaines d'Afrique noire', *Les Annales de la Recherche Urbaine*, Vol. 66, 13–21.

Mabin, A. (1996) 'A tyranny of difference: multiple traditions in South African urban planning law and problems of urban reconstruction', Paper presented to PIR-Villes Seminar on Urban Research in South Africa, Paris.

Mabogunje, A. L. (1992) 'Perspectives on urban land and urban management policies in Sub-Saharan Africa', Report submitted to World Bank, Washington, DC.

Marulanda, L. and F. Steinberg (1991) *Land Management and Guided Land Development in Jakarta*, Institute for Housing and Urban Development Studies (IHS) Working Paper no. 1, Rotterdam.

Mosha, A. C. (1993) *An Evaluation of the Effectiveness of National Land Policies and Instruments in Improving Supply of and Access to Land for Human Settlement Development in Botswana*, Habitat, Nairobi.

Nientied, P. and J. van der Linden (1990) 'The role of government in the supply of legal and illegal land in Karachi', in P. Baross and J. van der Linden (eds), *The Transformation of Land Supply Systems in Third World Cities*, Avebury, Aldershot, 225–42.

PADCO (Planning and Development Collaborative International), National Housing Authority and Asian Development Bank (1990) *The Bangkok Land Management Study. The Land and Housing Markets of Bangkok: Strategies for Public Sector Participation,* PADCO-NHA-ADB, Bangkok.

Payne, G. K. (1988) *Unregulated Urban Housing Submarkets in the Third World: A Review of the Literature,* CENDEP, Oxford Polytechnic, Oxford.

— (1997) *Urban Land Tenure and Property Rights in Developing Countries: A Review,* Intermediate Technology Publications and Overseas Development Administration, London.

Pienaar, J. (1996) 'Obstacles to housing delivery experienced at local level in South Africa', Paper presented to PIR-Villes Seminar on Urban Research in South Africa, Paris.

Royston, L. (1996) 'Urban land issues in contemporary South Africa: land tenure regularisation and infrastructure and services provision', Report submitted to PIR-Villes, CNRS, Paris.

Schübeler, P. (1996) *Participation and Partnership in Urban Infrastructure Management,* Paper no. 19, World Bank, Washington, DC.

Singh, G. (1992) *Land Laws, Land Policies and Planning in Malaysia,* UMP, Kuala Lumpur.

Skinner, R. J., J. L. Taylor and E. A. Wegelin (eds) (1987) *Shelter Upgrading for the Urban Poor: Evaluation of Third World Experience,* Island Publishing House, Manila.

Tomas, F. (1995) 'Mexico: tous propriétaires', *Les Annales de la Recherche Urbaine,* Vol. 66, 72–9.

Tribillon, J.-F. (1993) *Villes Africaines: Nouveau Manuel d'Aménagement Foncier,* ADEF, La Défense.

— (1995) 'Contourner la propriété par l'équipement dans les villes africaines', *Les Annales de la Recherche Urbaine,* Vol. 66, 118–23.

UMP (UNDP/World Bank/UNCHS Urban Management Programme) (1994) *Manejo del Suelo Urbano,* UMP Regional Office for Latin America and the Caribbean, Quito.

UMP and Ministère des Affaires Étrangères (1993) 'L'accès des pauvres au sol urbain: nouvelles approches en matière de politique de régularisation dans les pays en développement', Preparatory documents for International Seminar (Mexico, February), Ministère des Affaires Étrangères, Paris.

UMP and Ministère de la Construction et de l'Urbanisme (Côte d'Ivoire) (1994) *Formulation et Conduite d'une Politique de Restructuration de l'Habitat Spontané,* UMP/ Ministère de la Construction et de l'Urbanisme, Abidjan.

UMP, Ministère des Affaires Étrangères, Ministère de la Coopération and Deutsche Gesellschaft für Technische Zusammenarbeit (1995) 'Gestion foncière urbaine, politiques de régularisation et développement local en Afrique et dans les États Arabes', Preparatory documents for International Seminar (Abidjan, March), Ministère des Affaires Étrangères, Paris.

UNCHS (United Nations Centre for Human Settlements/Habitat) (1992) *Global Strategy for Shelter to the Year 2000 – Improving Shelter: Actions by Non-Governmental Organizations (NGOs),* Habitat, Nairobi.

— (1993a) *Améliorer les Systèmes d'Information Foncière et de Reconnaissance des Droits sur le Sol dans les Villes d'Afrique Sub-Saharienne Francophone,* Habitat, Nairobi.

— (1993b) *Evaluación de las Políticas Nacionales del Suelo e Instrumentos para Mejorar el Acceso y el Uso de la Tierra Urbana en América Latina*, Habitat, Nairobi.

— (1994) *National Experiences with Shelter Delivery for the Poorest Groups*, Habitat, Nairobi.

UNDP (United Nations Development Programme) (1996) *Living in Asian Cities. The Impending Crisis: Causes, Consequences and Alternatives for the Future*, Report of the Second Asia-Pacific Urban Forum, UNDP, New York.

USAID (US Agency for International Development) (1991) *Regularizing the Informal Land Development Process*, USAID Office of Housing and Urban Programs, Washington, DC.

Van den Hoff, R. and F. Steinberg (eds) (1992) *Innovative Approaches to Urban Management: The Integrated Urban Infrastructure Development Programme in Indonesia*, Avebury, Aldershot.

Vanderschueren, F., E. Wegelin and K. Wekwete (1996) *Policy Programme Options for Urban Poverty Reduction: A Framework for Action at Municipal Government Level*, UMP Paper no. 20, World Bank, Washington, DC.

Von Einsiedel, N. (1995) 'Improving urban land management in Asia's developing countries', Paper presented to United Nations Habitat II Regional Policy Consultation on Access to Land and Security of Tenure, Jakarta.

World Bank (1983) *Learning by Doing: World Bank Lending for Urban Development 1972–82*, World Bank, Washington, DC.

— (1991) *Housing, Urban Policy and Economic Development. An Agenda for the 1990s*, World Bank Policy Paper, Washington, DC.

— (1993) *Housing: Enabling Markets to Work*, World Bank Policy Paper, Washington, DC.

CHAPTER 14

Law and the Future of Urban Management in the Third World Metropolis

Sérgio de Azevedo

This chapter discusses the complex issues facing metropolitan areas in less developed countries in a context of simultaneous globalization and fragmentation of economic activities. In this context, it is essential to rethink the role of law and the relationship between the public and private sectors if more democratic and efficient forms of urban management are to be achieved.

The chapter draws on the case studies presented in this book in its exploration of the future of law and urban management in the third world metropolis. It is divided into three sections. The first discusses some limitations on the action of the state in developing countries which can help to explain the generalized crisis in governance in recent decades. The second section assesses different forms of participatory management to explain why some policies are more readily accepted and/or successful than others. Finally, the third section evaluates the role currently played by law in the management of metropolitan areas and the tasks and challenges facing local government at the turn of the century.

Re-thinking the Role of the State in Developing Countries

A new relationship between the state and the market has emerged in both developed and developing countries in the past two decades. In less developed countries in particular, development models involving direct state intervention in the economy have fallen from favour. As a result, a range of proposals for the reform of the public sector has been formulated, favouring a halt to further growth or even a reduction in the size of the state. The current trend is towards a decline in the state's role as direct producer of goods and services and an increase in incentives to private sector investment in strategic or priority areas for development.

There is also an increase in the legal regulation of private sector involvement in these areas and in public–private partnerships (Osborne and Gaebler 1992).

The reasons for the political and economic crisis which has affected many developed and most less developed countries over the past two decades are the subject of great controversy. Neo-liberal analysts explain the crisis of the state in developed countries as a direct consequence of the welfare state policies adopted in Western democracies in the 1950s and 1960s (Offe 1984). Such policies created excessive demands on the political system, dominating the state agenda and leading to geometric growth in social expenditure outstripping the state's capacity for accumulation.

In the southern hemisphere (with the exception of Australia and New Zealand), however, the crisis of the state is attributed not to massive social programmes but rather to its developmentalist ambitions and massive direct intervention in the economy. Heavy state involvement in the productive sector, in the guise of state-controlled companies and para-statal organizations, led to chronic balance of payments deficits. The need to balance government accounts in the short term led to a gradual growth in both internal and external debt and to high inflation. Companies providing public services wasted public money through over-staffing, inefficiency and a failure to programme investment in anticipation of future demands. Privatization was the only way to stem the recurrent losses of these companies and to channel resources from the private sector into strategic economic areas. The proceeds of privatization would also help to reduce government deficits.

Neo-liberal thinkers prescribe privatization even for those para-statal companies which are profitably and professionally managed. They do so on the basis of two main arguments. In economic terms, they argue that even when such companies are profitable, the returns to the Treasury are usually less than the dividends private companies pay their shareholders. Politically, they believe that the state should not tie up resources in productive activities when they could be better spent on social investment, which is usually well below the minimum levels demanded by the population. In contrast to their Northern counterparts, neo-liberals in the South argue that as the state withdraws from the economic sphere it will increase its participation in the social sphere.

In contrast to this neo-liberal approach, a neo-Marxist school, drawing on 'regulation theory', views the current crisis in advanced capitalism as a consequence of the transition from a decaying Fordist model of accumulation (employing Taylorist production methods and regulated by the welfare state) to a new model of flexible accumulation (Valladares and Preteceile 1990). In addition to the need for reforms allowing the state to adapt to current circumstances, extending the conditions of governance, flexible accumulation brings about a change in the political balance between social actors such as traditional trade unions and the nation-state. Their room for manoeuvre is considerably reduced by the dual processes of globalization and fragmentation of the economy. Instead of the large factories and production lines of the Fordist model, the new accumulation model features small and medium-sized modern companies employing highly qualified workers and advanced technology. They are often linked to the informal economy and display great flexibility in responding to the demands of a fragmented and fast-changing market (Castells 1985).

Although the crisis of the state in developed and less developed countries is therefore the subject of competing explanations, most analysts agree that contemporary societies are going through a period of rapid restructuring.[1] Over the past two decades, the processes of economic change have exceeded the state's traditional regulatory framework. Therefore, even where there has been no formal deregulation of the economy, a significant part of the legal and institutional system has in practice become obsolete. One of the challenges facing contemporary societies at the turn of century is therefore the formulation of a new regulatory framework for state action that will be able to cope with their complexities and idiosyncrasies. After all, it was precisely in order to counter the negative effects of the free market that the state's sphere of influence was extended and its regulatory power strengthened over the course of the twentieth century, through anti-trust or labour laws and social security legislation for example (Petrella 1994). The current trend does not, therefore, imply a reduction in the importance of the state, as only naïve interpretations would argue. It requires, rather, a discussion of its new role and new institutional arrangements.

In the past two decades, internal or external pressures have led many developing countries to undertake structural adjustment programmes. In many cases, these have managed to stabilize or even reverse the acute economic crisis. In spite of significant successes in the economic field and the consolidation of democracy in many countries, however, most countries have not yet achieved sustained, secure, economic growth (Huntington 1991). Most states have lost at least part of their capacity for effective intervention, opening up the prospect of a permanent crisis of governance.

Some analysts argue that the limitations on the action of the state in the so-called 'new democracies' are of a structural character, although this is still little studied or understood. These countries share a common experience of democratic political reforms undertaken in the 1980s without corresponding reforms to the social or economic orders (O'Donnel 1993). Some consider that the instability of these states results from the 'incorporation of the masses into the dynamics of political competition before the rules of the political game have been fully institutionalized' (Santos 1988: 112).

Other analysts link the constant institutional crises in developing countries to the failure of presidentialism.[2] In addition, the long tradition of habitual violation of rules (through political immunity, corporatism, extortion and so on) undermines the credibility of law in the third world. It also means that attempts to formalize state intervention can have contradictory effects. The results are permanent unpredictability, a lack of fixed and reliable 'rules of the game' and 'praetorianism' (the rule of the strongest) (Huntington 1979).

It is important to stress that the role participatory management can play within local government, to be discussed in the following section, is subject to the complex considerations I have outlined above.

Participatory Urban Management: Potential and Limitations

In the complex and rapidly changing societies of most developing countries, political participation cannot be limited to traditional institutional channels of representation (the right to elect and to stand for election). It requires other, more direct, forms of democracy for citizenship rights to be fully realized, especially at the local level. In short, the management of public affairs is too important to be left to the government.

In recent decades, rapid urbanization and a process of late industrialization benefiting only a small part of the urban labour force have led to complex urban problems which most governments have been unable to tackle effectively. Access to land and housing have always figured prominently in the low-income population's list of demands concerning their environment (which also includes sanitation, a clean water supply, electricity and public transport). This is one of the reasons why most states have given housing a prominent place in their portfolio of urban policies. It also explains the limited scope and failure of most state intervention in urban areas.

Since the 1980s, economic recession and fiscal crisis have been reflected, in metropolitan areas, in the re-emergence of the rental slum, rising population densities in central areas and the growth of illegal settlements on the urban periphery. The consequences of the illegal occupation of public or private lands have varied significantly from country to country. In some cases illegal settlement entails constant conflict with the state; in others clientelism leads the state to turn a blind eye to the illegality of the process, as powerful political interests seek the approval and votes of the low-income population (see, for example, Chapter 7 by Pérez Perdomo and Bolívar, Chapter 9 by Azuela and Duhau, Chapter 6 by Santiago and Chapter 10 by Varley).

Another result of the economic crisis has been that some middle- and upper-class groups have chosen to meet their housing needs in enclosed condominium developments connected to the central areas via motorways, light rail or metro systems. In a few metropolitan areas, traditional popular neighbourhoods in central locations have started to be restored and gentrified, changing the symbolism of the urban landscape and creating new amenities which set these neighbourhoods apart from other inner-city areas.

Such housing strategies often lead to the creation of middle-class 'islands' in peripheral areas or popular neighbourhoods. At the same time, the population of well-consolidated illegal settlements and low-income neighbourhoods has continued to grow, partly as a result of vertical development in such areas. Together these processes lead to a 'perverse' decrease in spatial segregation. This more intensive 'forced co-existence' of middle- and upper-class groups with the low-income population, in a context of persistent social segregation and low economic growth, tends to intensify social prejudices and the stigmatization of the poor as the 'dangerous classes' (Ribeiro and Azevedo 1996).

To some extent, this middle-class reaction is an understandable response to the rise in urban crime and violence. However, the habit of regarding the 'other' (from a lower social group) as a potential enemy tends to reinforce ideological prejudices in the elite, undermining the search for broader economic and political solutions such as a reduction in the amount of absolute poverty, increased opportunities for social mobility and reform of the state. The middle and upper classes opt instead for short-term, individualist responses which address the symptoms rather than the cause of the problem. These create further difficulties for urban society as a whole and even, ironically, for their own quality of life: a disproportionate increase in private security services and the resulting service charges; people feeling trapped in their own homes; and an impoverishment of the life of the street as a space for adults and children to socialize and enjoy their leisure.

When evaluating urban policies, we need to ask some important questions about state intervention in the provision of public services and infrastructure. Given the historic role of the state in developing countries, a statist tradition often prevails. Only recently – when fiscal crisis has set clear limits to public investment – has collaboration between the state and civil associations or public–private partnerships been seen as having anything to offer. It is true that service provision by the state generally does too little to counter social inequality, since management tends to be inefficient, clientelistic and corrupt. I do not, however, accept some currently fashionable interpretations of the relationship between the state, the market and society: I still believe that urban social and economic problems can be solved only by the state and by complex, pro-active and democratic political and institutional arrangements.

It is important to stress that the process of economic globalization is mostly restricted to capital movements, as there is currently no prospect of free circulation of third world labour. On the contrary, draconian legislation has been enacted in both the USA and the European Union to prevent migration from less developed countries. We are far from what could be described as an embryonic world citizenship. Nor is there, in the short or medium term, any possibility of the formation of a supra-national regulatory organization capable of operating on a global scale, although gradual progress has been made throughout the century in achieving international agreements on specific issues.

In such circumstances, rather than dismantling the national state, the real challenge is to reconstruct it in such a way that it can become a flexible space for institutional representation of the diverse individual and collective interests of which society is composed (Reis 1994). In this context, retaining public control over the provision of services is crucially important. This does not necessarily entail public ownership of the agencies providing the services. New relationships between public authorities and the private sector can be established in a number of ways, and there are various strategies for involving the private sector in the provision of public services. Evaluating the different models of public–private relationships will surely become an important task for urban research in the near future. This subject also points us in the direction of another critical question, concerning the democratic management of the city.

The majority of the available literature on urban demand-making does not distinguish the type of collective action characterizing 'classic' urban social movements from other forms of organized action, of an in-strumental and short-term nature. From the sociologist's point of view, however, 'classic' social movements can be defined as forms of collective organization directed primarily towards goals of a normative or ideological nature, i.e. those concerning the basic values shaping the institutional order. Environmentalist, feminist, anti-racist and pacifist movements fit this description. This does not mean that they cannot by definition pursue specific instrumental gains or negotiable goals. The emphasis, though, is on collective, non-negotiable goals, such as gender or racial equality or the defence of the environment.

The majority of community movements in developing countries do not, however, fit the above description. They should instead be described as demand-driven movements (neighbourhood associations, organizations campaigning for better public transport and so on). Their objective is to force the state to develop strategies for improving the urban environment (Boschi 1987). They bring together those with an interest in the provision of collective goods such as housing, urban services, schools, nurseries or health centres. Their goals are therefore negotiable, as there are no questions of principle at stake as there are in classic social movements.[3] In the overwhelming majority of cases, even when these movements adopt violent tactics such as land invasion, they do not challenge the broader political and social system (Gohn 1982; Moises 1982). Success, on the contrary, is more likely to *increase* their integration with the existing social system (as, for instance, when illegal settlers are converted into property owners by tenure legalization).

It is important to stress that such movements have nevertheless contributed to widening the overall conditions of citizenship, although their contributions are more incidental than intentional (Azevedo and Prates 1995). In certain circumstances it is possible for a demand-driven movement to evolve into an urban social movement (Sader 1988), but this is the exception rather than the rule.

Over the past three decades, participatory planning has mostly been of a 'restricted' or 'instrumental' nature. Participation is restricted to communities that are to benefit directly from a specific project or local programme – providing labour, defining priorities at the micro-scale and allocating some resources. In developing countries such programmes have a variety of objectives: to involve the community in decisions concerning the application of limited resources, eke out those resources by using free or under-paid labour and increase government legitimacy (Azevedo and Prates 1995).

Community organizations participate in these programmes for pragmatic reasons, to obtain extra resources from the authorities. Such programmes, which have their virtues, also have many limitations.[4] They are at best palliative measures, such that their attractions to the low-income population would evaporate if government agencies fulfilled their legal objectives by providing a basic minimum of social services.

A very different form of community involvement may be described as 'neo-corporatist participation'. It entails the linking of residents' associations to form collective bodies, committees or councils. Such institutional arrangements enable the groups involved to influence, directly or indirectly, the definition of government policies and priorities. Popular participation in the formulation of local laws, master plans and budgets seems to hold out the possibility of a new social contract, a new relationship between the public and the private sectors, incorporating social groups that have traditionally been excluded from the public arena of negotiation.

The question is therefore how to replace corporatism – informal, non-institutionalized and biased towards the groups with the most economic or political power – with a new institutional arena, in which clear and transparent rules apply, where the interested parties can discuss a particular urban policy. A broad and eclectic forum of this kind would necessarily be more truly public, and less corporatist, since, in order to defend its priorities, each group would have to negotiate and abandon its non-essential objectives.[5]

Experiments with neo-corporatist participatory management in developing countries are still in their initial stages. There are two reasons for this. First, while public authorities are enthusiastic about instrumental participation, they do not welcome the neo-corporatist variety. Second, most community movements have little interest in playing this kind of role. Although it is well established in Western European countries, neo-corporatist participation has only recently begun to gain a foothold in developing countries. It has primarily been of interest to demand-driven movements with broad geographical coverage (regional and national federations and associations) and *sensu strictu* social movements (environmentalist, anti-racist, feminist). This kind of participation is usually of little interest to local demand-driven associations (residents' or neighbourhood associations, or movements for nursery or public transport provision, for example, focusing on specific areas). Nor does it find much favour among social movements which do not see a given topic as a priority (for instance, participation in a municipal education or health council may not be a priority for trade unions).

Yet the creation of mixed councils of government and civil society representatives, with a real say in setting policy priorities in the fields of health, housing, transport or education, for example, and supervisory powers over the agencies providing such services, could become an important mechanism for the democratization and gradual incorporation of civil society into public administration and the management of collective services. If the low-income population stands to gain so much from participatory management, why has it been so difficult to gain its support for such initiatives? Why has it been so difficult to build effective, lasting alliances capable of ensuring the continuance of these initiatives?

Most analysts have explained this failure in terms of weak political leadership in local government and citizens' organizations and the population's low level of political awareness. The way forward, it is suggested, lies in better communications, emphasizing the practical contribution participatory management can make to the improvement of living conditions, to ensure that it is better understood by the population.

While acknowledging the importance of better communications, we must recognize that other factors hinder wider popular participation. Even government experts and professional politicians may find their powers of comprehension challenged by the complex legal and technical issues that must be addressed by consultative bodies discussing, for example, new master plans. This will discourage people from becoming involved; but even if most people were in a position to understand the technical issues raised, they would not necessarily be any the more willing to participate.

To understand why not, we must first appreciate that appropriate legal instruments and regulatory policies are required if the objectives of consultative bodies are to be made viable. In principle, such policies apply equally to everyone in society, but in practice they affect individuals or members of small interest groups rather than an entire class or other large social group (as would be the case with redistributive policies, for example). In other words, regulatory policies cross-cut society, affecting people from the same social group in different ways, and making it difficult to establish clearly defined, lasting alliances around them (Lowi 1964; Salisbury 1968).

Another problem is that most regulatory policies do not deliver immediate benefits, only the possibility that people will be able to benefit from them at some future point. This acts as a disincentive to mobilization, even among groups who may logically expect to benefit.

The lesson to be learned is that, in these circumstances, the implementation of a more advanced form of democratic management will depend on the government's willingness to take the initiative, providing strong and determined leadership in its pursuit of this objective. However, even if the government encourages more active participation in the formulation of policies which will eventually benefit most of the population, there is no guarantee that these policies will be successful. Regulatory policies often work against the interests of certain individuals and small but powerful groups, who therefore oppose them. When these groups have access to significant economic and political resources with which to pursue their objectives, they can sabotage participatory policies. A relatively small interest group or specialized public agency can often block a popular policy from which the majority of the urban population would have stood to benefit.

In summary, we can conclude that local demand-driven movements are generally willing to contemplate direct participation in policy formulation only for specific projects of limited general relevance. *Sensu strictu* social movements and demand-driven movements with a broader geographical coverage (city-wide, regional or national federations) are more open to the idea of becoming involved in the formulation of urban policies offering less immediate benefits to their members. Attempts to involve local demand-driven movements in the formulation of broader regulatory policies usually result in their representatives constantly diverting discussion to highly specific issues relating to their own immediate concerns.

The institutionalization of neo-corporatist participation can be an important step forward in the search for the effective exercise of citizenship and popular control over the state. If, however, the chosen strategy is miscalculated, it may produce the opposite effect from that intended, undermining urban management and jeopardizing rather than strengthening the democratic process (Jacobi 1990; Azevedo and Prates 1995).

The Challenges Facing Urban Law in the Third World Metropolis

Far from being monolithic, the state consists of a range of institutions with different and possibly incompatible objectives, histories and cultures.

Their access to human and financial resources varies, and they form unofficial alliances and rivalries in their competition for power and resources. This frequently results in confusing and contradictory urban legislation (see Chapter 4 by Razzaz, Chapter 11 by Mitullah and Kibwana and Chapter 6 by Santiago). From the outset, public policies often have ill-defined or contradictory goals, and their objectives then change in response to wider social and institutional changes. The success or failure of individual policies depends, *inter alia*, on their internal idiosyncrasies, the status of the agencies responsible for their formulation and application, the size and degree of organization of the constituencies to which they are addressed, and the power of the parties whose interests are likely to be affected by them.

In addition, policies have unforeseen results which can sometimes prevent them from achieving their objectives. This is partly a consequence of their interaction with other policies: some are complementary or overlap; others contradict each other. Sometimes the potential benefits of different policies have to be traded off against each other. Decision-making is therefore extremely complex, and there is no 'universal logic' capable of distinguishing infallibly between alternative courses of action (Santos 1994).

In these circumstances, the most appropriate option for cities in developing countries is 'strategic' or 'adaptive' planning (Cintra and Andrade 1978), or 'situational' planning (Matus 1993). This means retaining a broad perspective on a limited number of variables and issues considered to be of strategic importance, focusing on certain crucial aspects, but giving up any pretence of regulating everything in minute detail. This approach to planning starts from the recognition of the enormous heterogeneity of the public sphere. It acknowledges that institutions develop at different rates, and that planning should, when necessary, give a push to agencies in need of special help. It also means acknowledging the existence of different institutional agendas, using negotiation to arrive at a basic minimum of shared aims and objectives.

Bearing in mind these general principles, there are two main dimensions to strategic planning in third world metropolitan areas. The first of these is the city government's function of institutional co-ordination. It should use its planning agency to co-ordinate the actions of the different administrative agencies, designing and collaborating in the implementation of official programmes and policies. This aspect of planning should concentrate on the interface between different agencies and policies. Planning should neutralize or reduce the negative externalities of the different policies, ensuring economies of scale and a more efficient use of government resources. The time has passed when government agencies were supposed to speak with a single voice. If the planning process achieves a bare minimum of agreement between different agencies – even though they all speak with a different accent – it will be a major step forward.

In other words, the planning agency should not try to 'go it alone', nor, conversely, be content to stack up sectoral plans without seeking to integrate them in any meaningful way. Attempts to go it alone hark back to the outdated technocratic dream of comprehensive, 'global', planning, which has been shown to be unsuitable for developing countries (Waterston 1969; Mattos 1988).[6] Sectoral planning without any concern for overall policy coherence has been observed in cases where the failure of global planning has led to a ritual presentation of plans lacking any real purpose, serving only to meet legal requirements and existing commitments.

The second, equally important, aspect of city governments' planning role is to set social and economic priorities and objectives for the coming years. Greater efficiency and the creation of opportunities for real change require more than the co-ordination of state activities as described above; they also require the rest of society to become more involved and share more responsiblity with the state. In complex societies the local state is simply not capable of defining, alone and unaided, the path that cities should take. It does, however, have an essential leadership role, bringing together different interest groups to sort out a basic policy agenda, and creating coalitions which will be strong enough, and enjoy sufficient legitimacy, to see through major changes in the different areas for which the city government is responsible.

Despite the importance of legal regulation in shaping the future of third world cities, it should be stressed that the state faces three major difficulties in this respect.

The first difficulty arises from structural constraints. Globalization increases the gap between the economic decision-making process, which often reflects an international entrepreneurial logic, and political decision-making by national-states and regional or local governments, which refer only to their own territories. This means that extremely important economic projects, such as a new car plant, may demand major changes in infrastructure and servicing patterns, rendering many urban planning laws and regulations obsolete.

The second difficulty arises from the large number of variables involved in urban planning laws and regulations, most of which go undetected by specialists and law-makers. As a result, urban legislation usually has a significant number of unanticipated effects (see Chapter 4 by Razzaz). Although some of these have positive consequences, the majority do not. This is one of the major reasons for the failure of much urban legislation to achieve its intended objectives.

The third difficulty arises from an apparent paradox: the existence of an enormous number of legal instruments in a social context in which *effective* regulatory power over most urban activities (construction, the letting or sale of property, the use of public spaces, commerce and so on) is extremely limited – especially in the 'illegal city' where much of the population lives. In the major cities of developing countries, then, the crisis of governability cannot be explained (as it often is for developed countries) in terms of 'an excess of social needs and demands outstripping the state's capacity to respond', whether we are talking about its capacity to manage the city finances, run local government effectively, or devise appropriate urban laws and regulations. It is obvious that the arsenal of legal instruments for urban management cannot be effective without the political support needed to guarantee implementation of the laws in question. In other words, even the most sophisticated and democratic legal regulations cannot make a real difference if the wider social and cultural environment is not conducive to change (see Chapter 6 by Santiago). It is not realistic to expect standard urban policies to meet the requirements of each and every city, especially in developing countries suffering from major regional disparities. This is one of the reasons why it is so difficult to transfer first world models to developing countries. Much of the so-called 'formalism' identified in developing countries is the result of frustrated attempts to copy legal instruments and policies that have been successful elsewhere – either in other countries or in the more developed regions of the country in question.

The fact is that in developing countries law serves to distance the 'legal' from the 'illegal' city, increasing the value of the former (see Chapter 12 by Berrisford and Chapter 8 by Fernandes and Rolnik). The areas in which the law is implemented effectively are those that house the machinery of government, modern economic activities, and the homes of the middle and upper classes. By contrast, the unregulated parts of the city suffer from low levels of infrastructural investment and poor access to the means of collective consumption, and they house the poor and marginalized sectors of society. In extreme cases these areas became ghettos, totally set apart from the 'legal' city (see Chapter 12 by Berrisford).

The expansion of the legal sphere depends on the political pressure the 'have-nots' can bring to bear on the authorities, and on the trading of legal integration – tenure legalization or the approval of building plans, settlement layout, commercial activities – for electoral support and political legitimacy (see Chapter 7 by Pérez Perdomo and Bolívar, Chapter 10 by Varley and Chapter 9 by Azuela and Duhau).

We should not seek to enforce the law at all costs, as legislation in some areas can be so inappropriate that its non-enforcement is essential for the very survival of the low-income population (see Chapter 7 by Pérez Perdomo and Bolívar, Chapter 11 by Mitullah and Kibwana and Chapter 5 by Perry). Such legislation was not, as some schools of thought in vogue in the 1960s would have it, dreamt up by the rich to oppress the poor. On the contrary, it was the work of progressive urban planners seeking to ensure acceptable living conditions for all the city's inhabitants. Unfortunately, their efforts all too often led only to greater social and spatial segregation.

In other areas, however, effective implementation of existing laws could bring about a significant improvement in living conditions for the urban poor[7] – although doing so would run the risk of undermining informal alternatives which serve the poor reasonably well (Santos 1993; see also Chapter 7 by Pérez Perdomo and Bolívar).

In conclusion, although the illegal city may solve the immediate housing problems of the low-income population, in the long run it has negative consequences both for residents (for example, when they occupy areas that are unsafe) and sometimes for the city as a whole (for example, when illegal settlement harms the environment – see Chapter 3 by Yonder). There are, then, no standard recipes for improving urban law, and we should be wary of taking up dogmatic positions on the subject. In some cases new laws are needed; in others, effective enforcement of the existing legislation would be enough.

Finally, it should be stressed that the challenges facing city governments in developing countries are extremely complex. While economic restructuring may be necessary to enable countries to cope with globalization, every effort should be made to improve the living conditions of the urban poor. This means promoting economic activities capable of providing jobs at the unskilled end of the labour market, and making services and other urban amenities available to the residents of the illegal city.

Notes

Translated from Portuguese by Edésio Fernandes and Ann Varley.

1. In Latin America, some structural adjustment programmes (in Mexico, Chile, Argentina, Peru and Brazil) have enjoyed a certain degree of success, but their social and political context, timing and strategies were very different. Although the social costs have been considerable, the countries in question have to a greater or lesser extent managed to reduce and control inflation and pave the way to economic growth. Between 1980 and 1990 Latin America none the less experienced an estimated 10 per cent decrease in per capita incomes (Sagasti and Arevalo 1994). Despite this generalized economic crisis, however, and possibly because of greater popular pressure on newly democratic governments, a significant improvement in social indicators took place in comparison with the previous decade in Brazil (Medice and Agune 1994) and other Latin American countries (Coragio 1994).

2. Critics have argued that presidentialism denied governments the necessary parliamentary support for the controversial measures required to address the economic crisis, and also encouraged the legislature to act in isolation from the executive. Research comparing eighty-six countries gaining their independence between 1945 and 1979 has shown that none of the countries opting for pure or mixed presidentialist systems in their first year of independence managed to maintain uninterrupted democracies between 1980 and 1989 (Stepan and Skach 1993).

3. A third type of organization, including mothers' or old people's groups, sports or leisure associations, has objectives which are internal to the group (Costa 1991; Scola 1995). They can generally achieve their objectives without direct reference to the state, but may in certain circumstances evolve into demand-driven movements.

4. Restricted participatory planning is criticized for dressing up traditional clientelistic practices in a modernizing rhetoric and for increasing the exploitation of labour. An ingenuous and idealistic defence of this kind of participation in housing policies can be found in the classic works of John Turner (see, for example, Turner and Fichter 1972). From the opposite extreme, Emilio Pradilla (1983) provides a sectarian Marxist critique of this position. A critical analysis of both positions is offered by Azevedo (1987).

5. The supporters of this type of participation acknowledge that there is no easy answer to a number of difficult questions it raises: how the membership of collective bodies should be decided, whether or not their role should be purely consultative, how possible conflict with conventional democratic bodies should be resolved, or how the interests of population sectors which do not have organizations to speak for them should be taken into account (see Azevedo and Prates 1995).

6. When, in the mid-1970s, critics started to attack global or 'integrated' planning, some authors went to the opposite extreme, recommending one-off interventions which might be described as 'putting out fires'. In practice, such 'incremental' planning simply reinforces the *status quo*, as the state is towed along by market forces. This is a very conservative position, as the state renounces, *a priori*, its stated objectives, leaving the market to set its priorities. Taken to its logical extreme, this would have disastrous consequences. Although proponents of incrementalism rightly criticize the shortcomings of global/integrated planning (particularly in developing countries), they get the solution wrong when they renounce any sense of vision for planning (cf. Caiden and Wildavsky 1974).

7. An excellent example comes from São Paulo, where the 'Popular Front' municipal government in power from 1989 to 1992 insisted that the rental contracts used in the 'legal city' should also be used in the city's rental slums (*cortiços*).

References

Azevedo, S. de (1987) 'Housing policies in Latin America', *Political Science*, Vol. 20, no. 4, 895–901.

Azevedo, S. de and A. A. Prates (1995) 'Movimientos sociales, acción colectiva y planificación participativa', *EURE: Revista Latinoamericana de Estudios Urbano-Regionales*, Vol. 21, no. 64, 103–20.

Boschi, R. R. (1987) *A Arte da Associação*, Vértice/IUPERJ, São Paulo.

Caiden, N. and A. Wildavsky (1974) *Planning and Budgeting in Poor Coutries*, John Wiley, New York.

Castells, M. (1985) 'Reestructuración económica, revolución tecnológica y nueva organización del territorio', in M. Castells (ed.), *Metropolis, Territorio y Crisis*, Asamblea de Madrid, Madrid, 39–62.

Cintra, A. O. and L. A. G. Andrade (1978) 'Planejamento: reflexões sobre uma experiência estadual', in A. O. Cintra and P. R. Haddad (eds), *Dilemas do Planejamento Urbano e Regional*, Zahar, Rio de Janeiro, 15–50.

Coraggio, J. L. (1994) 'A construção de uma economia popular como horizonte para as cidades sem rumo', in L. C. de Q. Ribeiro and O. A. dos Santos Jr (eds), *Globalização, Fragmentação e Reforma Urbana*, Civilização Brasileira, Rio de Janeiro, 221–60.

Costa, S. (1991) 'Política para quem precisa de política: movimentos urbanos, participação e democracia', Unpublished MSc dissertation, Universidade Federal de Minas Gerais, Belo Horizonte.

Gohn, M. da G. (1982) *Reivindincações Populares Urbanas*, Cortez Editora, São Paulo.

Huntington, S. P. (1979) 'Preterionismo e decedência política', in F. H. Cardoso and C. E. Martins (eds) *Política e Sociedade*, Editora Nacional, São Paulo, 160–72.

— (1991) *The Third Wave: Democratization in the Late Twentieth Century*, University of Oklahoma Press and Scott Meredith Literary Agency, New York.

Jacobi, P. (1990) 'Descentralização municipal e participação dos cidadãos: apontamentos para o debate', *Lua Nova*, Vol. 20, 121–43.

Lowi, T. J. (1964) 'American business, public policy, case studies, and political theory', *World Politics*, Vol. 26, 677–713.

Mattos, C. A. (1988) 'Estado, processos decisórios e planejamento na América Latina', in P. S. Edler and P. R. Haddad (eds), *Estado e Planejamento: Sonhos e Realidade*, CENDEC, Brasília, 101–35.

Matus, C. (1993) *Política, Planejamento e Governo*, IPEA, Brasília.

Medici, A. and A. Agune (1994) 'Desigualdades regionais na década de 80: o Brasil não é mais o mesmo?', Paper presented to Annual Conference, Associação Nacional de Pós-Graduação e Pesquisa em Ciências Sociais, Caxambu.

Moises, J. A. (1982) *Cidade, Povo e Poder*, CEDEC/Paz e Terra, São Paulo.

O'Donnel, G. (1993) 'Sobre o estado, a democratização e alguns problemas conceituais', *Novos Estudos CEBRAP*, Vol. 36, 123–46.

Offe, C. (1984) '"A ingovernabilidade": sobre o renascimento das teorias conservadoras da crise', in C. Offe (ed.), *Problemas Estruturais do Estado Capitalista*, Tempo Brasileiro, Rio de Janeiro, 236–61.

Osborne, D. and T. Gaebler (1992) *Reinventing Government – How the Entrepreneurial Spirit is Transforming the Public Sector*, Addison-Wesley, New York.

Petrella, R. (1994) 'Litanies de Sainte Compétitivité', *Le Monde Diplomatique*, no. 479, 10–11.

Pradilla, E. C. (1983) *El Problema de la Vivienda en América Latina*, Centro de Investigación CIUDAD, Quito.

Reis, F. W. (1988) 'Consolidação democrática e construção do estado: notas introdutórias e uma tese', in F. W. Reis and G. O'Donnel (eds), *A Democracia no Brasil: Dilemas e Perspectivas*, Vértice, São Paulo, 13–40.

— (1994) 'Cidadania, mercado e sociedade civil', in E. Diniz, J. S. L. Lopes and R. Pradi (eds), *O Brasil no Rastro da Crise*, ANPOCS/IPEA/HUCITEC, São Paulo, 328–49.

Ribeiro, L. C. de Q. and S. de Azevedo (eds) (1996) *A Crise da Moradia nas Grandes Cidades: Da Questão da Habitação à Reforma Urbana*, Editora da Universidade Federal de Rio de Janeiro, Rio de Janeiro.

Sader, E. (1988) *Quando Novos Personagens Entraram em Cena*, Paz e Terra, São Paulo.

Sagasti, F. R. and G. Arevalo (1994) 'A América Latina na nova ordem fracionada', in J. P. Velloso and L. Martins (eds), *A Nova Ordem Mundial*, José Olympio, Rio de Janeiro, 227–48.

Salisbury, R. H. (1968) 'The analysis of public policy: the search for theories and roles', in I. Sharkansky (ed.), *Policy Analysis and Public Policy*, Markham, Chicago, 151–75.

Santos, W. G. dos (1988) 'Gênese e apocalipse: elementos para uma teoria da crise institucional latino-americana', *Novos Estudos CEBRAP*, Vol. 20, 110–18.

— (1993) *Razões da Desordem* (2nd edn), Rocco, Rio de Janeiro.

— (1994) 'A trágica condição da política social', in S. Abranches, W. G. dos Santos and M. Coimbra (eds), *Política Social e a Questão da Pobreza* (3rd edn), Zahar, Rio de Janeiro, 33–64.

Scola, G. T. (1995) 'Movimentos urbanos e poder local em São João Del Rei', Unpublished MSc dissertation, Universidade Federal de Minas Gerais, Belo Horizonte.

Stepan, A. and C. Skach (1993) 'Quadros metainstitucionais e consolidação democrática', in B. Lamonier and D. Nohlen (eds), *Presidencialismo ou Parlamentarismo*, IDESP/Edições Loyola, São Paulo, 218–44.

Turner, J. F. C. and R. Fichter (eds) (1972) *Freedom to Build: Dweller Control of the Housing Process*, Macmillan, New York.

Valladares, L. do P. and E. Preteceile (eds) (1990) *Reestruturação Urbana: Tendências e Desafios*, Nobel/IUPERJ, Rio de Janeiro.

Waterston, A. (1969) *Planificación del Desarrollo*, Fondo de Cultura Economica, Mexico City.

Index

Acquaye, Ebenezer, 40
acquisition of land: compulsory, 11, 32, 40–4, 90, 208 (compensation for, 42–3; in Africa, 41; in India, 40); laws, 109–10
administrative simplification, 243
Africa, urban land issues in, 36–44 *see also* Sub-Saharan Africa
African reserves: in Kenya, 196; in South Africa, 218
Aguilera Gómez, Manuel, 183, 184
Alleyne, Marva, 42
Alliance for Progress, 21
amnesty: for unauthorized buildings, 56, 59, 64; regularizations of land tenure, 240
Ankara, creation of, 56
anthropology, 30; legal, 20, 26
apartheid, 14, 213, 217, 221, 225, 226, 249; city based on, 214–15
Archer, Arthur, 42
Asante, Samuel K. B., 36
de Azevedo, Sérgio, 14, 16
Azuela, Antonio, 7, 9, 13, 26, 44, 47

Balachandran, M. K., 32
Bangalore: National Games Housing Complex, 95–101; official private residential development, 92–3; public housing developments, 90–2; Town and Country Planning Act, 98; unofficial private residential development, 93–5; urban change in, 12, 89–103
Bangalore Development Authority, 98, 99, 242
Bani Hasan tribe, 70, 71, 74, 76, 84
bantustans, 218, 219, 221, 222
Barbados, relocation of squatter settlement, 42
Barriadas Law (Peru), 24–5
barrios, 9, 25; conflict in, 135; founding of, as political action, 126; growth of, 129; in Caracas, 12; planning in, 129;

specialized housing companies, 135; violence in, 133, 136 *see also* police
Benin, 251
Benninger, Christopher C., 35
Bentsi-Enchill, Kwamena, 36
Berrisford, Stephen, 14
Bijlani, H. U., 32
Bolívar, Teolinda, 12
Botswana, 251
Bowen, Olukunke A., 47
Brazil, 8, 250, 252; Civil Code, 145–6, 150; Constitutional Congress, 146–9; Federal Law no. 6,766, 146; law and urban change in, 140–56; Master Plan Law, 147–8; National Urban Reform Bill, 143; Popular Amendment on Urban Reform, 146; regularization amnesty in, 240
Brookfield, Harold, 28–9
Bruton, Michael J., 34
building standards and regulations, 15, 205, 207, 208; relaxation of, 209
Burman, S., 47

cadastral systems, 59, 251
Cameroon, 251
Caracas: *barrios* in, 25; legal pluralism in, 123–39
Castells, Manuel, 5
Centre for Urban Studies, India, 32
Chalco Valley, Mexico, 161, 167, 168, 182
Chaturvedi, T. N., 32
Chihuahua, Mexico, land invasions in, 177
Chile, 247, 250; illegal settlements in, 234
citizenship, in developing countries, 3–17
city: in context of legal studies, 8–10; in developing countries, 3–17; right to, 7–8, 10, 151, 245
CIVIC organization, Bangalore, 96
clientelism, 253, 261, 262
colonias populares, Mexico, 167, 168
common law *see* law
conflict situations, resolving of, 135, 136
Congo, 251